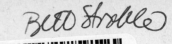
A Critical Handbook
of Literature for
Young Adults

Rebecca J. Lukens
Miami University

Ruth K. J. Cline
University of Colorado

■ HarperCollinsCollegePublishers

To my students, who continually awaken me to the worth and meaning of literature.
Rebecca J. Lukens

To young adult literature enthusiasts of all ages.
Ruth K. J. Cline

Acquisitions Editor: Chris Jennison
Assistant Editor: Shadla Grooms
Project Editor: Janet Frick
Cover Design/Design Supervisor: Mary Archondes
Production Manager: Mike Kemper
Compositor: RR Donnelley Barbados
Printer and Binder: Malloy Lithographing, Inc.
Cover Printer: Malloy Lithographing, Inc.

For permission to use copyrighted material, grateful acknowledgment is made to the copyright holders on pp. 201–202, which are hereby made part of this copyright page.

A Critical Handbook of Literature for Young Adults

Copyright © 1995 by HarperCollins College Publishers

Library of Congress Cataloging-in-Publication Data

Lukens, Rebecca J., 1922-
    A critical handbook of literature for young adults / Rebecca J.
  Lukens, Ruth K.J. Cline.
        p.   cm.
    Includes bibliographical references and index.
    ISBN 0-06-501108-2
    1. Young adult literature, American—History and criticism
–Handbooks, manuals, etc.   2. Young adults—United States—Books and
reading—Handbooks, manuals, etc.   I. Cline, Ruth K. J. II. Title.
PS490.L84   1994
809'.89283—dc20   93-45468
                                                          CIP

94 95 96 97   9 8 7 6 5 4 3 2 1

Contents

Preface

The focus of this text is learning to make critical judgments about literature for young adults—those between the ages of 12 and 20—to determine what is worth reading, worth discussing, worth buying, worth acquiring for the library. My hope is that the book will be useful for teachers of literature, for librarians and media specialists in junior high and secondary schools, and for those who wish to join these professions.

"Like a trapeze artist," psychologist Erik Erikson has said, "the young person in the middle of vigorous motion must let go of his safe hold on childhood and reach out for a firm grasp on adulthood depending for a breathless interval on a relatedness between the past and future." Youthful fictional characters, "in the middle of vigorous motion," provide interesting and profitable subjects for understanding; good literature provides the best possible clues about the nature of this age group. For young adults themselves, literature serves both as a mirror for them to observe themselves and thus to understand themselves better and as a lamp for them to observe others, singly and in groups.

Simultaneously, these opportunities afford readers great pleasure as well. The textbook *A Critical Handbook of Literature for Young Adults* examines in depth a large variety of novels with youthful protagonists, including lasting work from the twentieth century as well as recent fiction published for this age group. The critical analysis is based on formalist criticism: character, plot, theme, setting, tone, point of view, and style in many works, from the rather recent *The Chocolate War* by Robert Cormier, now a classic, and *Roll of Thunder, Hear My Cry* by Mildred D. Taylor. The much castigated novel *The Catcher in the Rye* by J. D. Salinger is occasionally used as example, but more strongly defended in Appendix A. Emphasis is always placed on the best, but less successful novels are occasionally used as contrast.

The best of these novels include "vigorous motion" of several kinds: the pull toward acceptance into groups and the universal human and vividly significant struggle between individuality and social identification. The stories present a spectrum of issues facing young adults in the process of coming of age, and when read in the light of adolescent concerns, they illuminate the issues and quests of the age group. The first chapter, "Literature and the Young Adult," explores what literature can do to provide pleasure and to increase readers' understanding—readers of any age. In addition, literature for young adults helps them to explore and to understand their own typical concerns. Fictional examples used throughout the following chapters are taken from books that exemplify superior literary quality, with character development and themes that enlighten readers about the issues that concern youth. The chapter on poetry sets up criteria for judging the genre; in each case, examples are taken from poetry open to the pleasure and insights of youth.

The *Critical Handbook* is based on the premise that literature for young adults may differ from that which focuses on adult issues in the depth and complexity of a topic or its treatment, but need not be inferior in literary quality. The definition of literature occasionally mentioned in the text is basis for the textbook organization: "Literature is a significant truth expressed in appropriate elements and memorable language," a definition that alludes to theme or truth and the elements of character, plot, setting, point of view, and tone, as well as memorable language or style. The protagonists are youthful; their concerns are their anxieties, experiences, and relationships as well as their efforts to emerge from childhood into adulthood. The negative qualities of literature for this age—shallow character portrayal, oversimplified conflicts, and preachy themes, among them—do little to bridge the transition for young adults. Because poor literature may, in fact, set readers back in their understanding of self, others, and society, such examples are useful as contrast to the good.

Some would say that no age group is so difficult to teach as adolescents; indeed some might say it *is* in all ways the most difficult age group—and make no further comment. No matter what the teacher knows of psychology, or how many case studies have been analyzed, flesh and blood young adults, like people in general, are different from the bare bones of case study narratives. Ideally, we hope to know all we can about our fellow beings, hoping that by such understanding of others we may understand ourselves better; but since living in the skins of others is impossible, discovering how they think and what they feel is not an easy task. The vicarious experience of literature helps.

Teachers of young adults, then, work with the most diverse and constantly changing group of students anywhere, each student stretching toward adulthood in different ways at different paces, with emotional and physical growth spurts and plateaus, with changes either minuscule or at times explosive. Such differences account for varying tastes and interests, but at no time is their literature beyond critical appraisal.

The *Critical Handbook* goes beyond the teacher to the student. Skills in the evaluation of literature will grow as students meet and talk about the best. They will see themselves in sound character development, relevant and credible conflicts, significant themes, consistent points of view, and stylistic excellence. And as lovers of literature know, one of its great pleasures is growth in understanding people by seeing them face challenges and adventures, make and live with personal choices, and connect with others.

In recent years new emphasis has been placed on literature in all aspects of the educational process, as part of the "whole language" curriculum or curricular philosophy, a term that Kenneth Goodman describes as freeing "the minds and creative energies of pupils for the greatest gains in their intellectual, physical and social development." Building on Dewey's age-old reminder that we start "where the learner is in time, place, culture, and development," the statement suggests that the process of decoding has meaning for young readers if—once they are able to have the experience of reading—they find attractive *what* they can read and enjoy.

Recently Louise Rosenblatt, a pioneer in insisting that the best literature should be a basis for reading, again emphasized her earlier thesis that reading is a transaction, and that the "aesthetic experience" (thinking, feeling, experiencing during the reading) of literature must be recognized. My own terms for this transaction or aesthetic experience can best be described as the experiences of pleasure and understanding. Thus, Rosenblatt and I agree. To this experience she adds another: "efferent" refers to the acquiring of information through the reading, an effect that also reinforces my own thinking. Despite differing terms, Rosenblatt and I take readers where they are with what they have experienced. For example, most students when reading *Roll of Thunder, Hear My Cry* react to the understanding of emotions, thoughts, and behavior of the Logan family. Another, perhaps a single student in a class, might limit the same story only to examination of a segregated school in the South during the Great Depression, noting, for example, the location of the schoolhouse and the system of distributing textbooks. In Rosenblatt's terms, the group stresses the private aesthetic experience of understanding the family and their struggle, and the single student focuses on the efferent or informative one. In either event, literature that speaks to young adults gives great pleasure as it encourages their involvement and growth in insight.

During the planning stages of *A Critical Handbook of Literature for Young Adults,* I faced establishing criteria for judging literature based on its form, and I hoped to avoid writing a forbiddingly long or a teaching methods book. As examples of excellence I have chosen primarily two touchstones, books by which we may judge others. The first, *The Chocolate War* by Robert Cormier, reveals the principled Jerry Archer who will not at first give in to the Vigils with their mayhem and dishonesty. Jerry's courage and determination serve him for a time, but at no point does the reader gain a false impression of ease in such a battle. Furthermore, Jerry's determination flags when he is subjected to beating. The second fictional work, *Roll of Thunder, Hear My Cry* by Mildred D. Taylor, also treats the universal struggle of growth to understanding of adult views, but Cassie Logan's family is black, and many of their problems result from their color. In addition, many current titles are used as examples of fine literature, some of them "current" because although they may have been around for a time they are still read, and others "current" because they are newly published.

In concert with self-recognition and understanding of others, whether separate or in social groups, the focus of the *Critical Handbook* is the developing of critical standards for judging the multitude of new books published for young adults. These books are judged not only by how well they address the interests and concerns of this age group but also on literary criteria: First of all, does the story give the reader pleasure of some kind—and there are many kinds of pleasure. Then, are the characters believable human beings that the reader cares about? Is the conflict, whether internal, against another being, or against nature or society, believable and significant? Is the thematic point of the story worth considering, even though it may not be euphorically happy-happy? Is the story told from a consistent point of view that leaves readers with clear understanding of people? Is the style of the story personal, distinctive, suited to the characters and situation? Does the reader see something about self and/or others that has meaning?

These are the questions that determine for us whether the book is worth talking about, worth recommending and passing on, or worth buying for the library or classroom. Gaining skills in making these judgments is useful to classroom teachers, media specialists, and parents, all of whom review, purchase, recommend, and talk about books.

Literature for children and young adults gets better and better. When I first began working on the *Critical Handbook of Children's Literature* almost 20 years ago, my search for the truly fine was far less rewarding. Now, that handbook is in its fifth edition and this new one about literature for young adults simply cannot mention all of the many that please and satisfy. Instead, I must confine myself to mentioning just a few of the multitudes of fine books published for the young. For assistance in making choices, I have relied on the Honor Sampling found in *Literature for Today's Young Adults,* Third Edition, by Kenneth L. Donelson and Alleen Pace Nilsen (HarperCollins). The librarians of Lane Library, Oxford, Ohio—particularly Nancy Weitendorf—have been absolutely invaluable. I can only hope that the works I have selected are representative of the best. Once readers become interested in making judgments based on the criteria discussed in these pages, they will wish to add their own titles.

I also owe a great debt of gratitude to those critics who read the manuscript in an extremely rough first draft, and who then made helpful comments: Jan Dressel, Central Michigan University; Anne Hildebrand, Kent State University; Alleen Nilsen, Arizona State University; and John Rutherford, Radford University.

Rebecca J. Lukens

One of the goals of any reading/English program is to help young adults become independent readers. Every program should have self-selection as an essential element. If the teacher always makes reading recommendations or assigns reading lessons, young readers will be denied the experience of choosing books for their own reading pleasure. Teachers and librarians should be available to assist their young readers since libraries can be confusing at first. But the most meaningful assistance will be limited to how to select books, not which ones to select.

Teachers and librarians will benefit from reviewing Margaret Early's Stages of Reading Development. The *unconscious enjoyment* stage is essential for getting readers hooked on the act of reading. At this stage, readers are lost in a book or a story. Mother calls them to dinner, friends want them to come out to play, but the readers have to finish the page, the chapter, or the book to be satisfied. If young people have never been so engrossed in a book, chances are it will be difficult to get them to care about reading anything else. Material read at this stage often includes series books such as Nancy Drew, the Hardy Boys, the Baby Sitters' Club, or comics.

As young people read more and more at this stage, always wanting "one more book just like this one," they become aware of the formula that is the basis for these books. The characters and plot are predictable, and at this stage predictability sustains enjoyment.

The next stage is *self-conscious appreciation;* it is the result of careful guidance by a teacher who helps readers see the contrast between the characters in the series books and the characters in books like *Roll of Thunder, Hear My Cry* (Taylor) or *The Chocolate War* (Cormier). That is what *A Critical Handbook of Literature for Young Adults* is all about: helping teachers and librarians to discuss critical elements of literature with their young readers. Conversations about these elements can help a young person acquire the language to talk about literature. Appreciation of literature will be heightened because of insights and knowledge gained from these discussions. Students will deductively arrive at issues of quality based on *their* reading experiences.

Early's third stage is *conscious delight* and it is this stage that inspired many English majors to pursue teaching. Readers at this stage have a mastery of criteria. They don't need reviewers or professors to tell them what to think about the selection, the character development, the use of language, or the resolution of the plot. An almost intuitive understanding of the criteria is basic to their enjoyment of literature.

The interesting insight here is that teachers can not expect all students, especially middle or junior high students, to reach the "conscious delight" stage. Teachers need to determine when their students have moved beyond the *unconscious enjoyment* stage. Some students may require longer exposure to "formula" literature before moving to the next stage. The teacher provides indispensable assistance in helping students move from one stage to another.

Teachers and librarians who work with young people are aware of the many distractions in our society that draw people away from reading. The list of such distractions includes television, movies, sports activities, arcades, malls, jobs, cars, sex, computer games, studying for other subjects, and "hanging out." Young people accustomed to TV sit-coms that resolve all issues in a half-hour often find that books move very slowly by comparison.

There are many ways to "grab" the interest of reluctant readers. Reading aloud is effective for all grades and ability levels. Stopping at a suspenseful point in the story may encourage some readers to finish the book independently. Using a segment from a video movie with a plot, setting, characters, or theme similar to a designated book could inspire some readers. Discussions with the class on some aspect of the book before reading it may create interest.

Teachers, parents, and librarians are an alliance working together to help young adults become independent, thoughtful, motivated, and critical readers. *The Critical Handbook* is a valuable resource for this worthy goal.

Ruth K. J. Cline

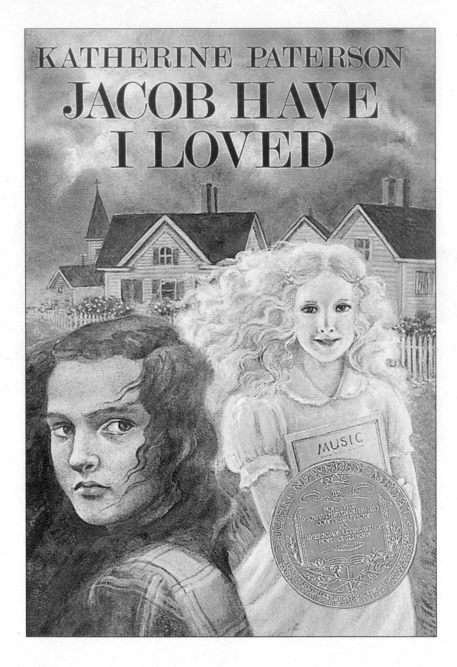

_1_

Literature and the Young Adult Reader

Those who enjoy reading know the distinction between reading strictly for information and reading for the pleasure of discovering ourselves and others. Although we cannot deny that there is pleasure in the discovery of information, whether in an article, an encyclopedia, or a trade book on a particular subject, the pleasure is of a different kind. In our search for information, we do not seek preachments or lessons but the pleasure of learning. In literature, poetry, and fiction, we seek another pleasure, that of entertainment and even escape into other lives and places. If we discover no pleasure, we put the book aside. Sad to say, however, we sometimes expect the young to find pleasure where we do not, in preachy messages, in stilted or repetitive language, or in boring stories where nothing happens or where nothing that seems relevant to their lives is described or explored. Surely if we seek pleasure, we can expect those younger than we to look for pleasure as well. Sometimes that pleasure occurs through laughter, sheer nonsense, the unexpected, or even the ridiculous. _Pleasure,_ then, is the first function of literature for any age group.

A second reward results from literature: _understanding._ Here young adults find a multitude of different kinds of pleasure stemming from exploration of what it means to be human, to be both unique and also part of the universal category of life called human beings. Enough preachments—the "shoulds" and "oughts" of life—are available without encountering them in pleasure reading. Instead, they search for the discoveries and observations about people and their inner lives, their relationships, their struggles that result in triumph or failure, or that end in denial or acceptance: "How does this story relate to me, my own real or imagined

1

triumph, failure or acceptance?" The same can be said of the expectations of all readers.

With these qualities in mind, note the definition of literature: **Literature** is a significant truth expressed in appropriate elements and memorable language. Consider what the best literature can do for readers of all ages, as well as how the nature of young adulthood influences that age group. It behooves us to remember what it is like or was like to be a young adult. We need to recall from the recent or distant past what we were concerned about and preoccupied with during those years of ups and downs so characteristic of that period in life.[1]

Characteristic of young adults is the feeling of being different, or unlike others, and of feeling isolated because of such feelings. *Literature shows human motives* by giving glimpses into the minds of the characters, what they think and feel as well as what they are unaware of in their subconscious minds. In literature young adult readers can find the effects of those thoughts, probe the depth of their feelings, and experience the significance of their imaginings. At times readers see what the less self-aware character does not. As they observe, they come to understand themselves better, as well as those around them whose actions had earlier mystified them. Young adulthood is a time of questioning, of wondering "Why did she say that?" or "What made him do that?" or even "What made me act that way?" Being inside the mind of another person might offer the perfect answer to such questions—assuming of course that the person knows the reason for her or her own behavior—but in real life that is not possible. Following the behavior of fictional people and seeing the reactions of others to them gives answers to some questions. But even more explicit answers derive from reading the interpretations and comments of an omniscient writer who knows, for example, what past experience has initiated a certain memory in the character and caused the resulting flare of emotion.

Literature provides form for experience. The sequence of events in people's lives is random; effect does not always follow closely upon cause. "What ever brought that about?" "I've no idea why that happened." Young adults recalling the high spots in their lives may not know their larger meaning beyond merely great fun or keen disappointment; they may see only the random disorder of successive events. To a young adult, hearing a parent reminisce about a small-town childhood may have its own interest. But when that reminiscence is juxtaposed with an event of the fictional present, it may have greater significance. "Oh, maybe *that's* why they think Susan did the wrong thing." Literature can illuminate experience by showing the relationships of one moment to others, or one experience to later events.

Literature reveals life's fragmentation. Like everyone else, young adults may feel at times that only their own lives lack the coherence that they'd like to think working toward a goal might accomplish. Most people wish at some time to see life more whole, to see how it all adds up. But life for everyone is made up of fragments. Even daily experience is fragmented by multitudes of pressures or questions. "What will the summer be like?" "Where should I apply for a job?" "Will I always dread meeting new people?" "Will my roommate and I lose touch once we graduate?" But literature sorts life experiences into disparate segments so that young adults and other readers can identify and examine them: haste, friendship, greed, advice, love, defeat, aging, disability, vanity, commitment, snobbery. Because everything is within the province of literature, each of these may be set before young adults for exploration. Events of yesterday may seem to have no bearing on those that happened today, or on the contrary may seem disproportionately causal in relationship.

But at the same time, even while people see life's fragmentation, *literature helps readers to focus on the essentials.* The "chaos of life," as novelist May Sarton calls it, is most easily observed and understood when art makes order of that chaos. Sarton asks as she writes, "Of all that I have observed, what is truly significant, and what can it possibly mean?" Minor details and irrelevant experiences do not distract the writer in the story-telling process; ignoring them highlights the essentials. Without the distance of time, each detail seems disproportionately significant or insignificant. Literature, however, sorts out the events. By focusing on the essentials, literature can tell readers that life is fragmented and simultaneously provide a sense of life's meaning.

As people live within the restrictions of society's institutions, they often fail to see the whole. *Literature can reveal the institutions of society.* With less experience than older people, young adults may feel a personal frustration about "ridiculous" unwritten dress codes in the school environment, "unreasonable" traffic laws in their quiet neighborhood, "useless" protocol in introducing youth to adults, and vast numbers of other restrictions that may make little sense to them. But when seen in fiction as necessary to the smooth workings of human relationships or to society's order, people easily concede. Some of society's institutions are rarely if ever examined aloud; a community's prejudice against those of other religions, races, or sexual orientation, for example, is sometimes taboo for discussion—although the prejudices are so prevalent they are in fact "institutions" of a social group. But in literature such issues, such biases or bigotries, can be examined to see how people come to espouse them, what their effects on both the bigot and the victim can be, why the issues are kept quiet and not discussed, what shame or embarrassment they may bring to friends. Other institutions like war or politics or family are revealed as the reader follows fictional examples. Young adults may be assisted in accepting conditions or choosing their battles because literature shows circumstances and situations that require struggle or compromise; it shows those for which agreement or consensus is the only solution.

Living as people do in the heated and cooled environments of their own urban or rural lives, it is possible for them to be unaware of nature as a force, but *literature can reveal nature as a force in human life.* Literature can take them to the southwestern desert for a year, to the tropical beach for a week, or to the Arctic wilderness for a day, where they can discover the impact of the natural world upon human activities, aspirations, and motivations. When literature posits a cataclysmic change like a nuclear blast, readers can observe not only the cold facts of radical alteration in seasons, mean temperatures, and precipitation, or changes in sea levels and elevation, but also what changes human beings are forced to make, are powerless to make, or refuse to make. Of course, people can read information about nature as a force in life as it is known in the earth's hemispheres, or can speculate about its effect upon people through nonfiction. But when a writer of fiction shows a group of people or an individual human being struggling with monumental change, the reality is quite different. Now readers see how that change brings emotional impact, disrupts relationships, or causes anxiety that leads to irrational behavior or impulsive violence. The effect is vastly different.

Literature supplies vicarious experience for readers. Young adults seek new experiences, the normal push of human curiosity to see "what's out there." Wish as they may, they can live no life but their own in no other place or period than that which they occupy. They might wish to know what it would be like to go to sea on a troop transport, to be left an orphan without parents or siblings, to travel with a band or be tutored on a movie set. Looking to the past, youth may be curious about what it was to be a prospector for gold in the days of the Klondike rush, an itinerant lawyer during the Civil War, or the wife of a president during colonial times. Fiction can give them a glimpse of such experiences. Through one novel they live as recent immigrants from Asia, through another they experience life as the child of an alcoholic parent, and in a third they experience religious ostracism. The vicarious experience of literature adds new dimensions to their understanding of "what would it be like if. . . "

And finally, *literature introduces readers to a writer-creator* whose medium—words—they know; whose subject—human nature—they live with; and whose vision—life's meaning—they stretch to understand. The skilled writer makes of readers passionate followers: "I want to read everything written by—" From the many discoveries, young readers gain understanding they wish to share, and pleasure they wish to urge upon others: "You really would love what this one writes."

For all readers, literature can accomplish these things. Young adults often wonder if they are "normal." Those who remember their own youth clearly, or who have been parents, may have some ideas about what makes this period in life different from others. Psychologists and psychiatrists have defined for us the nature of this period, descriptions that should prove useful as we look at literature for young people. When we search for books that may interest and give pleasure to them, it seems wise to consider their concerns as well as their wish to experience vicariously now what they may experience later in their lives, or may never experience but would like to know about.

Most of us hope to gain some understanding of other people, whether these people act as individuals or participate in the behavior of a whole group. We often shake our heads over the behavior of others, saying, "I just don't understand." If it doesn't matter, our admission is sufficient, but if we wish we might understand so that we could be helpful or sympathetic or even merely comfortable with the behavior, then we pursue the matter further. As we physically notice and emotionally "see" causes that precede effects and thoughts that influence actions, we may understand more clearly our own likes or dislikes, opinions or prejudices. Through reading about others, we now see how they think and feel as individuals or as parts of a group, and through that process discover more about ourselves. Literature opens for all readers new realms of discovery and understanding.

Summary

Literature can provide many kinds of pleasure, and many sorts of understanding. These contributions are brought to the reader because literature explores a **theme** or significant truth through such elements as **character, plot, setting, point of view,** and **tone** by means of **style,** language that is individual and memorable, suited to the situation, characters, and events.

Note

1. Because we believe J. D. Salinger's *The Catcher in the Rye* is the most accurate literacy portrayal of the concerns of young adults, a discussion of that much accused and foolishly castigated novel is included in Appendix A. Fortunately, despite adult misreadings and disapproval, the novel is still read by young adults. Obviously it speaks to generation after generation. Erik Erikson was among the first psychologists to acknowledge the special concerns of adolescence and to describe it in any detail. Appendix A therefore relates Erikson's description in *Identity: Youth and Crisis* to Salinger's novel, showing how one after another of the significant issues of young adults is acknowledged and convincingly explored. No novel so thoroughly explores these issues as they relate to both males and females. Carson McCullers's less read story *Member of the Wedding* and Doris Lessing's *Martha Quest* are somewhat successful, the former about a girl on the early edge of puberty and the latter about a young adult beginning a life of independence. Sylvia Plath's *The Bell Jar* touches on many of these issues, but because Esther Greenwood is suicidal, her story may seem eccentric rather than universal.

— 2 —

Character

Character as the term is generally used in life means the aggregate of mental, emotional, and social qualities that distinguish a person; in literature, it means the persons in the imaginative work. In life, character development implies the growth and change that results in what we ultimately are. In literature, however, the term **character development** means showing the character in various facets of complexity.

People are all three-dimensional, with a multitude of qualities. In fact, we are insulted when told, "Oh, you *always* do that" or "say that," as though we have no breadth, no flexibility or varied qualities that enable us to make individual judgments or behave according to situation rather than to internal programming. None of us is completely just, completely evasive, completely generous; each of us has limitations, and both virtues and flaws. In literature, the responsibility of the writer is to create whole characters who are composed of a variety of traits, characters we come to know and count on, just as we come to know and count on people. In fact, we might construct a relevant axiom regarding character development: Only the reality of the character can convince us of the reality of the action.

As the reader follows the central character or **protagonist** throughout the story, the writer has an obligation to make credible the actions, thoughts, and speeches of that character. The issue is simply stated: The closer the character is to the central conflict, the greater the necessity for us to see human complexity. Robert Cormier's *The Chocolate War,* for example, is Jerry Renault's story, and the reader comes to know him well. As the action and conflict move further away from Jerry himself, less important or minor characters participate, and because we have no need to know them well, Cormier has less obligation to show them in detail. Brian Cochran, for instance, merely keeps the record of chocolate sales and is minimally known to us; that is sufficient. Cassie of Mildred D. Taylor's *Roll of Thunder, Hear My Cry* is the principal character, and the reader knows her well. Here, too, as the action moves further away from the central character, less important or minor characters participate, and because it is not necessary to know them, the writer has less obligation to portray them fully. The author may show these less important people as two-dimensional, and in some cases may even show a character by a single trait or the traits of a class: The more the character functions merely as background, the less likelihood that the character needs to be developed.

As we have noted earlier, young adults often feel that "no one else in the world has ever thought and felt the way I do," an idea or feeling that appears in books from a variety of cultures. Thinking themselves sentenced to isolation, some may believe there is no group where they can feel at home, that will either admit them or accept their less-than-total conforming. Or they may feel they are adrift and will never feel anchored to a group whose set of values is similar to their own. Without opportunity to experiment, they may adopt a total life-style before they can evaluate all that it involves. To a great degree, understanding is gained through experience, of course, but understanding of who one is or is not is also enlarged through seeing human nature in its complexity revealed through literature. As young adults read, absorbed in what a protagonist is experiencing, they can harmlessly join that experience. They can vicariously view their options and the results of choosing one option or another, and thus consider which is the most right for them. As they discover in which groups they are comfortable or uncomfortable, their self-awareness increases. In situations arising out of normal needs, literature for young adults can be invaluable to them, but particularly when its solid and truthful character development assists readers in discovering what others like or unlike themselves experience.

Watch a young adult enter a new school. Fitting in academically may seem far less important than finding a group of friends. For example, Jennifer arrives dressed as she had dressed in her former school, looks around for another dressed like herself, and believes she has found someone who might be compatible. She watches her chance, and if she has the courage, speaks, although she may wait to be spoken to. Within a few days the tentative reaching out may have helped her connect with a new friend. Follow her for a few more weeks or even days, however, and notice that she has drifted away from the first friend or group; she has discovered that although they may look like the friends she has left behind, their ways of dealing with academic pressure or with dating behavior are vastly different from her own. She now faces a choice: conform to the new group, go through the uncertainty of finding another with which she feels more at home, or choose to be distinctively herself. Here Jennifer's extensive reading may help her. If she has met the character of

Sarabeth in *Silver* by Norma Fox Mazer, for example, she can vicariously experience the loneliness of isolation and feeling different, the uncertainty of the search for friends, and the realization that the isolation may not last forever, as well as the additional discovery that any school is a universe of varied groups with varying values. Having found a convincing portrayal of character in the novel has increased Jennifer's understanding of her own situation.

Follow Mike through another experience. With his family, he has moved from one home to another, entering a new school where he is met either with silence or with offers of friendship that puzzle him. The necessary part-time job cuts into leisure time, and he has no relationship with his father, who is on a lengthy overseas assignment. The vicarious experience of such a story as *Across the Grain* by Jean Ferris suggests to him the possibility of closeness with an older man who is not his real father, but who welcomes him, understands his puzzlement, and by asking the right questions assists Mike in evaluating the offered friendships. Through his leisure reading that can both verify and expand his experiences, Mike has vicariously experienced the difficulties of making personal choices. He has come to see that by his choices and his behavior he takes a risk, and that any decision must be his own.

Literature at its best is not intended for use as therapy but for the exploration and revelation of what it means to be human, either alone or in groups. Although Jennifer and Mike do not retreat into literature, they do find understanding that sees them through uncertain times.

Revelation of Character

When we meet people, we make judgments about them, either consciously or unconsciously. When first we meet another person at a party, for example, we take note of what she or he is wearing, whether quiet or mousy in color, flamboyant and attention-seeking in style, or expensive and conservative in fabric and fit. We listen to the conversation, noting the speech characteristics of a region or the signs that English may be a second language. Sometimes we make judgments about a New Englander, for example, based upon speech patterns, or about a member of a cultural group different from our own, only to find that these judgments are not verified in any way. Then we note the newcomer's behavior at the party. She is loud and rowdy, he is stiff and aloof, she is warm and friendly, he is open and comfortable with himself. Furthermore, if we find the newcomer is known to a friend, we listen to the friend's comments and add this new information to the bases for our judgment. All these pieces of information we absorb and assimilate, although we may never know how the new acquaintance really feels or thinks.

In literature readers get acquainted with characters in the same way; how the character looks, what she says, how he behaves, and what others say about her or him influence our judgments. In literature, however, readers have an additional means of knowing a character. The author, who can do what we cannot do in real life, may inform readers of what the character is thinking and feeling, may give judgments of character, or even tell about the character's past or future.

Look for example, at the characters in Robert Cormier's *The Chocolate War*. Readers come to know them in a variety of ways.

By Actions

Actions help the reader to understand a character. When first the reader meets Emile, "he was siphoning gas from a car, watching it flow into a glass jug. Emile giggled." He is getting his "gas for the week." Cormier tells us Emile is "an animal, and he doesn't play [football] by the rules." He "reaches" people by "whistling softly so that it got on the teacher's nerves, a barely perceptible whistle that could drive a teacher up the wall. That's why Emile Janza reversed the usual process. Wise guys usually sit in back. Emile didn't. He chose seats near the front where he'd be in better position to harass the teacher. Whistling, grunting, belching, tapping his foot, stirring restlessly, sniffling. Hell, if you did that kind of stuff from the back of the room the teacher wouldn't notice."

But Emile doesn't harass only teachers. He has found that the world is full of willing victims. Emile learned early in life that "you could take a kid's lunch or even his lunch money and nothing usually happened." His actions help to describe his character: Emile is a bully. If this were Emile's story, we would know more about him, even why he is a bully, but for Cormier's purposes in a story that is essentially Jerry Renault's, Emile serves as a bully.

By Speech

Speech also reveals character. Archie is the leader of the Vigils, the secret organization that rules not only the student body but the Trinity staff as well. He has called a meeting to assign Goober his destructive task. Goober, a meek kid who tries to please everyone, is cowed into servility and forced to call Archie "sir," as if he were in the Army. While Goober trembles as he stands before the leader of the Vigils, notice Archie's side of the conversation:

> "Tell me," Archie said, "why you're here." He allowed a bit of impatience to appear in his voice.
> "For . . . an assignment."
> "Do you realize that there's nothing personal in the assignment?"

The Goober nodded.

"That this is tradition here at Trinity?"

"Yes."

"And that you must pledge silence?"

Archie's persistence in pursuing his question, his insistence on being addressed as "sir," his use of painful, even unbearable pauses between questions, and his condescending tone suggesting to Goober that he is stupid—everything awakens the reader's suspicions that Archie is a ruthless tyrant, one who "let himself be caressed by the laughter of admiration."

By Appearance

The way we look says something about us, and the same is true of characters in fiction. Goober's appearance prepares us for his status; he has the "look of a victim": "Despite his height, he was easily six-one, he reminded Archie of a child, someone who didn't belong here, as if he'd been caught sneaking into an Adults Only movie. He was too skinny, of course. And he had the look of a loser. . . Vigil bait." So frightened he is "white-faced" while standing there "spellbound," Goober nods his head, "accepting the assignment like a sentence of doom," and "in bewilderment, looking as if he were going to cry."

By Others' Comments

Just as flesh-and-blood human beings comment on each other, characters also comment on others. Jerry pities his father, who after his wife's lingering death seems "like a puppet being maneuvered by invisible strings." Jerry himself feels part of the football team, but wonders, "what was his father part of?" Because his father works staggered hours, Jerry often finds him asleep on the sofa and surmises that his father feels his life to be empty. Jerry wonders what can be interesting about his father's job at the pharmacy—is there nothing exciting? Observing his father drag himself along from day to day, Jerry comments to himself, "Was this all there was to life, after all? You finished school, found an occupation, got married, became a father, watched your wife die, and then lived through days and nights that seemed to have no sunrises, no dawns and no dusks, nothing but a gray drabness."

Through what Jerry says about his father the reader sees clearly portrayed a grieving husband and distracted father. At the same time, however, these comments reveal something of the grieving Jerry and his attitudes and concerns about his own future. The writer tells the *why* of

Jerry's actions; knowing this, the reader may judge whether or not Jerry deserves our sympathy.

By Author's Comments

Real life allows no comments by an author, but Cormier knows what his characters are thinking and feeling, and does not hesitate to let the reader know. In the opening chapter, readers meet Jerry Renault, who weighs only 145 pounds and is small for football but is determined to play. He knows the coach is "looking for guts." "I've got guts, Jerry murmured, getting up by degrees" from the ground. As the coach glares at him, "Jerry hung in there, trying not to sway, trying not to faint." He says to himself, "I'm going to make the team. *Dreamer, dreamer.* Not a dream: it's the truth." At the bus stop, Jerry leans against a telephone pole, watching the Hippies and Flower Children. Cormier tells us Jerry is "fascinated," envious of their ragged old clothes while he must wear the Trinity school uniform of shirt and tie. When accused of staring, Jerry, Cormier says, is "uneasy," hating "confrontations," and his heart "hammers." Again, when Brother Leon begins his daily harrassment of a student in the classroom, the writer tells us "Jerry felt a sense of dread and anticipation, both at the same time." As the harrassment intensifies, "Jerry's neck began to hurt. And his lungs burned. He realized he'd been holding his breath. He gulped air, carefully, not wanting to move a muscle. He wished he was invisible. He wished he wasn't there in the classroom. He wanted to be out on the football field, fading back, looking for a receiver."

Jerry has recently seen his sick mother linger and then suddenly die; not only his home life but all of his life is affected by her death, and it is thus important that Cormier tell the reader about Jerry's depression, and what motivates his furious efforts to "feel alive," and to "dare disturb the universe."

> Jerry was overcome with rage, a fiery anger that found him standing at her coffin in silent fury. He was angry at the way the disease had ravaged her. He was angry at his inability to do anything about saving her. His anger was so deep and sharp in him that it drove out sorrow. He wanted to bellow at the world, cry out against her death, topple buildings, split the earth open, tear down trees. . . .

Characters, then, come to be known by what they say, what they do, how they look, what others say about them, and, when the author chooses to be omniscient, by what the author says about them.

For another example of how readers come to know characters, note the way in which they are introduced to Lola, one of the orphans confined to *The House of Stairs,* the title of a fantasy or science fiction novel by William Sleator. In the opening pages of the story, Lola is described as small, with short dark hair and direct, penetrating black eyes, "standing with her feet apart and her arms folded across her thin chest." As she talks to Peter, Lola's voice is rough but distinctly feminine, and what she says is assertive: "No, I do *not* know" what the endlessly stretching stairs and bridges and landings are, "but I'm gonna find out pretty quick." She is "not gonna wait around in this . . . this . . . this *place* till some administrator out there remembers we're here. I'm gonna find the way out." Her assertive stance, her easy violation of orphanage rules about smoking, her giggles as she tells about her recalcitrance in the orphanage, and her relaxed posture as she sits comfortably on the open and interminable stairs are all actions of a self-confident, even cocky 16-year-old. Through the knowing author, Lola reveals her own attitudes as she thinks about Peter, at first her sole companion: "She had already typed him as one of those shy, sensitive creeps. . . . Why didn't he realize that the whole point was to get away with things, to prove that you were better." A game, a challenge, is the way she thinks of their confinement in the house of stairs. The reader draws conclusions about Lola from her appearance, her speech, her actions, and what she thinks.

Unity of Character and Action

In real life we are often changed by events. We are not surprised when some trauma like the divorce of parents, the accidental death of a good friend, or the burglary of one's home results in a person's being changed. In fact, we occasionally comment—thoughtlessly because we do not always *see* the changes—that a particular person does not seem to have been affected by bereavement or other trauma. We have come to expect that an experience—action—may cause change.

In less traumatic events, people may experience change as well. The reserved high school student urged to try out for a play and then chosen for a role finds that her busy life is very different, that she has a new group of friends, that she has skills or talents she didn't know about; the experience of acting in the school play, whether the role is large or small, changes her in some way. Or, to his surprise, the boisterous class clown finds himself in an advanced placement writing class. While he may remain gregarious and effervescent, he gains a new view of himself, a view that has impact on his friendships, his use of time, his relationship with his parents, even perhaps his choice of a girlfriend.

Although in real life we may or may not know the nature of or see the results of an internal struggle or its resulting change, in literature the author can reveal these feelings to us and demonstrate through the story's events how the action has affected the person to whom it has occurred. Character, or who and what the person is, influences action. And once involved in the action, the person may either experience change or remain unchanged. In either case character and action are inextricably woven together. As the novelist Henry James once said, "What is character but the determination of incident? What is incident but the illustration of character."[1] We might say that this unity of character and action over time sets up a causal chain: character in action leads to character change, which leads to new action, which may cause additional change. . . .

Look, for example, at *The Chocolate War,* and note how Jerry's character influences his behavior and how his actions in turn change him. After his mother's death, Jerry felt an emptiness, "a yawning cavity like a hole in his chest." He wonders at the boring routine of his grieving father's life, and the thought of being "a mirror of his father" makes him cringe. Such a fear fuels Jerry's desire to take action, to be quarterback, which in turn forces him to take terrible abuse on the field, abuse that sends him home exhausted and nauseous. But on the football field, he does not feel empty but "part of something." Very soon Jerry is given an assignment by the Vigils: he is ordered to defy Brother Leon and for a brief time to refuse to sell the chocolates that all Trinity students must peddle, then at a time set by the Vigils to reverse himself and agree to sell the chocolates. Jerry, who had been glad the terrible assignment of facing Brother Leon with refusal was now over, with the changed assignment now faces personal conflict. He hates the teacher's torturing of students in the classroom, hates the contest of wills as each day he defies Brother Leon, and sees hatred in Leon's eyes.

Weariness with the Vigil-forced contest of wills and with his own hatred forces him to a new kind of action. On his own and without Archie's approval, he says, "No. I'm not going to sell the chocolates." Jerry's conflict keeps him awake nights; he recalls the hippie's taunt at the bus stop, "You're missing a lot of things in the world," but sees his defiance as a way of refusing to "sleep his life away" as he believes his father is doing. Hero to some and fool to others, Jerry is acting out his answer to the message on the poster tacked inside his locker, "Do I dare disturb the universe?" and feels himself a stranger to the conforming classmates. Jerry's action is now a defiance of Archie and the Vigils and he faces punishment, first by being called before the Vigils. Jerry's determination to act and his actions themselves increase his self-confidence so that he can continue to defy the Vigils' orders as well as finally call the girl he has been admiring. He has dared to disturb the universe, and feels buoyant. Jerry's defiance causes others to lose their fear of Vigil control; to keep control, the Vigils initiate violence, including singling Jerry out for vicious attacks during football practice, harrassing him with phone calls, and stealing his homework. When, at Archie's direction, the Vigils step up the chocolate sales, Jerry is next challenged by those who had days before thought him a hero. He is accused of homosexuality, ambushed, and beaten; his locker is emptied; faculty and students treat him as though he does not exist; and he is finally beaten senseless by the bloodlust of the student body at the raffle-fight. Semiconscious, Jerry tries to tell Goober, "Don't disturb the universe, Goober, no matter what the posters say." There is no question that Jerry's character has determined his action, and brought about the retaliatory action of the school, which in turn has changed Jerry. Unity of character and action is clear.

Unity of character and action is further understood in the second touchstone, Taylor's *Roll of Thunder, Hear My Cry* as the reader observes Cassie, whose short temper gets her into trouble at school and brings down the wrath of the storekeeper, Mr. Barnett, when she insists that since she "was here first," she should be waited on before newly arrived white customers. When she refuses to move off the sidewalk for white Lillian Jean, and even defies Lillian's father, Cassie acts as her character dictates. When she cannily entices Lillian Jean to walk in the woods with her, then punishes Lillian for her arrogance, Cassie acts true to character.

Fonny of James Baldwin's *If Beale Street Could Talk* offers another example of unity of character and action, character that influences events and is then changed by them. When the powerful story begins, Fonny's girlfriend Tish says that he is beautiful, gentle, protective, an artist who wants to be a sculptor, a tender lover who has big dreams for the two of them. But Fonny is proud and defiant, too; when Tish is falsely accused of theft, he strikes out in her defense, making an enemy of the accusing police officer. Fonny's character shapes the events. Later, after being falsely arrested for rape by the furious officer, Fonny awaits trial in jail, sees Tish once a day, then is sent to solitary for refusing to be raped by fellow inmates. As he stares through the tiny opening in the cell door, Fonny fears he has lost track of everything, his mind "empty as a shell . . . rings, like a shell, with a meaningless sound, no questions, no answers, nothing." By the time Fonny has spent eight months in jail, he is lean, changed, hardened. He will never be the same Fonny. Tish says of him:

> . . . He looks straight at me, into me. His eyes are enormous, deep and dark. . . . He has moved—not away from me: but he has moved. He is standing in a place where I am not. He grins again, and stands, and salutes me. He looks at me, hard, with a look I have never seen on any face before. . . . He dares to look around him. He is not here for anything he has done. He has always known that, but now he knows it with a difference. . . . I bring him books, and he reads. We manage to get him paper, and he sketches. Now that he knows where he is, he begins to talk to the men, making himself, so to speak, at home. He knows that anything may happen to him here. But, since he knows it, he can no longer turn his back: he has to face it, even taunt it, play with it, dare.
>
> He is very far from me. He is with me, but he is very far away. And now he always will be.

Fonny's character has shaped the action, and the action in turn has reshaped Fonny.

Types of Characters

Certain terms describe the degree of character development, and others refer to change or lack of it in a fictional character. Briefly, a **flat character** is one readers do not know well, who has fewer traits. A **round character** is better known and has a variety of traits that make her or him believable. Within these two categories variations and degrees of "roundness" or "flatness" may exist. A character that changes is called a **dynamic character** and a character that does not change is called a **static character.**

Flat Characters

Flat characters, or those with few traits, appear in *The Chocolate War.* The school environment dictates the need for students other than Jerry, Goober, and Archie, students like Howie Anderson, Richy Rondell, Brian Cochran, and others, including Obie, who is under Archie's command; readers know little of these people and therefore can call them flat characters. Flat characters also occur in *Catcher in the Rye,* a story told entirely through the vision of Holden. Holden's neighbor Ackley, for example, is a flat character, a thoughtless and unappealing slob who imposes on Holden. Like all the other characters in the novel, Ackley is known to readers only through Holden's reports of what Ackley says and does; Salinger deliberately limits the character's delineation to what readers need to know for this story.

Look at some of the flat characters in *Roll of Thunder.* Avery is the white friend of Cassie's brother Stacey; he is quietly loyal and ignores the bus for white children so that he can walk to school with the Logans. No matter what he faces from other whites, he stays with them, and makes a whistle for Stacey's Christmas gift. He builds a tree house so that he can remove himself from his family, where his two scoundrel brothers hold sway. Big Ma, Cassie's grandmother, is a cautious woman who would rather give in to the unreasonable demands of the whites than challenge them. But she is proud of her two sons, the Logan family, and their landowning status; with the help of Mr. Jamison she wisely deeds the land to them so that Mr. Granger cannot manage to purchase it. Mr. Jamison is the principled white attorney who uses his profession, his money, and his personal courage to help the Logan family when pressures of income and the tax bill threaten to pull them under.

One kind of flat character is a **foil,** a minor character with few traits, but useful as a contrast to highlight the traits of the more fully developed central character. Goober in *The Chocolate War* might be called a foil; he is similar to Jerry in his hatred of the chocolate sales, but in contrast to Jerry is too timid and inhibited to defy the command of Brother Leon and the Vigils. In Madeleine L'Engle's *A Wrinkle in Time,* twins Sandy and Dennys are foils; they do not have Charles Wallace's extreme acuity nor Meg's moody sensitivity, but are totally normal children who build tree houses and comfortably accept Bs and Cs at school. To cite still another example, Bette Greene in *Summer of My German Soldier* shows Sharon as a foil, contrasting her to protagonist Patty. Patty is treated harshly, but her sister Sharon is the subject of their parents' bragging—her hair, her clothes, and her behavior are perfect at all times. Both parents bestow loving treatment on Sharon, but for Patty their mother keeps a vicious tongue and their father shows nothing but impulsive brutality.

Another special kind of flat character is the **stereotype,** one who represents a group by embodying its traits. Stereotypes are often useful as minor characters in carrying the action or illuminating an idea. Cormier in *The Chocolate War* uses a range of flat characters, among them the stereotypical bully, Emile Janza, who thrives on violence. Brian Cochran is a stereotypical good student who is afraid to speak up on his own behalf but is needed to keep the books on chocolate sales. Stereotypes of phoniness occur in *Catcher in the Rye;* for example, there is the stereotypical alumni who return to Pencey Prep, one to look for his carved initials on the stall door of the bathroom while he burbles on about Pencey as the best days of his life, and another who returns to talk at convocation, giving a "blowhard's" lecture to the boys about applying themselves.

Although a stereotype may adequately fill a need in plot or theme when used as a minor character, when given greater prominence, stereotypes can be highly destructive portrayals of groups of people. Thoughtful people know that skin color has nothing to do with characters' behavior or values. In the past, however, thoughtless writers presented stereotyped black families in thoroughly unjust and destructive portraits that showed, for instance, a Southern black family with a single parent and many troublesome children lacking education and living in slovenly poverty. But Mildred Taylor confronts and defies the stereotype of the black family in both *Roll of Thunder, Hear My Cry* and its sequel, *Let the Circle Be Unbroken.* The closely knit, landowning Logan family consists of an educated mother who teaches school, a hard-working father, and four clean and attractive children who are all good students. A churchgoing group, they are principled and caring, offering kindness and leadership wherever they are needed. Readers can respect and admire them. Taylor furthermore refuses to depict white families—either the poor or the more well-to-do in responsible positions—as stereotypically racist. Mr. Jamieson, a white attorney, is a compassionate and helpful man who endangers his own life to defend wrongly accused blacks, but Mr.

Grainger, a white plantation owner, treats the black community viciously. Cassie's white friend Jeremy Simms is a good boy who is ashamed of his older brother's lawless behavior. T. J. Avery, an impressionable black boy, is involved in theft, but the planning has been done by his false friends, his white contemporaries who blame it on T. J.

Round Characters

A **round character** is a complex person whose many traits the reader knows. For example, early in *The Chocolate War,* Cormier introduces his principal characters by giving each of them a brief chapter of his own. Chapters one, three, and six are about Jerry, the central character, two is about Obie, four and five Archie, seven Emile, eight Goober, and in nine and several others the reader is back to Jerry. Since Jerry is the protagonist, the reader must know him best; he is the football underdog, the exploited one who struggles to maintain his courageous stand against the power of the Vigils and of Brother Leon, the instigator of the chocolate sale. Jerry's grieving, his quiet home life with his depressed father, his insistence—so that he can feel alive—upon taking both bodily punishment and emotional blows, as well as his courage as he stands up to faculty and students are all aspects of Jerry's character. Jerry is a sexual being, a thoughtful boy protective of his father, good friend to Goober, a young adult with principles. During the concluding boxing match, Jerry shows his defiance is not superhuman but human when he realizes to his horror that his furious and premeditated lashing out is not merely self-defense but an act of revenge. Jerry sees he is no better than the Vigils: "A new sickness invaded Jerry, the sickness of knowing what he had become, another animal, another beast, another violent person in a violent world." Cormier's Jerry Renault is thoroughly human, a round and flawed being who lives in a flawed society; readers may recognize themselves or their own potential, a stirring recognition of human complexity. The reader also sees many traits within Archie, who knows he is hated and struggles wearily with the responsibility to invent new and vicious assignments for the Vigils; the reader becomes sympathetic to him as well.

Change in Character

A **dynamic character** is one that changes in the course of the story. When first readers meet Jerry of *The Chocolate War,* he is depressed by his mother's death and by what he sees as his is father's empty life. But when slightly built Jerry decides that he must take the challenge to "disturb the universe," he goes out for football; he takes terrible battering and abuse but stays with it. At first he accepts the command of the Vigils to refuse to sell chocolates, but when Archie changes the order, Jerry soon decides to defy both the Vigils and Brother Leon and to refuse on his own. Despite the abuse to which he is subjected, his determination to stand by his decision grows. But in the end, battered and bloody, he advises Goober not to stand alone, not to try disturbing the universe. The action of the story has changed Jerry, and he is therefore a dynamic character.

Change in the character of Cassie Logan is less apparent. At the beginning of *Thunder* she is impulsive and confrontational, as the situations with Lillian Jean and Mr. Barnett suggest. By the end of the novel, she has seen through the example of Uncle Hammer that confrontation often holds great danger. She knows that the pride of the Logan family consists not only in their being landowners among sharecroppers both black and white, but in their maintaining independence and dignity as well. "Doing what you gotta do," as Papa puts it, is essential to keeping self-respect.

Character change also occurs in *Shadow in Hawthorn Bay* by Janet Lunn. Scottish Mary, who grew up with her cousin Duncan in a mysteriously close relationship, has second sight and struggles to be true to her "gifts" but to rid herself of the malevolent psychic call of Duncan, who emigrated to Canada and drowned himself in Hawthorne Bay. Drawn to the Canadian wilderness by Duncan's spirit, Mary is nearly overwhelmed by the pull toward the shadow in the bay and self-destruction. Mary's growing love for Luke and for the new land, however, conflicts with and overcomes old loyalties, and she is finally free to embrace the new. She has changed and is thus a dynamic character.

Rob, the protagonist of Robert Newton Peck's *A Day No Pigs Would Die,* is another example of a dynamic character. Although Rob at twelve is accustomed to farm chores, feeding stock and milking cows, he is a boy who loves to roll in the grass with Pinky, his pig, to wander in the woods and splash in the creek. By the end of the novel Rob is a year older, and while he may not give up simple pleasures, he has faced the fact that Pinky is barren and must be killed for food, and has helped in the butchering of his pet. He has also heard from his father of the latter's approaching death, found him dead in the barn, and finally dug his father's grave and made the funeral arrangements. In facing such serious issues, Rob has changed, grown up. His diction is altered, his manner with adult farmers is that of an equal, and he is greeted by his adult neighbors as a peer.

Examination of other dynamic characters may be helpful. The protagonist of Chris Crutcher's *The Crazy Horse Electric Game* is Willie the athlete, whose father seems to live through him. "Willie's successes were Big Will's too; and likewise his failures." Big Will fosters in son Willie a feeling of indestructibility that prompts Willie to take chances, which result in a severe waterskiing injury. Willie struggles with brain damage and can no longer be a star player. His sense of humiliating defeat permeates all his relationships and activities, and even leads him to believe the deterioration of his parents' marriage is his fault. Willie's despair makes him run from home to find a place where he is unknown. The reader is aware first of Willie's sense of indestructibility, then his despair, his fear and doubt slowly growing to self-confidence as over time he becomes more optimistic and better able to manage his life. Willie is a round character whose change makes him a dynamic character.

A careful look at Tree in *Sweet Whispers, Brother Rush* by Virginia Hamilton reveals that she, too, is a round and dynamic character: loyal to her brother Dab, who is sick with porphyria, patient in helping him, faithful about her chores around the house, imaginative in her dealings with Brother Rush. Tree is nonetheless resentful that her mother gives her so much responsibility for Dab, and believes that her mother is not only shirking responsibility but is even selfish in her motives. With the help of Brother Rush, however, Tree comes to understand her mother's feelings about her sick son and is far more forgiving. Tree is changed, a dynamic character.

Although, if the action warrants it, a round character *may* change, if the character does *not* change, he or she is called a **static character.** Goober, for example, is a round character in *Chocolate War* who has the same qualities at the end of the story as he had at the beginning; he does not change and is therefore static. On the other hand, however, *flat* characters do *not* change: readers do not know them well enough to perceive their evolution from one kind of person into another kind. For example, Allie of *Catcher*, a flat character whom the reader knows little about, lived and died as an innocent. Little is known to us of D. B., a flat character who is a reader and a writer and is successful in Hollywood. If once he was innocent like Phoebe and Allie, then critical of human imperfections like Holden, the reader does not know because the reader witnesses no change.

In *Beyond the Chocolate War,* Cormier again writes of a group of characters in which the major ones from protagonist Jerry to Archie are round and complete in the drawing. Again, Cormier's omniscient narration creates sympathy for several boys in their struggle to elude Archie's control and the clutches of the group. Each feels fear when tempted to reveal the assignment or to retaliate against the unscrupulous Archie. Because the reader sees them clearly, entangled in the net that ensnares them all, concern for these round characters holds attention until the final page. Nonetheless, only Jerry clearly changes; the others are static.

To summarize, flat characters cannot change because readers know little of what they were like in the first place. It stands to reason, then, that foils or stereotypes, who are also flat characters, cannot change. They keep the same few traits throughout the story.

Number of Characters

No rigid rule exists about numbers of characters in a novel; the writer may use few or many. In such stories as *The Chocolate War* there are one principal and many others who illuminate the protagonist and contribute to the whole. In others a number of distinctive characters are essential to the theme and conflict in the story, each one well enough defined and known to avoid confusion. *Roll of Thunder* includes the Logan family of eight, several poor white families, and the powerful landowners and store keepers, as well as Mr. Jamison and various Klan members, to cite just a few.

Many characters also contribute to *Princess Ashley:* Richard Peck names a number of high school students and three sets of parents, all characters in the story of two years at Crestwood High. Readers can easily follow the action, because he makes only a few of these distinctive; the others remain background characters. Readers are well acquainted with Chelsea, the narrator, as they are with her sometime boyfriend, Pod. Ashley, the perfect, wealthy beauty whom Chelsea admires, seems less real, almost a shadow attached to the reality she craves for herself as beautiful trendsetter and leader. Chelsea is unaware that Ashley is merely a two-dimensional, go-along person wanting only to hang onto Craig, the flashiest boy in the class. When—partly through Ashley's failure to take a stand with defiant Craig, who seeks constant attention—student violence erupts and drinking results in a devastating accident, Chelsea comes to her senses and appreciates both her mother the guidance counselor and Pod the wisecracking nonconformist; she sees Ashley as someone who uses people for her own benefit. The multitude of characters in this case does not confuse or detract from the story.

A number of characters are shown in Kathryn Lasky's *Beyond the Divide,* a story that focuses on Meribah and her family, troubled by the "shunning" through which the Amish community is punishing her father for attending the funeral of a non-Amish friend. Meribah is a loving and concerned sister and daughter, unaware of the sacrifices she will have to make if she leaves the farm with her outcast father and the westward-moving pioneers. Members of the wagon train speak of her as "our innocent," "our unspoiled little girl." After the hardships of the Westward journey, Meribah is different, not an innocent girl but a young woman who has survived hunger, isolation, threat of rape, and loss of both friend and father. When she turns back alone to find again the valley where she has chosen to wring her living from the land, Goodnough the government cartographer

> watched her descend the east slope. He noticed the muscled grace of her movement as she quickly traversed the steep slope with her back-

pack. She walked with an easy balance, a confidence in her re-
flexes. . . . In her extraordinary presence, as he explained to her how to
take compass bearings and do certain calculations, he had felt smart but
not wise. He knew many things, but she knew something else . . . she
knew nature. He drew boundaries. She didn't. He measured. She invented. . . . [She] had mapped something besides the land. She had
mapped herself.

The reader has met many characters, those from Meribah's home, the
wagon train, and others along the way, each of whom adds to the story.
But at no time is the reader confused about the importance of one character or another. Numerous as the characters are, the story is a unified
whole.

But only two characters, both of whom Robb White describes in subtle ways, are needed for *Deathwatch*. Readers initially meet them
through a whispered argument between Ben the guide and protagonist,
who clearly knows his mountains and desert, and his hunting client
Madec, who seeks a perfect bighorn specimen. In three days of camping
and hunting, humorless Madec has laughed only after bragging about his
ruthless business deals: "It wasn't enough for Madec to outwit somebody,
outdeal a man in some tricky way, but the guy had to get really hurt, too."
Immediately the reader has hints about the kind of man Madec is. As he
huddles over his high-powered gun, the intensity in his eyes is far
stronger than that of a hunter: It is the look of a murderer. "I'd wait until
I saw some horns," Ben counsels Madec. After he shoots, Medac vows he
did see horns, but the brief dialogue that follows convinces the reader
that both Madec and Ben know this is a lie. Immediately Madec tries to
bribe Ben to continue hunting for the perfect specimen—if, as he says,
the one he has just killed has a nicked horn. Ben's moral strength is clear
as he rejects the bribe. When the two find that Madec has shot not a
bighorn but a prospector, honest Ben insists upon taking the body to the
sheriff for report, but Madec refuses. The way he viciously forces Ben to
hike to the highway without clothing, shoes, or water, and his methodi-
cal trailing, scouting, and shooting at Ben, and later his fabricated story of
Ben as killer are all consistent with the reader's first impressions of
Madec. Although Ben could have killed Madec in revenge, Ben remains
the principled young man. On the final page, Ben is offered the chance to
file charges against Madec for attempted murder but, true to his character, he declines, saying he had come only to report the original accidental
killing. The protagonist is a static character; despite all that has happened, Ben's integrity remains as strong at the end of the novel as it was
at the beginning. As for the story as a whole, the reader needs no more
than two characters.

Anne Burden, the protagonist in Robert C. O'Brien's *Z for
Zachariah,* is a round, or fully developed character, again one of just

two. One of the last survivors of a nuclear blast, she is an intelligent farm girl, husky and strong, one with experience in planting and cultivating the earth, gathering eggs, cooking and canning produce, and driving a tractor. She handles a gun comfortably, and knows the habits of farm and domestic animals. She is resourceful and independent, able to find her way around the countryside, to hide in the thickets, and to live off the land. She is a good student, one who loves literature and calls fragments of it to mind to help her deal with the loss of family and friends in the nuclear blast. The only other apparent survivor is Mr. Loomis, who devises one unsuccessful trick after another to trap Anne. What she must and does do to remain free seems monumental for a 16-year-old, but the reader, seeing and understanding Anne's character fully, is convinced that what she does is possible. Because of her intelligence and her understanding of her adversary Mr. Loomis, Anne manages to save herself, struggling to the point of physical combat against him. The battle, intense, suspenseful, and credible, is waged between just two characters.

What matters is the numbers needed for the story and its plot. Sometimes a whole society must be shown, as it is in *The Chocolate War* and *Roll of Thunder*. At other times, a story is complete with two characters, and another might conceivably be complete with just one.

Evaluating Character

Because the function of literature is to give pleasure and understanding, credibly developed characters are essential. By seeing and living vicariously the lives of "real people," the reader's understanding of self, others, and society is enhanced. An examination of a few additional novels and the ways in which their writers have handled characterization may clarify for us the necessity to make judgments about character development.

Some young adults enjoy the easily read series books, stories focused on the same characters in similar situations, many of them with predictable flaws. Sometimes these protagonists are stereotypes, as in *Hostage!* of the Sweet Valley High series. Elizabeth is sixteen, beautiful, and smart; Jennifer, her twin, is equally beautiful but interested only in trivial things. Bruce is handsome and rich; Regina, his girlfriend, is deaf and shy. Matt, son of the villain, is "a hunk" and good. While these qualities are perhaps within reason, real people have more than two traits, and by the end of the novel readers should know these characters far better than they actually do. The novel lacks not only characterization, but also a unifying idea and distinctive language; plot is all. When readers weary of the improbable action, nothing remains to sustain interest. More importantly, however, readers have gained no new understanding of human beings.

When science fiction first became a popular genre, plot and a strong—though cautionary—idea were everything, but science fiction has changed in recent years. Some devotees of the genre are disappointed, believing that it has become "too much like other fiction" because characterization, style, and more universal themes have grown in importance. Readings in the Tom Swift series—*The Negative Zone,* for example—reinforce what was once the general truth about science fiction: action is everything, and characters are flat and two-dimensional. *Contamination* and *Time for Yesterday* of the Star Trek series, however, show more whole human beings. The characters of Ensign Kirk, Mr. Spock, Admiral Morrow, and others are defined and described far more clearly; the series demonstrates that science fiction loses nothing when it abandons character stereotyping or total reliance on plot to carry story. Plot remains highly significant but characterization is also important—evidence, some would say, that science fiction *is* becoming more "like other fiction."

Writing of a social group easily susceptible to stereotyping, Gillian Cross has written a fast-moving novel, *Chartbreaker,* based in the interaction of members of a rock group called Kelp. Cross, however, avoids stereotypes. Finch, a singer with the group, is a hot-tempered seventeen-year-old whom readers come to know well as she defiantly refuses to be controlled by her mother's husband-to-be, or by Christie, the leader of Kelp. Her short fuse and tough demeanor are significant keys to her successful interaction with Christie, the male singer to whom she is attracted. His cool, detached management of the band is finally broken when Finch in her anger gets through to him. The plot is effectively developed, the characters of other band members distinctive, and suspense carried primarily by keen interest in the character Finch.

Stereotypes, which as noted above can be highly useful as background figures, are not always dealt with effectively. Consider M. E. Kerr's novel *Gentlehands,* which concerns Buddy, the son of a policeman, who falls in love with a wealthy summer resident. The two families are starkly and stereotypically different: the policeman's home and family are simple and conventional, their conversation without refinement, and their interests ordinary. Skye's wealthy family has an exotic home, extravagantly expensive cars, and ostentatious parties; Skye herself has a cultural veneer of knowledge about literature, music, language, and travel. What little readers know of the two families is meant to show and explain Buddy's effort to deny his own simple home life for the sake of feeling acceptable to wealthy Skye. Because the families are so flat, however, their depiction fails to set up the conflict in values facing Buddy. There seems little reason to choose either.

Another of Kerr's novels, *I'll Love You When You're More Like Me,* also falls into a stereotyping trap. Charlie, who is well over six feet tall and has just come out of the closet to admit he is gay, says that life was simpler when the media did not try to defy homosexual stereotypes by revealing the name of every muscular athlete who is gay. While seeming to decry gay stereotyping, Kerr then describes Charlie as having a "high-pitched sibilant voice," and a "strange, small-stepped, loping walk." Wally's father, furthermore, tells him that you can tell what a girl will look like as an adult if you just look at her mother. Lauralei Rabinowitz's mother "had blond streaks through her wiry black hair, wore long, thick false eyelashes, and favored red and orange dresses gussied up with fur capes made from the skins of tiny animals." Wally thus assumes he can expect adult Lauralei to exhibit these traits, an extension of the unfair stereotype of older Jewish women. Stereotyping has set back the reader's understanding of people.

Look next at *Tiger Eyes* by Judy Blume, who has again written a story with events and problems that appeal to young adults, her greatest strength as a writer. But once again her novel is short on character development and therefore lacks the needed unity of character and action. Although Davey, the principal character, tells the story in first person, we do not know her well enough to understand the motivation for her actions. The same lack of clear motivation is true for others; for example, after Davey's father is killed in a robbery in his 7-Eleven store, her Aunt Bitsy and Uncle Walter come for the funeral, stay a few days, and take Davey, her mother, and her brother Jason back to Los Alamos with them. None of the five, however, express feelings of ambivalence or pain, or explain the rationale for uprooting the family. Davey, the most developed character, seems hardly more than a shadow; her grief keeps her at home as she sleeps time away while missing school, time that passes with little mention of her feelings. Once enrolled in school in Los Alamos, she quickly finds a friend in Jane. Jane says her life isn't easy and she drinks during and after school, but we are never given reason to understand either action or motivation. Very soon Davey wins a leading role in the school musical with little difficulty.

Readers are told that the reason Davey and Wolf—whom she meets by chance in the canyon—find themselves to be soul mates is that their fathers are dead or dying, but we do not actually witness their discovery of each other. Given the minimal conversation between the two, Wolf at a more mature twenty seems unlikely to connect effectively with Davey at an immature fifteen; if readers knew of some meaningful conversation between them, however, they might be convinced. The device of having Wolf give his father a windup bear (a toy with unknown significance), which his father then wants Davey to have at his death, is a contrived way to connect the three, or even the two characters. Davey's mother tells her in the last pages that Uncle Walter is a rigid person, but there is no evidence, no action demonstrating his rigidity, the cause of it, or even why it matters. Davey's mother seems a grieving shadow who for many months keeps to her room, then after a few sessions with a counselor comes out to take a job and to find a boyfriend who soon wants to marry her. When, in abrupt action without involvement of character, the family of three returns to Atlantic City, readers have not seen them arrive at the decision. Instead, the widow is remarkably healed, they say goodbye, and all take off for home, miraculously changed merely by time and distance. There are no personal conflicts, anxieties, or actions resulting from traumatic experience and leading to convincing new self-awareness or supplying reason for further action to convince the reader. Without believable characters whose behavior is influenced by their personal traits, the story is contrived, merely a disappointing series of events that makes no contribution to the understanding of human beings.

As noted above, novels vary in the numbers of characters involved in the story. In some stories there may be one or two principal characters and several others of lesser or very minor importance. In others, a number of distinctive characters are essential, each one significant, defined well enough and known to us. If a writer chooses to use many characters, the reasons for their inclusion must be clear. In Margaret Mahy's *The Tricksters,* however, there is a family of seven: mother Naomi, father Jack, older son Charlie, younger son Bennie, older daughter Christobel, protagonist daughter Ariadne (confusingly called Harry), and younger daughter Serena. Seven guests arrive to spend a New Zealand Christmas with the family: single mother Emma and toddler Tibby, Anthony from England, Christobel and Charlie's friend Robert, and three supernatural strangers who seem to be parts of one person and are named Felix, Ovid, and Hadleigh. Because interest is divided among the many characters each with a small part to play in the story, the novel lacks clear focus for character and action.

Summary

We discover great pleasure in reading about beings that are similar to ourselves or like people we know, beings who may seek peaceful or adventurous lives, who find peer relationships easy or difficult, who struggle with decisions and disappointments, and whose progress to maturity, like our own, is sometimes three steps forward and two steps back. As we read of them, our understanding of ourselves and others increases.

In fiction as in life, people are different. In life we learn to know people by their appearances, what they say, what they do, and what others say about them. In fiction, we have the additional advantage of the author's remarks about what characters think and feel, as well as views of past experiences. Flat characters have few traits, round characters many. Two particular kinds of flat characters that also serve as background figures or contrasts are stereotypes and foils. Central characters in the action are round, so that by believing in their reality we are led to discover something about humanity; this discovery convinces us that conflict in life, like that in the story, is significant. Flat characters do not change, but round characters may or may not change or be dynamic; if characters change, however, we expect that change to be believable and the result of action.

Like Jerry Renault and Cassie Logan, young adults are often in conflict, may see issues as either right or wrong, and may refuse to compromise or to accept others' choices as valid. The experience of a good work of fiction assists them in recognizing themselves as part of humanity as well as seeing humanity in themselves. If literature is to help them in the discovery of the nature of humankind, nothing—neither intricate plot nor breathtaking suspense, exotic setting nor terrorizing tone, hysterical laughter nor sentimental tears—nothing can substitute for solid character development in the creation of satisfying literature for young adults.

Note

1. Henry James, *The Art of Fiction* (New York: Oxford University Press, 1948), p. 13.

Recommended Books Cited in This Chapter

Baldwin, James. *If Beale Street Could Talk*. New York: Dial, 1974.

Cormier, Robert. *Beyond the Chocolate War*. New York: Knopf, Dell, 1986.

———. *The Chocolate War*. New York: Random House, 1974.

Cross, Gillian. *Chartbreaker*. New York: Dell, 1986.

Crutcher, Chris. *The Crazy Horse Electric Game*. New York: Dell, 1988.

Ferris, Jean. *Across the Grain*. New York: Farrar, Straus & Giroux, 1990.

Greene, Bette. *Summer of My German Soldier*. New York: Dial, 1973.

Hamilton, Virginia. *Sweet Whispers, Brother Rush*. New York: Avon, 1983.

Lasky, Kathryn. *Beyond the Divide*. New York: Macmillan, 1983.

L'Engle, Madeleine. *A Wrinkle in Time*. New York: Farrar, Straus & Giroux, 1962.

Mahy, Margaret. *The Tricksters*. New York: Macmillan, 1987.

Mazer, Norma Fox. *Silver*. New York: Morrow, 1988.

O'Brien, Robert C. *Z for Zachariah*. New York: Macmillan, 1975.

Paterson, Katherine. *Jacob Have I Loved*. New York: Harper & Row, 1980.

Peck, Richard. *Princess Ashley*. New York: Dell, 1988.

Peck, Robert Newton. *A Day No Pigs Would Die*. New York: Knopf, 1989.

Salinger, J. D. *The Catcher in the Rye*. Boston: Little, Brown, 1951.

Sleator, William. *House of Stairs*. New York: Dutton, 1974.

Taylor, Mildred. *Let the Circle Be Unbroken*. New York: Dial, 1981.

———. *Roll of Thunder, Hear My Cry*. New York: Dial, 1976.

White, Robb. *Deathwatch*. New York: Dell, 1973.

Permanent Connections

Sue Ellen Bridgers

—3—

Plot

When asked about a novel most readers, whether old or young, will respond with a summary of plot—what happens. Perhaps plot is not the most important element in the novel, but it is the easiest element to talk about. We use action verbs and active adverbs, vivid adjectives and specific nouns. Readers expect things to happen. The order in which things move and events happen in a story is called **narrative,** the sequence of events showing characters in action. In *The Chocolate War* the Vigils rule Trinity school and order Jerry Renault to refuse for two weeks to sell the 200 boxes of chocolates. Jerry refuses to accept the order passively, and at the end of two weeks continues to refuse. The Vigils and Brother Leon are infuriated by his defiance and with midnight phone calls, ambush, and football violence try harrassing Jerry to force his submission. When he is adamant, the Vigils punish him by beating him mercilessly. Unlike the random sequence of events in our lives, the ordering and planning of action in a plot is no accident but is the deliberate choice of the writer, the sequence best able to tell the author's story. If the writer plots the story carefully, the story will also include conflict, tension, and action to arouse and hold interest. This total is then more than narrative; it is **plot.**

Most readers want the same thing: happenings, questions needing answers, answers to fit the varied questions, outcomes both unhappy and happy, the growing, shifting, and turning of events. Young adults, however, are in the period of the greatest change in life, and that constant change leading to mature adulthood involves vast numbers of serious concerns and possible outcomes both gratifying and frightening. One of the ways in which they discover themselves is through following the circuitous trails and seemingly arbitrary switchbacks in the lives of credible fictional characters. The great question of youth is "What if. . . ?" The great question that literature addresses is also "What if. . . ?" The variety of accompanying questions is endless, just as the variety of situations is endless.

Types of Narrative Order

In addition to creating characters, one of the great privileges of the writer is that of ordering existence, arranging events, creating any kind of order. A work of fiction may focus on a single day, or a single hour, and yet for pages and chapters involve a reader intensely in that brief time span. The single hour may be so heavily charged with significance that everything in the protagonist's life changes—health and mobility, future career plans, relationships with parent or siblings, school, home, and country. Meanwhile, the writer may ignore or summarize great segments of time in the protagonist's life because they have little bearing on this particular piece of action. Selectivity and purpose determine what is to be included.

Narrative order, or the sequence in which events are related, may follow any of several patterns, but the most common is a chronological arrangement. Throughout this chapter, kinds of order and elements of plotting will be discussed.

Chronological Order

Of course, people live their lives in simple **chronology,** May 5 followed closely by May 6, classes followed closely by exams as night follows day follows night. If a story relates events in the order of their happening, it is chronologically recounted. Moving from place to place does not disturb time order, nor does showing action in one place then showing action in another, although the actions are occuring simultaneously: "Meanwhile, in biology class. . . " Although one event may follow another in the telling, they are occuring simultaneously, occupying the same moment of time; the action is still chronological. The touchstones chosen for close examination in this text, *The Chocolate War* and *Roll of Thunder, Hear My Cry,* move in **chronological order**, showing one event following another.

A great many novels are told in a strict chronological order, such as *A Circle Unbroken* by Sollace Hotze, the story of Rachel stolen by Indians at ten and returned to her white family seven years later. Others use variations, like the one found in *In Lane Three, Alex Archer* by Tessa Duder, the story of a New Zealand girl competing in the national swim tournaments in order to qualify for the Rome Olympics. An italicized page of Alex's thinking precedes each chapter, which in turn follows the last in chronological order of the action; although the chapter itself begins in action only mentally relating to swimming, each shows Alex's thinking as she acts, slicing through the water.

"Concentrate! One hand has brushed the cork loops that make up the lane ropes. That might cost me a hundredth of a second, and the race. . . ."

"Looking ahead through my bow wave, I see the glint of blue tile. . . ."

"If you're ahead after the turn, don't let up. . . ."

"I am! I can, Andy. I'm closing the gap. . . ."

Pam Conrad has also chosen an interesting variation in chronological narrative order for her story *My Daniel.* At eighty Grandmother Julia Summerwaite has come east to visit her son and her grandchildren and to see the Natural History Museum, which houses dinosaur bones from Nebraska. As she and the two children move slowly from floor to floor, noting each display along the way, she stops to rest and take off her shoes. At each rest stop, Julia recalls a bit more of her childhood and the reader is swept into moments from the past that now become immediate action: on the Nebraska prairie as she and her older brother, Daniel, dream of finding dinosaur bones, meet exploring paleontologists, in guarded secrecy actually find the skeletal parts and notify the authority who comes to excavate and ship them back east. Each bit of the immediate present as the group moves through the museum is far less significant than Julia's vivid memories that in their own chronological order include her relationship to her dearly loved brother, the excitement of the discovery, his death by lightning, and the salvaging of the skeleton.

Some writers make use of a plotting device in narrative order called a **frame,** opening and closing the story with the same incident. S. E. Hinton's *Rumble Fish* uses a frame effectively. The first chapter occurs on a California beach where Rusty-James meets his friend Steve of six years past; Steve is on vacation from college, and Rusty is "just bummin' around." Steve is excited about their meeting and wants to reminisce over dinner about the old days of drinking, knife fights, and the Motorcycle Boy, but Rusty-James, who has spent several years in the reformatory, is reminded only of his brother's violent death and the unhappiness of the old days. Chapter two begins the story of the two boys' friendship and loyalty during a time of violence, terror, and precarious survival. The final chapter returns to the meeting on the California beach, showing Steve pursuing a normal life and Rusty-James, although no longer involved in violence, not yet set on a road to a happy or productive life.

Two stories about the Viet Nam war era also use a framing device. Bobbie Ann Mason frames her story *In Country* by using chapters at beginning and end that show action occurring in the final car trip to the Vietnam Veterans' monument. Theresa Nelson's *And One for All* begins with a prologue set on Easter Sunday, 1968, in which Geraldine is riding the bus from White Plains to Washington, D.C., to find Sam, her brother Wing's best friend, to tell him that Wing has been killed. Then the story moves to 1966 and 1967 to show Wing's high school days with Sam, his being suspended and barred from playing basketball, his disgust with his school record, and his enlistment at 18. The two final chapters return the reader once again to Geraldine's bus trip and her finding Sam, who is leading a peace march; the novel then concludes with Wing's funeral and a reconciliation between war protester Sam and the family of soldier Wing.

Robert Cormier's second book for young adult readers, *I Am the Cheese*, has a complex plot of interwoven levels and chronologies lacing together the story of Adam's psychological search for his father with his search into his memories and his cycling through fantasies. Describing the plot complexity of the novel is difficult, no substitute for reading. The novel's central enigma concerns what Adam Farmer, once Paul Delmonte, knows about his past, and perhaps more importantly, who needs to find out—Adam for his return to mental health or the government for its witness relocation program. Adam's father, an investigative reporter, had uncovered and exposed important evidence of corruption, been given a new identity, relocated with his family, and lived in terror of discovery. Adam, who learns something of his parents' secret before their mysterious deaths, must now live as a stranger without a past.

The story revolves in circles around Adam's continuous and frustrating struggle to recall his fear of real memories, mysterious Mr. Grey and his visits, sudden "vacation" trips, and the terrifying car that seems intent on running down the family. Readers later discover that Adam's bicycle trip in search of his father, a second plot level, is unreal; his repetitious circling of the sanitarium grounds on his bicycle is a trip that cannot end but perpetually revolves as the novel opens and closes with the same paragraph: "I am riding the bicycle and I am on Route 31 . . . on my way to Rutterburg, Vermont . . . the wind like a snake slithering up my sleeves. . . . But I keep pedaling, I keep pedaling." Interspersed is still another vein of narrative, Adam's interrogation—by a psychiatrist—in order to help? by a government agent in order to determine the degree of risk from Adam's "knowing too much"? The novel, like the child's continuous game "The Farmer in the Dell," moves in circles. The last verse, sung in the final pages when psychologically damaged Adam, whose parents have been killed in a violent gangland murder—or perhaps by the government, concerned lest they reveal too much?—sings to himself, "The cheese stands alone. . . . I am the cheese."

Young people are often reticent and isolated, but Adam's discomfort is exacerbated by fear, puzzlement, distrust, even terror. As the story moves in and out of Adam's bicycle ride, through his fantasies and his memories and the dialogue with the psychiatrist, the actual events of his past life are revealed and his present life in an institution becomes clearer. By the story's final pages, we surmise that Adam is not being psychologically healed; the interrogation is merely politically expedient. In the government records, all characters are mere numbers, and Adam will never be free of the entanglements of his past nor of the recorded interviews, but will merely be a designated number, a series of digits in a government file. The intricate plot is skillfully written; readers are intrigued, puzzled, and kept in breathless suspense by a master storyteller who leads them through time sequences that collide, mingle, and separate in a complex narrative order.

A plot summary is never the story. Once again a description of narrative order does not do justice to another Cormier novel, *Fade,* in which plotting is similar in complexity to that in *I Am the Cheese,* and equally absorbing. In succession from uncle to nephew, the power to fade into invisibility is passed on and used for innocent nosiness as well as for murder. As Paul Roget recounts his transformation from a gentle, inquisitive thirteen-year-old who only uses his power to fade out of curiosity, to a vicious but invisible avenger willing to murder, his efforts to control the fade are halfhearted. But when Paul's own little brother dies for no apparent reason, Paul firmly decides to control the personality-changing fade. Part two focuses on Paul's niece Susan, who years later has found fragments of Paul's novel and tries to separate reality from fiction. She questions the story of Paul's fading as autobiographical. The third part of the novel, another fragmentary account of Paul's struggle with the power, is followed by Ozzie's story: Paul's nephew Ozzie can fade, a trait that has seized this miserably unhappy boy and turned him into a criminal. Paul seeks to warn him of the dangers of fading. The debate about behavior while invisible occurs within Ozzie, but when the evil force is in ascendance, Ozzie attacks Paul. The final pages return to Susan's speculation about her uncle's real life. Again, the story's suspense is gripping; it forces the reader to wonder about the possibility that knowing one is invisible or unidentifiable might encourage one to depravity.

Flashbacks

Fiction occasionally makes use of **flashbacks** in which the writer chooses to interrupt chronology to recount some event out of the character's past, perhaps showing how that event influences the character's response to an occurence in the present. Or the writer may show a past event that caused the present one. In any case, the writer chooses to juggle time to make a point about the character and the story. Margaret Mahy's novel *Memory* is filled with suspense periodically broken by flashbacks. Jon Dart searches for an explanation that would clarify why Bonny, his dead sister Janine's best friend, made false statements at the time of Janine's death. The story begins at midnight as Jon approaches the Rivendell Community and walks in on an unfamiliar group at Bonny's house. Her distrustful mother appears and scolds him for drinking. Jon, muddled as he is, goes back in time to Janine's death. *"Through the flawed glass of memory he saw Bonny and Janine, crouching on either side of a circle of daisy beads, watching intently as Bonny cast the* *cards with pictures on them up into the air. . . ."* Jon is sent home, then awakens close to a taxi stand and begins *"to go in and out of the old memory which he knew by heart, but which to him was always extraordinary. . . . Once again Janine fell. For a moment Jonny, seeing her feet leave the ground, had believed she was actually beginning to fly. . . ."* A few pages later, the flashback of memory recurs: *"The first test was always the same. Climbing past the danger sign under the chain fence. . . ."* All of these and the subsequent flashbacks are memories printed in italics; each one brings the reader a bit closer to the answers Jon seeks.

Many other examples of flashback occur in literature for young adults, who easily follow shifts in time and recognize cause and effect relationships. Stella Pevsner in the novel *How Could You Do It, Diane?* moves in and out of chronology and flashbacks as Bethany tries to understand her sister Diane's reasons for suicide and recalls moments with her. Flashback is also the device used by Zibby O'Neal in *A Formal Feeling;* it shows Anne's relationship with her mother before she died contrasted with her present relationship with her father's second wife. The flashback reveals how different the two women are, and thus illuminates the difficulty Anne has in adjusting to the second wife, who wisely does not try to be mother. Flashback in all its varieties is a useful plotting device.

Types of Conflict

More than mere narrative order or story line is involved in a plot. Plot also involves **conflict.** A group of other terms might be used to describe conflict: tension, friction, alternatives, forces, excitement and suspense, discovery, resolution, all elements of conflict. **Conflict** occurs when the **protagonist,** or central character, struggles against some kind of **antagonist,** or opposing force. When conflict is added to order, the result is plot.

Primarily four kinds of conflict occur in literature: person-against-self or internal conflict, person-against-person, person-against-society, and person-against-nature. Sometimes a novel has elements of more than one kind of conflict. Look now at each of them.

Person-Against-Self

The touchstone *The Chocolate War* has a strong **person-against-self** or **internal** conflict, since Jerry's brave wish to defy the Vigils conflicts with his fear of their increasingly furious attacks on him. As noted earlier, Jerry is challenging himself to defy the universe, but the effects of his defiance are brutally vicious and psychologically scathing as he struggles to hold out. *Catcher in the Rye* offers another example. Holden Caulfield, a young adult torn by the discrepancies between the real and the ideal, is in conflict about wealth, prep schools, life goals, love, sex, homosexuality, concern for his parents, the wish to keep children innocent, and a host of other issues.

Internal conflict also holds interest in Cynthia Voigt's *A Solitary Blue*. At seven Jeff is left with his father after his mother's departure. Following a visit with her several years later, Jeff maintains a fantasy that she loves him, her spontaneity and beauty somehow holding him ransom. But after another visit with her, his many unanswered letters finally persuade him that she does not care about him. Love for a birth mother is strong even in an abandoned child; Jeff struggles with his guilt over no longer loving his mother until at 17 he is able to tell her honestly that he no longer loves her nor wants to live with her.

The conflict in Rosa Guy's *The Friends* is also internal. Phyllisia Cathy, a new immigrant from the West Indies, is struggling not only with the process of integration into the Harlem school system, but also with a clarification of her values. In the harsh and unfamiliar school environment she desperately needs friends to help her get along, to protect her and to educate her about how to be smart without being resented. The girl who befriends Phyllisia does not fit her mental image of the desirable friend: Edith is not clean or well-dressed or totally honest, nor does she speak well. She lives in a dirty apartment, often skips school, and is solely responsible for a number of equally untidy siblings. As Phyllisia endures her father's prison-warden rules and his deceptive bragging about his exotic restaurant that she soon finds to be a modest and even sleazy cafe, and observes her mother's death, a class ambush, and a riot, she finds that in each case Edith is her only loyal standby. Phyllisia comes to see that she has overvalued middle-class niceness. When misfortune comes to Edith, Phyllisia lacks the courage to disobey her father and seek out Edith to show compassion for the big family whose father has disappeared, whose eldest brother has been shot by the police, whose youngest has died for lack of medical care, and who are now dispersed to the orphanage. As Phyllisia recognizes her materialistic values, she also recognizes that Edith's values of friendship and loyalty to family and friends are those that matter to her. When she returns to ask Edith's forgiveness and promises to stay in touch, her internal struggle is resolved.

A similar person-against-self conflict exists in Linda Crew's *Children of the River,* a story of a young immigrant's struggle to adapt to a new country, new customs, and new friends without losing the approval of her immigrant fellows. Sundara, who has left her own family behind and now lives with the family of her aunt, has come to Oregon from Cambodia and is attracted to the American Jonathan. Although she knows her family would strongly disapprove, she has lunch with him, walks with him in the halls, and even lies to her aunt about meeting his family. When her aunt finds out that, honest and open as Sundara and Jonathan are, his white skin has touched Sundara's hand, she is angry, claiming that now she will never find a husband for Sundara; she forces Sundara to promise never to talk with Jonathan again. Jonathan cannot understand the Cambodian restrictions, and the promise is extremely difficult for Sundara to keep, her wish to continue to see him strong. Her internal conflict is intense: keep her promise and lose Jonathan, or talk to him, defy her culture, and lose her roots within the family and community.

Even quiet novels like *The One-Eyed Cat* by Paula Fox rely upon conflict. *Cat* concerns Ned's internal conflict about his guilt; tempted by the rifle given him by Uncle Hilary, he fires one forbidden shot before his father stows the gun in the attic. The appearance a few days later of a half-blind cat convinces him that his shot is responsible. Ned's secret fills him with guilt that is unresolved until with his mother he sees the one-eyed cat playing in the "cat moon" moonlight with her kittens. When he learns that his mother has known all along that he had fired the gun, and hears about how she too had been unable to be perfectly good, he is reassured.

A final example of internal conflict is another quiet story. *The Island* by Gary Paulsen is told through Wil, who has reluctantly moved with his family from the city to northern Wisconsin. Wil spends days and nights alone on a small island, watching the loons, fish, and turtles and "going into himself" to discover who he is, to consider what his forebears were like, and what his values are. As he writes and paints and watches, he achieves a serenity that allows him to return home a more self-aware fifteen-year-old.

Person-Against-Person

Z for Zachariah by Robert O'Brien exemplifies a **person-against-person conflict.** The story plunges immediately into suspense. Anne Burden's journal begins, "May 20./I am afraid./Someone is coming." The someone turns out to be the only other known survivor of nuclear radiation who tries in every way to control or even enslave Ann. O'Brien masterfully sustains the suspense throughout the novel as Anne, who had thought herself the only survivor of the nuclear blast, nurses Mr. Loomis through his radiation sickness and watches him as he grows increasingly intent upon controlling her, regulating not only the farming efforts but every aspect of her daily life, and finally assaulting her so that she must flee.

> And then it happened. To my absolute astonishment, he . . . reached over and took my hand. "Grabbed" would be a better word. He took it very quickly and hard, pulled it to his chair, jerking me toward him so that I almost fell over. He held my hand between both of his.
>
> . . .
>
> After that I felt embarrassed, awkward. . . . Awkward because, the way he had pulled me, I could not sit right in my chair, but was leaning

> off balance. And afraid, finally, because when I tried to pull away he
> just tightened his grip.

When Mr. Loomis shoots her in the ankle, Anne realizes he wants her as
his prisoner. As these events occur, however, Anne's journal records the
many ways in which she reassures herself by finding herself at fault, or
thinking she misreads Mr. Loomis's motives. As she calms her fears, the
suspense ebbs briefly until once again she is assaulted by his trickery, and
her anxiety—as well as the reader's—is heightened. Clearly, Anne's conflict is with Mr. Loomis, another person.

A second example of person-against-person conflict, a life-and-death
struggle, occurs in Robb White's *Deathwatch,* in which Ben serves as
wilderness guide to Madec. When Madec shoots impulsively and acciden-
tally kills an old prospector, Ben insists that the body must be turned over
to authorities, although he willingly agrees that the death was accidental.
Madec, however, afraid that he will be arrested for murder, can think of
only one way out—killing Ben. When Madec, who has stripped Ben of
food, water, and protective clothing, stalks Ben in the huge expanse of
desert, the struggle is clearly person-against-person.

Person-Against-Society

In addition to the person-against-self conflict for Jerry, Cormier in *The
Chocolate War* shows a second conflict, this one **person-against-society.** The reader is plunged immediately into the action and conflict:
"They murdered him," reads the first line of page one; the use of "they"
suggests that this is not a one-to-one combat but person-society conflict.
By the end of paragraph three, the reader knows that Jerry is being tested
by the football coach and players, and can guess that this kind of testing
will continue throughout the novel. The complexity of Jerry's conflict results from his standing up against the pressures in Trinity school. When
the Vigils single him out, ordering him first to refuse to sell the candy and
then to consent, Jerry first yields, but later decides on his own to "disturb
the universe" by defiance. The Vigils try coercion through nighttime
phone calls, football violence, gang assault, locker ransacking, and finally
resort to the brutal fight.

Cassie of *Roll of Thunder* is in conflict with herself as she learns to
control her impulsiveness and to understand the Logan pride that allows
them to be strong and independent without being foolhardy. But the additional conflict is person-against-society, as Cassie fights her personal
battle with the oppressive white society, including being forced off the
sidewalk, ignored in the general store, splattered with mud by the white
children's school bus, and other ignominious treatment. A combination
of conflicts also engages the reader in Jessamyn West's novel *The Massacre at Fall Creek.* The person-society conflict is between the protagonist Hannah allied with her justice-loving community of settlers versus

the group of five who massacre the Indian "trespassers." Hannah wants justice for the Indians, but some of the settlers regard the Indiana territory as theirs and the Indians as lawless trespassers. Readers sensitive to character watch Hannah's own internal conflict as she must choose between the two young attorneys, one who defends the Indians but exploits Hannah, and the other a kind man who defends the white marauders.

Person-Against-Nature

Island of the Blue Dolphins by Scott O'Dell exemplifies the **person-against-nature** conflict. Karana, left alone to survive on an island, knows the fish and vegetation her people have subsisted on. Yet she encounters problems as, for example, she tries to harvest food safely without losing her life to the stranglehold of the octopus, or builds a shelter to protect herself from the wild dogs that had killed her brother. She is alone and lonely, her life filled with the struggle for survival. One night a rumbling sound awakens her and she sees that the tide is incredibly low; an earthquake is in progress, soon followed by a tidal wave.

> The air was suddenly tight around me. There was a faint sound as if some giant animal were sucking the air in and in through its teeth. The rumbling came closer out of an empty sky, filling my ears. Then beyond the gleam of the beach and the bare rocks and reefs, more than a league beyond them, I saw a great white crest moving down upon the island.
>
> It seemed to move slowly between the sea and the sky, but it was the sea itself. . . . In terror I ran along the sandspit. I ran and stumbled and got up and ran again. The sand shuddered under my feet as the first wave struck. Spray fell around me like rain . . . filled with pieces of kelp and small fish.
>
> . . . Water was already rushing around my knees, pulling from every direction. The cliff rose in front of me and though the rocks were slippery with sea moss I found a hold for a hand and then a foot. . . . I dragged myself upward. . . .
>
> I stood facing the rock, with my feet on a narrow ledge and one hand thrust deep into a crack. . . . The first wave was trying to reach the sea and the second one was struggling toward the shore.

For several more paragraphs, O'Dell describes the rush of the waters and Karana's struggle with the tidal wave, a fight to cling to the rock long enough for all to subside. A tense battle ensues in which her courage and will are finally rewarded with safety. Karana has battled the force of nature and has survived still another threat to her life.

Not strictly a *person*-nature conflict but rather a protagonist-nature conflict is vivid in Whitley Strieber's *Wolf of Shadows*. Bonds slowly grow between the wolves and the human survivors of a nuclear blast. The black wolf, the central character, cautiously adopts a human mother and her child for mutual support as with death dogging their footsteps they find their way south from the epicenter, the "water country" of Minnesota. Nuclear winter is upon them, fleeing human bodies have died in their cars, human predators have killed others to steal their food, then have starved and frozen. Wildlife is almost nonexistent as food for them all. The conflict of protagonist against nature is vividly described.

> The rain agitated Wolf of Shadows, for it was colder than it should be. It was also unlike any he had ever smelled before. It was full of fire-scent and the color of the lake shore mud. It came in driven drops, spattering the trees and the rocks, making everything gray.

> Wolf of Shadows shook himself and then went off toward his hill, intending to see the extent of the sleet. On the way up his claws clattered on ice. When he reached the top a vicious wind struck him. The sleet stung his face, making him turn his flank to the storm's fury.

> The days passed without counting, a seasonless twilight of ice and brutal wind. The sleet changed slowly to hard-grained snow and then to ice as fine as sand. The cold clutched them more and more tightly. Whenever Wolf of Shadows thought it could not get worse the wind rose again and the ice seemed to penetrate not only his fur but his skin, and finally his bones and blood.

Although not as common as other kinds of conflict, such stories are often highly suspenseful. Using a true occurrence as starting point, Arthur Roth in *The Iceberg Hermit* follows Allan Gordon from shipwreck to his return to Aberdeen, Scotland. When he is the sole survivor of a whaling boat wrecked in the Arctic fog, Allan faces attack by two polar bears, fifty-below-zero temperatures, and the threat of his iceberg crashing into another or cracking apart.

Several stories for slightly younger readers show conflict with nature. Harry Mazer's *The Island Keeper* tells of Cleo's deliberate retreat to an island in Lake Michigan, and of her growing skill in living off the land as she manages to survive and to grow into an independent young woman. In *The Cay,* Theodore Taylor tells of a shipwreck in the West Indies during World War II. Blinded by a head blow as well as by the brilliant Caribbean sun, Phillip—but not Timothy, his black companion—survives alone on the arid island, tested by the need to find food, to fish, to climb the palms for coconuts, and finally to survive the hurricane, despite his sun-blindness. Jean George's novel *Julie of the Wolves* offers another example of a person-nature conflict, survival in the Arctic reaches in which the wolves are helpful to Julie. The three pets of Sheila Burnford's *The Incredible Journey* act as protagonists and survive a struggle with the

Canadian wilderness as they make their way back to their original home. Such conflicts in books for readers of any age require that the writer convey not only the intensity of the struggle but also a clear picture of nature, the antagonist. O'Dell, Roth, Mazer, Taylor, George, and Burnford have all effectively fulfilled that requisite.

Patterns of Action

Plot is more than the conflict or the sequence of action. In plotting a story, the writer must prepare the reader for the action by telling of events or circumstances relevant to the rest of the story. Depending upon the story, the writer must include varying amounts of information. In *Tex,* for example, S. E. Hinton prepares the reader for the action by providing **exposition,** or background information. This early exposition shows that Tex and Mason live alone, that their father left to ride in rodeos several months ago, that their mother is dead, and that Tex stole a car at 12. The brothers are struggling financially, so poor that basketball star Mason has had to sell their two horses. The house is near collapse, the barn merely a lean-to with two stalls. This exposition sets the stage for Mason's ulcer, his need for a college scholarship, and the many possibilities for Tex's getting into trouble with drugs, alcohol, or wild driving. The first pattern of action might be diagramed as a straight horizontal line, represented, for example, by *Catcher in the Rye.* Events follow one another chronologically without coming to any high point. Flashbacks do not occur; past action is reported through Holden's meandering narrative.

To cite another example, exposition in Katherine's Paterson's *Jacob Have I Loved* also occurs throughout the first two chapters, enabling us to see Wheeze's competition with Caroline, her twin whose talents, ambitions, and manner differ from Wheeze's own. We observe the family dynamics as we see the particular attention paid to sickly Caroline by her parents and note the reasons for Wheeze's feeling left out. We watch Wheeze's competition with her sister, the impact of the difficult grandmother on them all, and Caroline's success in everything she tries, even to finally marrying Call after he returns from the army. Wheeze has meanwhile fought to be as different as possible from Caroline, early on setting her heart on becoming a waterman, a career Caroline would never consider. In a quiet climax of conflict resolution, Wheeze is reconciled to leaving the island, to becoming a nurse rather than a doctor. The story ends by revealing that Wheeze marries an older man with children and lives a quiet but productive life as a nurse-midwife in rural Appalachia. Her parents' admission that they will miss her even more than Caroline, her satisfying marriage, and her own compassion for sick children and their caring parents is the brief conclusion.

A second pattern of action, a **progressive plot,** is one in which the conflict moves suspensefully to a peak. If the pattern for *The Chocolate War* were diagramed, a line ascending from left to right, beginning to end, would stop abruptly at the highest point. The opening line of the novel, "They murdered him," presents conflict and arouses interest. Throughout the early chapters, the exposition acquaints readers with Jerry and the other characters, and introduces Jerry's feeling that his father's grieving has made him an unfeeling automation whose life is empty and meaningless. Jerry decides he will not succumb to such paralysis, and is tempted to "disturb the universe" of Trinity. **Complications,** part of the increasing tension, soon follow, as Jerry at first refuses to sell the chocolates, then defiantly challenges the power of the Vigils, who devise ingenious means of intimidating him. In several chapters of **rising action** that move toward the high point in the plot, the reader inches down Brother Leon's roll-call record of boxes sold, naming students in alphabetical order from Malloran to Parmentier to Renault, who by his defiance faces threats. The Vigils' harrassment of Jerry ends with the brutal boxing match, stopping abruptly at the high point when Jerry is badly beaten. Jerry lies battered, semiconscious, and floating in pain, trying desperately to tell his friend Goober not to defy the universe. And Cormier leaves it at that

A Hero Ain't Nothin' But a Sandwich by Alice Childress proceeds in similar mounting tension, and at the high point leaves readers with a question: will Benjie show up at the detox center? As Butler Craig, his stepfather, waits patiently, moving from the entranceway to the steps and ultimately to the curb so Benjie cannot miss him, he says, "Benjie, I believe in you . . . I'm waitin' right here . . . I'm waitin' for you. . . ." Left here, readers don't know whether or not Benjie will come. An **open ending** results, one without definite answer but that leaves issues or actions unresolved. In a similar ending, Sue Ellen Bridgers's *Permanent Connections* leaves readers not knowing whether Rob will return to Montclair or stay in Tyler Mills, committed to staying with his father's family until Uncle Fairlee's hip is healed and Rob is no longer needed. Despite the open ending, readers are certain that Rob has changed sufficiently to be comfortable with either choice. Another story with high suspense that leaves the reader wondering about the final outcome is O'Brien's *Z for Zachariah:* readers do not know whether Anne will survive and live her dream of teaching school children. Perhaps she will be caught and enslaved by Mr. Loomis, or perhaps despite her suit of radiation-proof fibers she will die.

The third pattern of action, again a progressive plot, is more complex. Here action ascends to a climactic peak and briefly descends; diagramed, the long line of plot would peak, then drop briefly as the last questions are answered. The story gives needed background information or exposition and moves with complications and rising action to a climax in which the conflict is resolved and the knotted situation is now "untangled" in a **denouement**—or as others might put it, all loose ends are neatly tied. The effect is a **closed ending** that shows outcomes.

Suspense

The term *suspense* has been used frequently up to this point, on the assumption that its meaning is clear. Stories with action that rises to high points rely on **suspense** or uncertainty that makes readers read on. Some adventure stories rely almost entirely upon suspense as the device to keep readers reading, but the novel that is concerned about human beings and their interactions creates believable characters involved in interesting conflict that makes a point about human behavior. These novels may also use suspense as a means to keep readers reading, but they rely on thematic significance and other kinds of complexity for what, to many readers, is a more satisfying story.

Few novels manage to hold readers in suspense more successfully than those of Robert Cormier, whose secret lies in developing characters readers care about and whose well-being is in question. *The Chocolate War* once again serves as clear example. Suspense can be examined in terms of questions that need answers. Line one of page one gets us started: "They murdered him" on the football field. Is someone out to get Jerry? He wants desperately to make the team as quarterback. Will he make it? The Vigils meet. Will they single out Jerry for a hard task? Brother Leon asks the cooperation of the Vigils in the chocolate sale. Will Archie cooperate, and if so what kind of assignments will he set up? Brother Leon is a vindictive tyrant in class. Will Jerry be his victim? Jerry gets his Vigil assignment. Can he hold out against Leon's sneers and biting comments? Once he has completed his assignment, will Jerry knuckle under and sell the chocolates? Does he have the strength and determination to "disturb the universe"? Will the ransacking of his locker change Jerry's mind? The attack on the way home? The nightly phone calls? Because readers must know the answers, they continue to read to the last page, wondering if slightly built Jerry can stand up to the bludgeoning of Emile and the crowd at the raffle boxing match. Readers care about Jerry's survival, about whether and how the Vigils are punished. Cormier never lets his readership down with obvious answers or too-neat solutions. Suspense holds readers to the last page, where they hear Jerry tell Goober that disturbing the universe is just not worth it.

The Cliff-hanger

Years ago movie theatres often included with their Saturday matinees a serial story, each weekly episode ending with a question that might literally show a character hanging from a cliff. This **cliff-hanger,** or suspenseful ending, hooked the audience into returning for the sequel. In fiction, suspense is often heightened by the use of cliff-hangers at the end of a chapter.

Richard Peck makes effective use of cliffhangers in his novel *Are You in the House Alone?*, the story of occurrences leading up to a rape, the rape itself, and subsequent events. Consider the following chapter endings.

> But we went out to the lake . . . to that empty cottage that Steve's dad used for a fishing shack. . . . The only place where we thought we were alone.

> Yes, I said almost out loud. *I'm home now, whoever you are.*

> It was the middle of the next week when I got the second note. And it was the last one.

> But it wasn't Steve [at the door]. No, the time was all wrong. It couldn't have been Steve.

> . . . The last thing I remember is the poker in Phil's hand and the way the muscle rippled in his naked shoulder when he brought his arm back in a sportsmanlike backhand just before he swung it down at my temple.

Even when these final chapter sentences are read in isolation, suspense is undeniable.

Foreshadowing

In a work of fiction the clues along the way that point to eventual happenings are called **foreshadowing.** Readers may recall having finished a mystery and marveled at the outcome, saying to themselves "I would never have thought . . . " In such a case, either the writer has neglected to plant the necessary clues or the reader has missed the hints dropped along the way. By contrast, an unskilled writer may make the clues too obvious, and readers may say with some disappointment, "I knew it all the time." Readers who read one mystery story after another often develop skill in recognizing foreshadowing.

Foreshadowing assists readers in following the action in *The Chocolate War*. In chapter two Obie hates "that bastard" Archie, and yet hates the way he simultaneously admires Archie, a foreshadowing of the evil for which Archie is consistently responsible, and the hold he has on others. Brother Leon's cruelty in class foreshadows his bargain with Archie and predicts the kind of pressures ahead. The introduction to Emile the bully as he siphons gas foreshadows his total viciousness; it is no surprise that it is he who finally beats Jerry into bloody misery. Jerry's locker poster, "Do I dare disturb the universe?" coupled with his feeling that his father's life is deadly dull foreshadows his defiance of the Vigils and Brother Leon. The brutality of football practice foreshadows the kind of ruthlessness Jerry is subjected to in the final showdown. Cormier's novel is a well-constructed whole with foreshadowing and suspense balanced to keep readers reading, wondering about outcomes and worried not only about Jerry's physical survival but also about the strength of convictions.

Readers are well prepared by early foreshadowing for the appearance of a harsh and even brutal father in Bette Greene's *Summer of My German Soldier*. On the second page Patty sees the porter from her father's store waiting in the crowd for the arrival of the German prisoners of war; as she approaches him, he cringes, assuming he is to be reprimanded for being away from work for a few minutes. Three pages later she waves to housekeeper Ruth and without hearing any accusation, protests, "I didn't do a single thing wrong!" At Ruth's suggestion, Patty says grace before lunch, thinking, "I think maybe I worry too much. After all, it's just plumb silly to think of him walking in on us right in the middle of our prayers. . . . The nerve at his temple would pulsate. Shouts of 'God damn you,' directed at me and maybe at Ruth." Although "him" has not yet been clearly identified, Patty's fears have foreshadowed the violence to come and suggested that Patty's father will be its source. Ruth has told Patty to "'keep our jubilee in easy reach.' Why can't it be that way with my mother and father?" Patty wonders. Ruth asks Patty to tell her why others use affectionate terms for their parent, but "you is always talking about your father when all the other young girls be talking about their daddies?" By page 58, foreshadowing has prepared readers for the brutal beating Patty gets from her father with "hate that gnarled and snarled his face like a dog gone rabid."

Richard Peck, too, has carefully planted foreshadowing throughout *Are You in the House Alone?* by giving evidence that shows Phil capable of rape: He is a playboy, affluent, indulged, and accustomed to having his own way. He seems to spy on Gail, even over the dinner-table centerpiece. He is a strong young man, an athlete of unusual skill. The threatening, anonymous note Gail finds on her locker agitates Alison, Phil's girlfriend, who has hinted earlier that his view of sex is that it is dirty and unconnected with love. Such hints point toward Phil's latest actions.

The Climax

The **climax** is the point at which the conflict is resolved and readers know the outcome of it all. The climax is sometimes called the peak or turning point in the story. Throughout the plot, from first recognition of the conflict through the essential turns and twists, the discoveries and reversals in the protagonist's life, readers have been concerned about how things will turn out for the protagonist. The climax, then, is inextricably linked to conflict. In each novel with strong conflict, there comes a point at which tension is high and the outcome uncertain. In fact, if foreshadowing has been too heavy-handed and readers have "known it all the time," the story has lacked suspense, and the climax is scarcely the high point of the plot.

Look at the climax in *The Chocolate War.* The reader has watched as the Vigils made Jerry miserable by their dogged punishment for his defiance. The extreme revenge is "a raffle like no other in Trinity's history," a chance, Archie says, for Jerry to get revenge. On the isolated athletic field the school gathers, as Jerry meets Emile Janza, his primary physical opponent, expects a fair fight but soon sees that nothing can possibly go his way, and that he cannot back down. Cormier further heightens the suspense by telling the reader of the hatred each of the Vigils feels toward Archie and his plan, then introduces the possibility that Archie could draw the black marble and so be forced to be one of the fighters. Students designate the kind of blow Janza is to inflict, with the chance of winning a big prize if the blow is the knockout. Jerry's first blow is ineffective, but Janza's connects: "He struck Jerry with all the force he could summon, the impact of the blow coming from his feet, up through his legs and thighs, the trunk of his body, the power pulsing through his body like some elemental force until it erupted through his arm, exploding into his fist." Jerry is shocked at the viciousness of the blow, which is closely followed by another. He strikes back with all his hatred of the Vigils, only to receive a totally illegal blow to the groin, followed by Emile's blow upon blow as he senses "a kill." Jerry, nearly unconscious and "broken," has lost his battle. This is the climax, the high point, the resolution of the conflict.

Denouement

Once the climax has been reached and the conflict resolved, most readers wish for a sense of completion, of closure, of knowing how everything else turned out. This completeness is called **resolution** of the conflict. The **denouement** or **falling action** begins at the climax, at the point where the protagonist's fate is now known. Depending upon plot complexity, the denouement may take more or less time, but it follows the climax. Jerry, with Goober's help, struggles to stay conscious, knowing he has something he must say to Goober, a discovery he has made.

> . . . He had to tell Goober to play ball, to play football, to run, to make the team, to sell the chocolates, to sell whatever they wanted you to sell, to do whatever they wanted you to do. He tried to voice the words but there was something wrong with his mouth, his teeth, his face. But he went ahead anyway, telling Goober what he needed to know. They tell you to do your thing but they don't mean it. They don't want you to do your thing, not unless it happens to be their thing, too. It's a laugh, Goober, a fake. Don't disturb the universe, Goober, no matter what the posters say.

Few questions are left unanswered. The last two pages describe Archie's confrontation with the brother who had turned off the floodlights to stop the murderous fight, but he, too, is under Brother Leon's control. The final line of the novel, "The ambulance's siren began to howl in the night," leaves the reader knowing that nothing has really changed.

Questions are answered in the denouement of *Roll of Thunder, Hear My Cry*. At the climactic point, angry white people form a lynch mob and pursue T. J., who they believe killed Mr. Barnett while robbing his store. Mr. Jamison's intervention slows their action, but only when the cotton catches fire—fire set by Papa, not by lightning—and everyone must rush to save the fields is the crowd distracted so that T. J. can be saved from the mob and taken to jail. This final cooperative effort resolves the conflict, at least temporarily, and the story leaves no immediate questions unanswered.

As is usually the case, the denouement follows the climax with high speed as it does in *Taming the Star Runner* by S. E. Hinton. A terrifying thunderstorm frightens Star Runner, the untamable pony that challenges all of Casey's training skills; he jumps the fence and is off. In the Jeep, safely insulated from lightning strike, Travis races with Casey after wild Star Runner. In their frantic chase, the Jeep overturns, leaving the two stunned on the ground. All that is known of Star Runner's fate is suggested in brief paragraphs.

> There was nothing. Just the windswept pasture, the overturned Jeep, and the line of trees. The acrid smell of electricity, the smell of something burning . . . flesh burning.
> Nothing. He gazed at the empty pasture.
> It was raining now, harder. It felt like tears, it felt like blood, on his face.

When the reader is assured that all is well—or at least that the questions are answered—the story is said to have a **closed ending.** In Hinton's book, the reader knows everything necessary. True, the ranch may be a long time selling and there is a possibility that Ken and Teresa, who love their child Christopher, may not reunite. The focus, however, has been Travis, his book, his adjustment to country life, his loneliness now gone, his hoping for a girlfriend who returns his feelings, and his amicable relation to his mother, who had once seemed to favor his stepfather but who now stands up for him. Everything seems to be moving in the right direction for Travis. Optimism is in the air at the point of closing.

Inevitability

Inevitability is the quality of "it had to be." Given these people with their character traits in this environment and involved in these events, there could be no other outcome. The author's plotting skill is praised when the reader can say firmly of the conclusion, "It was inevitable." Clear portrayal of character as instrument of action convinces the reader. Character as well as skillful foreshadowing have prepared the reader for the denouement of *The Chocolate War.* Jerry has been intent on standing firm, aware that his holding out before the powerful and vicious Vigils could bring to him nothing but serious damage of some kind. *Catcher,* too, has an inevitable ending. With growing acceptance, Holden has commented on how children change; each year as they see the same museum exhibit, they are different people who must be allowed to make mistakes and to change. In *Roll of Thunder,* Papa's frequent comment that "you do what you gotta do" has prepared readers for the inevitable—his setting fire to his own cotton crop in order to stop the mob from lynching T. J. The story that leaves readers feeling the ending to be inevitable has for most readers a satisfying closing.

Types of Plots

Two principal types of plots, plus a third combination of the two, hold a story together. The plot of *The Chocolate War* and *Roll of Thunder,* with a central climax followed by a denouement, is called a **progressive plot.** It seems logical that people must always have liked stories with suspense and climax; the plot structures of many folktales or stories told and retold in societies relying upon oral rather than written story-telling are often in this plot form. Although different ethnic groups do vary the story forms, folk tales with progressive plots, each with its own suspense and climax, exist in many cultures.

Episodic Plot

A striking contrast to the novel-length progressive plot is the **episodic plot,** in which episodes are usually related to one another by a central character; often they make a significant point about a way of life in a particular area. Jim Wayne Miller's *Newfound* is a growing-up story about Robert Wells, who lives in Appalachia. Here Miller gives readers the flavor of life in the Appalachian hills as they follow Robert from ages 12 to 17. Each of the 29 chapters has its own focus; events and nonevents follow one another in what may seem to be a haphazard manner. Chapters are separate stories and yet make up a whole. If summarizing titles were given to each of the chapters, the first few might be described in this way: Dad quits his job and Mom is mad; Dad starts his cement-block-making business; Dad pays the store bill with blocks; Dad starts another mysterious business; Mom threatens to leave; Dad leaves; Mom and Dad got married; moving to Mom's parents' house; Mom seems to be studying something; beekeeping and tobacco cutting; two Christmases. . . .

Instead of a central conflict with tension leading to a climax, the episodes of quiet living among the same family are strung together with unity provided by characters and setting. Interest is held by the lives of these people in this environment where families are of two kinds, "the good livers" and the "sorries," those who manage and those who drift from job to job and live from hand to mouth. Anecdotes and tall tales punctuate the whole; one set of grandparents dominates one chapter and the other set holds the next one together. With Robert, the reader visits Dad's fishing-hole business, explores Grandma Wells's attic, hears about her education at a rote-learning "blab school," listens to Grandpa Smith's quiet poetry recitation, and watches retarded Velma through the binoculars as she plays on her front porch. If the chapters are successful they hold our interest through their own slight tension.

Similar structure holds together Robert Newton Peck's *A Day No Pigs Would Die,* the story of a Vermont Shaker boy's love for his father. Once again, listing the focus for each of the chapters, the reader sees such topics as Robert delivers a calf; is badly bitten by the cow; is rewarded with Pinky, a baby pig; trains his pig; gets his report card; cares for Pinky; goes to the graveyard; listens to gossip; goes to the fair—and on with typical rural activities until Robert's father dies and Robert must dig the grave, responsibilities for the farm now resting on his young shoulders. The father's explanations of the natural world taken from the Book of Shaker, as well as the love and respect between father and son, hold the story together. Still another story of father and son is Graham Salisbury's *Blue Skin of the Sea,* the first-person episodic plot consisting of eleven chapters about Sonny Mendoza growing up in a Hawaiian fishing village. Chapter One tells of Sonny's father lowering the terrified six-year-old into the ocean to learn to swim; the final chapter shows Sonny at 19 testing his courage by swimming in shark-infested waters. Between these are nine other chapters about the extended family's life in the Islands.

Myths and legends of other cultures and times are occasionally the basis for plot. King Minos, cruel and warlike king who worships the bull Minotaur and relishes bloodshed, is the evil father of Ariadne in Brian Keaney's *No Need for Heroes.* With the arrival at Knossos of Daedelus and Icarus and their mysterious and deadly box, Ariadne is more trapped than ever in a repressive society. When Theseus of Athens arrives, however, Ariadne by her wise planning becomes his savior. The story departs from the early Greek myth and yet retains the serious tone. British writer **Alan Garner** uses as basis for *The Owl Service* the Welsh legend of Blodeuwedd from the Mabinogion; the resulting story combines horror and evil as contemporary young people confront situations similar to those of the legendary past. Internal conflict holds interest in Diana Wynne Jones's *Eight Days of Luke,* a story with mythological relationships in which the protagonist David meets Luke—actually Loki, the god of mischief—who is being sought by other Norse gods for the accidental death of the god Baldur. In the course of the story, David struggles with his wish to rescue Luke in the face of the angry gods Tew, Woden, Thor, Frey, and Freya (from whose names come the days of the week), all called by contemporary names related to their Norse origins.

The success of television's plot-heavy programs may be having some effect on the expectations of young adult readers. Each episode of an adventure series has its own plot and tension; movies, furthermore, are action-packed, as the ads proclaim. In fact, films with focus on relationships and quiet lives rather than tension and climax are often shown only in the "little theaters" because crowds of interested people are not expected. In films and television we have little or no chance to meander along with the central character, tasting life with him or her, getting acquainted with another generation, perhaps finding out what it used to be like, and being intrigued both by the differences and the universalities of life here and there, or then and now. Perhaps there will be a revival of such stories, or perhaps some day it will happen that only older readers have the patience to read such slow-moving stories held together by so unsuspenseful but satisfying an element as theme or character.

Evaluating Plot

Coincidence

Flaws in the plotting of a novel are of several different kinds. **Coincidence** occurs when the writer has not prepared the reader for an event by earlier foreshadowing. The event "just happens." In an otherwise well-plotted structure, S. E. Hinton's *Rumble Fish* resorts at one point to coincidence. When Motorcycle Boy, Rusty-James's brother, disappears and returns from California with news of their mother, he is asked how he came to find her. He says he saw her in the audience while he was watching the Academy Awards on television. Not only is there no foreshadowing to prepare us for her involvement in the movie-making world, but from what is known of her life since leaving husband and family, Motorcycle Boy's spotting his mother in such a way and then being able to track her down seems farfetched.

A variety of strengths can be found in *Song of the Buffalo Boy* by Sherry Garland, but unfortunately coincidence distracts from the author's stated purpose of showing how "a war goes on affecting people's lives many, many years after it is over and how often it is the most innocent— the children and the women—who suffer the most." Perhaps in order to avoid sentimentality, the author provides no easy "everything always turns out well" ending in which Amerasian Loi and Khai, her Vietnamese husband-to-be, are relocated in America; instead, at the last moment, all obstacles to marriage in their native village are miraculously removed and their love will win in that way. The customs of the country and the poverty of its inhabitants are clear, and Loi's plight arouses our sympathy. Coincidence intrudes, however, because of sudden solutions to enormous obstacles: the ostracism of Loi and her family for her American blood and her mother's prostitution; threats against her uncle, who had taken her mother in; the dogged opposition to marriage from Khai's family; Loi's severely injured foot with symptoms of blood poisoning now cured by a single inoculation, the two young lovers finding one another among four million Saigon citizens. Plot resolution relies far too heavily upon coincidence.

Sentimentality

Sentimentality in a story robs the reader of a feeling of legitimacy; when feelings have been exaggerated, a thoughtful response is lost. Sentimentality is not sentiment; that difference must be understood immediately. Sentiment is a natural concern or feeling for another person. **Sentimentality,** however, occurs when our capacity for emotional response is used to squeeze from us emotion well beyond any that is legitimate, given this situation and these occurrences. Look first at a personal example: Suppose your little sister has run her tricycle into the side of a moving car and is injured. The accident would rouse in you strong feelings of love and concern—legitimate sentiment; this is your little sister and you love her. Suppose, on the other hand, that you become so entangled with the life of a soap opera child—despite your knowledge that the story is staged and untrue—that you are tearful and preoccupied with his misfortune, not just for the moment but over a period of time. That is sentimentality.

To cite another example, oftentimes viewers struggle with their tears in the movie theater. Sometimes as they move out onto the street wiping their eyes they may even say to a stranger waiting in line, "It's good. Really good." They are unashamed of their tears because tears are legitimate response to a moving story. At other times moviegoers may wish to hide their teary eyes, knowing that the film does not justify tears and that they have been hoodwinked into crying over a story without real substance. That is sentimentality.

Although the potential for sentimentality in Cynthia Rylant's novel *A Kindness* is high, Rylant never falls into the trap. Told through fifteen-year-old Chip's point of view, the story concerns his learning that his divorced mother, Anne, with whom he lives, is pregnant. At first Chip feels a furious anger that Anne will put him through the humiliation of her carrying the baby to term and keeping it, as well as an anger that an unknown man could be both responsible and irresponsible. He feels displaced from his comfortable relationship with his artist mother, a relationship in which he takes care of practicalities and she of homemaking while earning a living from her painting. But Chip comes to love the baby he has named Dusky, and Anne continues to keep her agent, Ben, from knowing he has fathered the child. Anne manages her own life, keeps her new status from being a burden to Chip, and continues to make a warm and loving home for both of her children. Such a story might easily have lapsed into sentimentality: Chip might have been burdened with baby care, his normal high school student life totally disrupted by Dusky and Anne's demands. Anne might have fallen apart and been unable to support the family. She might have married unwisely, someone, anyone to provide a man in the home. She might have blackmailed Ben and his family, demanding money and recognition. But none of these plot scenarios develops and the story successfully avoids sentimentality.

Lack of Conflict

Although Peck carefully plots *Are You in the House Alone?* and his effectively planted foreshadowing creates conflict and suspense, it is nonetheless appropriate to comment that the plot unrealistically downplays another conflict. It suggests that a rape victim, usually severely damaged psychologically as well as physically, can return her life to its old security in far too brief a time. Rape cannot be put aside or otherwise dealt with quickly and cleanly by means of a few psychotherapy sessions. It may so thoroughly affect the victim that the internal conflict lasts a very long time. As research clearly shows, the effects of rape may last for years, affecting not only the woman or girl's relationships with her family and friends, her husband or boyfriend, but also making a full relationship with men extremely difficult even for years to come. Good psychotherapy over a long period of time may be her only way of returning to a normal life. To the thoughtful, mature reader, the novel's conclusion is inadequate in one respect: Peck denies readers the opportunity to watch as the protagonist struggles over time with the various effects of rape. Although the novel is noteworthy in many other ways, the ending raises false hope and expectations about speedy recovery from one of the worst events of a victim's life. Peck's story suggests furthermore that rapists are mentally ill,[1] a suggestion that to some extent exonerates the rapist as not guilty by reason of insanity. After the second rape, however, Gail does say explicitly, "We . . . [try] to protect ourselves as individuals and families instead of organizing to make everybody safe. There are more Phils out there, you know," and suggests that in order to protect women and society as a whole, we must have the courage, despite the unpleasantness, to file charges and press for conviction, to see that justice is done. "That's the way we are, isn't it? . . . We keep everything locked up tight inside us because . . . because one little leak might cause an explosion and we'd all go flying apart." Although Peck's novel is not sentimental, the protagonist's internal conflict following her rape is oversimplified.

Inadequate Foreshadowing

Occasionally a writer creates what appears to be a closed ending, but it may instead challenge credibility because it is too neat, or because fore-shadowing is inadequate. Such is the case in Julie Reece Deaver's *Say Goodnight, Gracie,* a novel based on a close friendship that ends with Jimmy's death by car accident. In an effort to support her reasonable theme that it is possible to survive a devastating loss with the help of psychotherapy and a stiff upper lip, Deaver has weakened the plot by making the healing too rapid, almost miraculous. Trauma does not just disappear. The reader sensibly expects that, along the way toward recovery, evidence or foreshadowing of healing will appear little by little.

Sensationalism

Dropping hints along the way creates for the reader not only a sense of inevitability, but also one of satisfaction. Writers who believe that plot is the single most important element in a story may resort to **sensationalism,**[2] or unrelieved anxiety and suspense created by horror or terror about outcomes. Such plotting often occurs in soap operas and in film. Readers hooked on violence or on adventure or spy stories may enjoy the breathtaking tension, while others may be bored by it, preferring instead that their interest be carried by credible characters or a point about human behavior or feelings.

The Mall offers a lurid example of sensationalism. "He's everywhere, waiting just for *her,*" proclaims the back cover. The story relies upon mistaken identity as three young men change appearances and jobs, and the reader knows that one? two? all three? have malevolent intentions toward Trish. Bloody hands around corners, disappearing clothing and store clerks, a head and neck pierced by an ice pick and found in the trash, subterranean passageways, dark loading docks, mysterious chambers, rattling freight elevators and pitch dark dead ends, threatening phone calls and too-loving notes, ringing phones with whispered messages, cars that suddenly won't start, and a feeling of being constantly watched all occur in the novel. The result is sensationalism.

Summary

The successful novelist weaves plot and character together inextricably, the natures of both protagonist and antagonist determining the complexities of plot. Order may be simply chronological or may rely on frames or flashbacks. In a progressive plot, suspense pulls the reader beyond exposition, through complications and rising action, and on to the central climax. Here the conflict, whether it be person against self, another person, society, or nature, is resolved in a manner foreshadowed and therefore inevitable. Final uncertainties are left unknown in an open ending, or settled in the denouement with closed ending. The episodic plot, however, is made up of chapters that may each have their own tension, and by means of idea or character combine for a unified whole. Without conflict or tension of some kind, the story is often dull, but the well-plotted story does not rely on sentimentality, sensationalism, or coincidence for resolution of the conflict. What matters is that, as we read, our interest is held by credible character involved in credible action.

Notes

1. The belief that anyone who commits rape must be insane is not unusual. Perhaps it stems from the believer's not knowing personally any man so irrational or so governed by a sadistic demand for power that he would be capable of such an act—an appreciative view of men that would be wonderful to accept in the universal.

2. Syndicated newspaper humorist Dave Barry gives a good example of extreme sensationalism in the *Cincinnati Enquirer,* June 3, 1992:

> . . . Phil just got out of prison after serving a sentence for a murder he committed when he became a drug addict because of the guilt he felt when his wife died in a freak submarine accident while Phil was having an affair with a nun, but now he's all straightened out and has a good job as a trapeze artist and is almost through with the surgical part of his sex change and just became happily engaged to marry a prominent member of The New Kids On The Block, so in other words he is fine. . . .

Recommended Books Cited in This Chapter

Bridgers, Sue Ellen. *Permanent Connections.* New York: Harper & Row, 1987.

Burnford, Sheila. *The Incredible Journey.* Boston: Little, Brown, 1961.

Childress, Alice. *A Hero Ain't Nothin But a Sandwich.* New York: Putnam, 1973.

Conrad, Pam. *My Daniel.* New York: Harper & Row, 1989.

Cormier, Robert. *The Chocolate War.* New York: Random House, 1974.

———. *Fade.* New York: Delacorte, 1988.

———. *I Am the Cheese.* New York: Dell, 1991.

Crews, Linda. *Children of the River.* New York: Doubleday, 1989.

Duder, Tessa. *In Lane Three, Alex Archer.* New Zealand: Oxford, 1987.

Fox, Paula. *The One-Eyed Cat.* Scarsdale, New York.: Bradbury, 1984.

Garland, Sherry. *Song of the Buffalo Boy.* New York: Harcourt Brace, 1992.

Garner, Alan. *The Owl Service.* New York: Dell, 1967.

George, Jean. *Julie of the Wolves.* New York: Harper & Row, 1972.

Greene, Bette. *Summer of My German Soldier.* New York: Dial, 1973.

Guy, Rosa. *The Friends.* New York: Bantam, 1983.

Hinton, S. E. *Rumble Fish.* New York: Dell: 1989.

———. *Taming of the Star Runner.* New York: Dell, 1988.

Hotze, Sollace. *A Circle Unbroken.* New York: Clarion, 1988.

Jones, Diana Wynne. *Eight Days of Luke.* New York: Knopf, 1975.

Keaney, Brian. *No Need for Heroes.* London: Oxford University Press, 1989.

Mahy, Margaret. *Memory.* New York: McElderry, 1987.

Mason, Bobbie Ann. *In Country.* New York: Harper, 1986.

Mazer, Harry, *The Island Keeper.* New York: Delacorte, 1981.

Miller, Jim Wayne. *Newfound.* New York: Orchard, 1989.

Nelson, Theresa. *And One for All.* New York: Orchard, 1989.

O'Brien, Robert C. *Z for Zachariah.* New York: Macmillan, 1975.

O'Dell, Scott. *Island of the Blue Dolphins.* Boston: Houghton Mifflin, 1960.

O'Neal, Zibby. *A Formal Feeling.* New York: Viking, 1982.

Paterson, Katherine. *Jacob Have I Loved.* New York: Harper, 1980.

Paulsen, Gary. *The Island.* New York: Orchard, 1988.

Peck, Richard. *Are You in the House Alone?* New York: Viking, 1976.

Peck, Robert Newton. *A Day No Pigs Would Die.* New York: Knopf, 1989.

Pevsner, Stella. *How Could You Do It, Diane?* Boston: Houghton Mifflin, 1989.

Roth, Arthur. *The Iceberg Hermit.* New York: Scholastic Point, 1974.

Rylant, Cynthia. *A Kindness.* New York: Orchard, 1988.

Salinger, J. D. *The Catcher in the Rye.* Boston: Little, Brown, 1951.

Salisbury, Graham. *Blue Skin of the Sea.* New York: Doubleday, 1992.

Strieber, Whitley. *Wolf of Shadows.* New York: Knopf, 1985.

Taylor, Theodore. *The Cay.* New York: Avon, 1969.

Voigt, Cynthia. *A Solitary Blue.* New York: Atheneum, 1983.

West, Jessamyn. *The Massacre at Fall Creek.* New York: Harcourt Brace, 1975.

White, Robb. *Deathwatch.* New York: Dell, 1973.

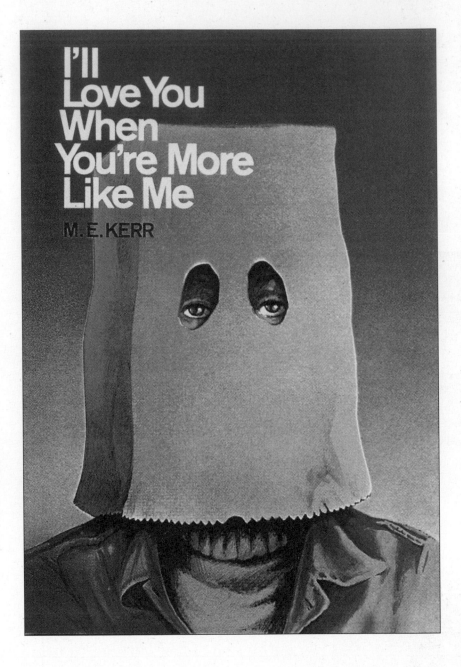

I'll Love You When You're More Like Me

M. E. KERR

—4—

Theme

We all try our hands at telling stories; sometimes we define them as anecdotes, or experiences, or vignettes, or perhaps jokes. We also know that
some storytellers have great gifts for narration, but that we dread seeing
others take the floor. The difference in their telling can be described
quite simply. Slender threads of chronology or association may be all that
holds a series of anecdotes together: "That was the same day that . . .
Later on we had another experience. . . ." Nothing seems related to anything else in any way other than that events happened in sequence. A
more successful storyteller may tell a story with greater complexity, or
use suspense to keep us guessing at the outcome. "You'd never guess
what she said. . . . The clincher was the arrival of. . . " Although boredom
arrives less quickly in this instance than in the first, at their best these storytellers hold our interest only briefly. A third narrator, however, tells of
experiences that hold us more successfully; the story makes a point, encourages us to think, invites us to consider thoughtfully our own experiences. This last storyteller has reached beyond narrative to meaning. We
may be encouraged to respond with stories of our own that demonstrate
a similar point, or explore the relationships between things that happen
and the people to whom they occur. The influence of this successful narrator may awaken in us ideas such as the impact of friends on our behavior, the need for close relationships, the difficulty of moving to another
community, and a vast variety of other thematic points.

"What happened next," the thread of the first storyteller, is a matter
of simple chronology or narrative order. "Why did it happen?" suggests to
us conflict and plot as the second teller keeps us in suspense. But when
we consider the question addressed by the third teller, "What does it all
mean?" we begin to discover theme.

Theme or Unifying Truth

Literature has been defined as "A significant truth expressed in appropriate elements and memorable language." **Theme** is the significant and unifying truth or truths of a work, the idea that holds it all together, the point of the story. Such a truth, idea, or point may relate to human behavior, human needs, the human condition, and to groups or society as human beings act and interact.

Ask young adults about their memory of the Nancy Drew books, a Tom Swift book, or a Gothic novel. In all probability, the fond memories will be about what happened, the barest outline of chronology or events. Ask them about *Roll of Thunder, Hear My Cry*, or *The Chocolate War*, however, and they will thoughtfully respond about the meaning of the stories. They remember characters, conflicts between characters, and soon go on to state "what the story means." Pride and commitment to self and others permeate *Roll of Thunder;* curiosity about their own courage perhaps coupled with fear about their possible behavior may haunt them as they remember reading *The Chocolate War*. There seems little doubt about the lesser impact of many other novels as compared to the significance of the latter two.

Writers frequently wish to help readers see something more clearly, some truth they are committed to, some insight into human behavior or the human predicament. Often writers express the view that good fiction is more helpful in explaining human behavior than is a textbook in psychology or sociology. Novelist Graham Greene maintains, furthermore, that the books read in childhood have greater influence on people than anything they read later on in their lives. Nina Bawden, British writer of books for both children and adults, comments that her childhood reading left her "free to go where [she] liked, be who [she] wanted to be." No barriers of time or distance, age, race, sex, or ticket availability were put upon her travels while she found out "the kind of person [she] was." Events in a story could be "more truthful" than the readers' dull lives, opening "their minds and imaginations" while taking child readers seriously. Bawden does not hesitate to admit that a theme may be a value judgment,[1] "helping [readers] to develop a sense of moral structure" but without the preachment often offered by the real adults in their lives.[2]

Clearly, character and plot are significant, but what Greene suggests and Bawden affirms is the need for some significance, "a point," called here "theme." The truth or theme goes beyond this story and relates in some way to human motivation, behavior, and life, perhaps staying with the reader long after the series of events has faded from memory. The significant truth—or truths—unifies and illuminates the story as it gives pleasure. The reader gains one pleasure from the discovery of the simplest of truths, and gains another pleasure from the discovery that truth is not simple.[3] Theme provides this discovery, this understanding, this pleasure of recognition.

But before examination of themes begins, individual differences must be acknowledged, differences in understanding, in experience, and in insight that allow one reader to single out one theme as "the most significant" and another to single out a second theme. What matters is, first, that the fictional piece possess a theme or themes that speak to readers, and, second, that each reader finds in the story specific events or words that can verify his or her choice of theme.

Types of Thematic Statements

Explicit and Implicit Themes

Our touchstone young adult books, *Roll of Thunder, Hear My Cry* and *The Chocolate War,* serve once again as examples from which to draw themes, supporting the choices from examples of statements or incidents found within the novels.

An **explicit theme** is one clearly stated in words within a work. In *Thunder,* as Mama explains to Cassie after Lillian Jean and Mr. Simms humiliate her, some people think they are better than others. But, says Mama, "White is something just like black is something. Everybody born on this earth is something and nobody, no matter what color, is better than anybody else." As Mama further explains to Cassie, "For him to believe that he is better than we are makes him think that he's important, simply because he's white." Uncle Hammer, chiding Stacey because he has let T. J. goad him out of his new coat, says that "as long as there are people, there's gonna be someone trying to take what you got and trying to drag you down. It's up to you whether you let them or not." Papa explains to Cassie and Stacey why their black neighbors have given up on the store boycott, saying that not everyone has their options; like the others, we must "keep doing what we gotta, and we don't give up." When the Klan's lynch mob comes for T. J., Papa faces a tough decision, and before he goes out in the storm to set fire to the cotton field, he says to Mama, "I'll do what I have to do, Mary . . . and so will you." Filled with grief that T. J. has died from his injuries, Cassie cries "Oh, P-Papa, d-does it have to be?" And holding her tightly, Papa replies, "it shouldn't be." In each of these cases, theme is explicitly stated.

In *The Chocolate War,* Caroni, the good student whom Brother Leon accuses of cheating, does not stand up for himself but says to himself that life is rotten and "there were no heroes, really, and . . . you couldn't trust anybody, not even yourself," an explicit theme reenforced by Jerry's discovery that his blows in the boxing match were not only self-defense but also that he "had become another animal, another beast, another violent person in a violent world." The poster in Jerry's locker suggests a primary and **implicit theme,** one implied though not stated precisely. Here theme is phrased as a question without an answer. "Do I dare disturb the universe?" He stares at the challenging graffiti by the bus stop: "Why?" asks one writer. "Why not?" asks another, and the reader ties these brief but conflicting questions to the issue raised by the poster. Taunted by a street person, Jerry hears that he is "middle-aged at fourteen," and reads it as a dare to disturb the universe. The subsequent action of the novel implies an answer to the poster's question, an implicit theme or restatement saying in declarative form: "Disturbing the universe takes great courage, is extremely risky, and may result in destruction." Some thoughtful readers, however, may believe that although Jerry stands up for what he believes, he is too naive about the consequences.

An implicit theme becomes clear when Emile's behavior reenforces the idea that it is safest to challenge no one with power, to make no waves. He can victimize others because he knows that "nobody wanted trouble, nobody wanted to make trouble, nobody wanted a showdown"; for good reason, nobody wanted to disturb the universe. Any number of incidents imply that this is a seriously flawed world, the veneer of civilization distressingly thin. As Archie says about the final boxing match, "You see, Carter, people are two things: greedy and cruel. So we have a perfect set-up here. The greed part—a kid pays a buck for a chance to win a hundred. Plus fifty boxes of chocolates. The cruel part—watching two guys hurting each other, while they're safe in the bleachers. That's why it works, Carter, because we're all bastards." As the crowd disperses, Brother Leon, having watched the bloody fight from the hill beyond the bleachers, condescendingly drapes his arm over the shoulder of his fellow teacher. "Leon was still in command, still in the position of power," indicates implicitly that trying to disturb the universe may change nothing. In the final pages of the novel, Jerry suggests a complementary but highly ironic theme as he mentally instructs his friend Goober, telling him "what he needed to know. They tell you to do your thing but they don't mean it. They don't want you to do your thing, not unless it happens to be their thing, too. It's a laugh, Goober, a fake. Don't disturb the universe, Goober, no matter what the posters say."[4]

Just as the number of truths about human beings is infinite, the variety of possible themes is infinite. Perhaps because of the common issues young adults face, their novels tend to group themselves around common kinds of themes. Insight into self that asks one to take responsibility for one's own behavior, for example, frequently holds a story together. A variety of other broad concerns include marriage and parenthood, fostering hope despite differences or difficult circumstances, becoming aware of interdependence with other people, learning to live with uncertainty, dealing with a sense of isolation, learning not to judge people by appearances, coming to understand the complex nature of society, and dealing with sometimes contradictory truths. All these themes recur in literature for young adults.

Common Themes

Becoming Self-Aware and Responsible for One's Own Life

More commonly explored in young adult literature than almost any other, the thematic idea of self-awareness is perhaps the central issue of the age group. The Socratic injunction to "know thyself" is part of the lives of most people, but is particularly significant to the emerging adult. The protagonist Tree in Virginia Hamilton's *Sweet Whispers, Brother Rush* is searching for acceptance of herself and who she is. Because she is most comfortable alone or with her sick brother, Dab, Tree hurries home after school, locking the door and retreating to care for him or to sketch in her own little room where she meets her phantom uncle, Brother Rush. The mystical glimpses of her early childhood and Dab's, of her very young mother, and the father who abandoned the family give her some sense of where she comes from, and what events have shaped her life, but she remains self-conscious with classmates and others. When in the hospital she confides to Silversmith that she is sometimes "ashame," he states an explicit theme: "One day you become a full-grown woman. And the more you come to know [yourself], the more you will feel good inside about knowing." This quest to know causes Tree to consider leaving home to search for her father, to find out why he left, and whether he loves her. She also wants to know whether she will die of porphyria, and why her mother M'vy leaves her alone with Dab all week. When Tree is finally surrounded by assorted family members that include her mother, a prospective stepfather and stepbrother Don, and the once homeless housekeeper Mrs. Pricherd, Tree knows not only something about her family and her earlier life but also about how secure her new life will be. M'vy, too, has learned something about herself; she had perhaps been misguided in seeking more money for her family and leaving Tree to care for her sick brother. Like Tree, M'vy—now that she knows more about herself and admits that parents make mistakes—"feels better inside."

A related theme often explored in literature for the young adult reader involves growth to independence and a sense of self-worth, as in Brock Cole's *Celine*. Celine is "always ready to believe anyone who tells [her she's] unreasonable and selfish." She thinks to herself, "That's what you are, you know. A kind of monster. . . . Why am I a monster?" and paints herself as a grotesque monster whom she calls Celine-Beast. Artist Paul Barker is a foil to Celine. He looks over his paintings, saying, "It was all wrong. I was too busy trying to please others, and forgot what I wanted to do myself." When Celine's friend gets into trouble for getting drunk at a party and losing her clothes, innocent Celine is blamed—and accepts the blame. "There is this about guilt. It makes you behave. I float through the remainder of the day in an insulating bubble of sorrow, trying to do everything right." When she achieves a level of self-respect that lets her reject Dermot, the two-timing hulk, she says of herself, "I think I will begin a new life. A quite different life. Take charge, as they say. I can be anything I want. Anything at all." Despite her being tossed from parent to parent to grandparent, Celine not only survives but finally convinces the reader she will indeed take charge of her own life.

Another novel that explores this important theme but with a somewhat different plot line is *Notes for Another Life* by Sue Ellen Bridgers. Wren and her brother, Kevin, live with their grandparents while their father is in a mental institution and their mother is elsewhere, finding a career for herself after having married very young. Both Kevin, whose great love is tennis, and Wren, to whom music is extremely important, meet their first girl- and boyfriends, feel very much in love, and think of continuing these relationships into marriage at a later time. But during the course of the year's yearning for their parents, both learn that they are not ready to commit themselves to permanent relationships, and that they must seek independence before they give over their lives to others.

The search for self is also implicit in Cynthia Voigt's novel *Sons from Afar.* Brothers Sammy and James seek competence and achievement and want to do what they do best—to sharpen their skills, and to show courage. Each one earnestly wishes to know "What am I?" and yet fears the social ostracism often awarded young achievers. Sammy doesn't know what he thinks of himself, and James sympathizes with that. In the boys' search, they fear finding in themselves the weaknesses they are discovering in their long-gone father. The most admirable trait they find in him is his independence: "He must have been *something,* our father. I mean, however bad he was, he went his own way. Nobody could make him do anything." He was himself, and they too would try.

In *One Fat Summer* by Robert Lipsyte, Bobby Marks explores the theme that no one can help with personal problems, in this case Bobby's weight, appearance, and timidity. After having been awed by Pete's muscles and his social poise, Bobby finally realizes that Pete is not perfect. Pete has encouraged Bobby to realize that "it's all up to you," and yet when Bobby fearlessly takes on and defeats the thug Willie Rumson, Pete moves in to further punish Willie—but *after* that defeat. The mystique is gone. By his own actions rather than instructions from friend Joanna, mother, sister, father, or Pete, Bobby has proved to himself that he can lose weight, gain self-confidence, and handle his own life. It was all up to him.

A similar theme of knowing oneself is explored in Virginia Hamilton's *A Little Love,* the story of a young adult who, because of her wish to find Cruze, her father, feels empty, an emptiness she continually tries to fill with the solace of food. Sheema, self-consciously overweight but loved by Forrest, fantasizes about her father, who, angry at the loss of his wife in childbirth, abandoned Sheema as an infant. She is brought up by loving

Granmom and Granpop, who encourage her search for her father. When with Forrest's help she finds him, Sheema finds Cruze doing well, but there can be no reconciliation. "She trembled with the grief of the child who had lost out. Hers was the rage of a stricken young woman who was at last learning to stand up for herself." On the return home, Sheema says to Forrest, "Funny, you think you love somebody. But what you been lovin is the *idea* of somebody. Idea of *Cruzey,* a great big dad that's gone to care about you like nobody else, that's gone to do for you. . . . But you don't really love someone unless he's there." Sheema, who had often thought her aged grandparents were "lunchin" or "out to lunch," now appreciates them in a totally new way. Sheema now "was getting right with herself inside. Felt she belonged where she was just for a little while. No thinking. No crying. No wanting. No hungering. Just safe in Granmom's nice old lap."

Gaining insight into self is once again shown as the dominant task of young adults in *The Dawn Palace: The Story of Medea* by H. M. Hoover, a story based upon the Greek myths of Medea. Here readers find the explicit statement "We create the roles we play in life, our character based on what we think we are, our actions on how we wish others to see us." At another point Medea sees that "as [our] awareness of [our] loneliness grows, so does [our] desperation at [our] inability to change what cannot be changed." Knowing this, she now sees that she has been waiting for someone else to take responsibility for her.

In high fantasy the conflict is between the forces of good and those of evil, conflict that can result in self-knowledge. Ursula K. Le Guin explores that conflict in *The Wizard of Earthsea,* in a profoundly moving battle within the protagonist Ged, who is told by his mentor that he must seek out what is seeking him. He "must hunt the hunter," confront the shadow that pursues him, the shadow that is the evil within himself. "As a man's real power grows and his knowledge widens . . . he chooses nothing, but does only and wholly what he must do." Less personal themes occur as well: "Need alone is not enough to set power free: there must be [self-] knowledge." "To hear, one must be silent." "Danger must surround power." "The wise man is one who never sets himself apart from other living things." Although the central theme explores the need for self-understanding, other explicitly stated themes abound.

One reader may respond powerfully to one theme of recognizing self, and another find it irrelevant. That may be the case in Mollie Hunter's *Cat, Herself,* which develops an explicit and distinctly feminist theme in the story of Cat from a family of Scottish "travelers," itinerants who follow the seasons and the roads, finding their living as they go. The travelers follow distinct traditions and male-female roles, but young Cat does not wish to be confined by subordination to the will of men. She expects to be herself. Trained by her mother to do all that is expected of a woman and by her proud father as well, she is unafraid to be called a "split mechanic," the travelers' term for a woman skilled in male tasks—pearling, poaching, fishing, dog training. As Cat's mother says, "Man, woman, or child, everyone has the right to make of their life what they want to make of it." And Old Nan chimes in: "Every single life has its own importance . . . which is why a body should always be free to live as one wants to live."

As psychologist Erik Erikson suggests, the young adult seeks a group to belong to, peers who accept but don't judge. M. E. Kerr's *I'll Love You When You're More Like Me* explores the theme of conformity across generational lines and within peer groups, a theme explicitly stated in the command to "Grab the reins!" Make up your own mind, rather than drift with others. In Richard Peck's *Princess Ashley,* this is the problem for Chelsea, new in a wealthy high school where her mother is a guidance counselor who knows all about everyone. Chelsea keeps her distance, refusing even to acknowledge her mother, and struggles to find a group of her own. The struggle results in Chelsea's submerging her values in order to be accepted, ignoring the illegal drinking and reckless driving she cannot condone, and refusing to recognize that she is being used by Ashley and Craig, "the beautiful people." Among the themes that emerge is one that says that it is difficult to hold to one's values, to act according to what one knows to be right, especially when others who are very different seem to have everything.

Understanding Marriage and Parenthood

Most young adults think about marriage and parenthood, some for the near and others the more distant future. Young adult readers may have the same illusions about how easy it is to be a parent that Sib has in Bruce Brooks's *Midnight Hour Encore.* Sib knows that at her birth her mother handed her over to Taxi, her father, so that she could pursue her own interests. Now 16, Sib meets her mother for the first time and finds she is no longer a hippie seeking to "find herself," but a successful businesswoman who assumes the accomplished and beautiful Sib will now live with her. The surprise of the story is Sib's discovery that she loves the one who has been her devoted parent, her father. In one discussion, Sib challenges Taxi about what is involved in being a parent, what he has lost by being a father to her, and a theme emerges: "Don't put words in my mouth, Sib—I haven't ever said you 'took away' from my life. . . . Your mother would have discovered, as I have, that you add a lot more than you 'take away.'" He describes the essential commitment of being a good parent, how parenthood dominates one's thoughts:

> The most noticeable thing at first, probably, is what happens to your attention. . . . It's suddenly got an object, and if you want to give any attention to the things you used to think about, you have to think about them on a second level. The way you would, say, eat a sandwich while

driving. The driving has your first level of attention, or it should; the sandwich gets what notice you can give it in quick bites.

Sib cynically asks how many minutes in the day he had to be attentive, and when she hears that it was "pretty much all the time" is still doubtful. Taxi, however, confirms the importance of being totally committed to parenthood: "I was *there* for you twenty-four hours. Babies need you when they need you. For lots of things."

In a time when divorce is a common occurence, it is natural that young adults whose families have broken up wish to read of others' similar experiences. Paula Fox's novel *The Moonlight Man* explores how the child of a divorce comes to a realistic view of the absent parent. During the years since her parents' divorce, Caroline has seen her father only briefly, over lunch or dinner, but this sixteenth summer he has planned a full six weeks for them together. Caroline had dreamed of an idyllic time, perhaps a permanent change in their relationship, a dream disrupted by her discovery that Mr. Ames is insecure, unreliable, and a heavy drinker, discoveries that alienate her from him. Caroline's disappointment prompts her boyfriend to say, "You have a life elsewhere." Caroline's father, without excusing his behavior, states an explicit theme, "Life's not all grand opera." And when they laugh with embarrassment over their discovery that the housekeeper's "little Jackie" is not her child but her dwarf husband, Mr. Ames makes a broader statement about relationships, saying, "Don't make excuses. . . . There's nothing funny about the way we all betray each other." The discovery of what living with her father is like helps Caroline understand and accept her mother's long-ago decision to divorce. When she says to her mother, "I can see why you must have cared about him. . . . I can see, too, why you couldn't live with him," Caroline shows that she better understands her parents. This statement in the closing pages of the story pulls it all together; it is a mature recognition that a love can be real and intense, and yet can disappear over time.

One implicit theme in *Rainbow Jordan,* by Alice Childress, explores the idea expressed in the dedication that one can find a loving parent in someone other than a birth mother. Another theme might relate to mother Kathie's difficulty in settling into a satisfying motherhood because of having had a baby at 15. Because Beryl, Rainey's pregnant friend, has given in to her boyfriend's pressures for sex, her life will be disrupted just as Kathie's was, but, because Rainey by the end of the novel has found the strength to resist too-early sex and possible pregnancy, a more complete life is open to her. Being saddled with a child too early in life—as Kathie has been and as Beryl soon will be—prevents one from growing up in a normal way. The cycle does not change. Because both Rainey's mother and her 57-year-old foster mother lose their husbands to younger women, and Rainey loses her boyfriend to a young rival who will have sex with him, another implicit theme emerges: At any age, one may suffer loss. The story, short and accessible, addresses a number of strong thematic issues significant to young adults.

Human beings often struggle with how they feel about parents as it conflicts with how they think they ought to feel. *A Formal Feeling* by Zibby O'Neal implies that our true feelings may be disguised in just that way. Anne believes that she loved her mother intensely, and after her mother's death and her father's remarriage, she cannot love his new wife, Dory, who is so different. When Anne returns from boarding school to face the new wife, she must also face the fact that her own mother was a demanding perfectionist who was not particularly loving, and that Dory is a more relaxed, affectionate, and comfortable wife for her father; she is a woman who wants to love and be loved.

Themes sometimes turn the expected into the unexpected. An unusual twist on the single-parent situation occurs in Norma Klein's *No More Saturday Nights,* the story of 17-year-old Tim Weber, who takes on the rearing of his infant son born during his senior year in high school. Having been raised by his self-pitying widowed father, Tim thinks that he could care for Mason better than his own father had cared for him. Tim experiences what the single female parent might experience, but with the added element of people's shocked reaction to a boy's taking on the responsibility of a baby. As a scholarship premed student at Columbia, Tim must keep up his grades and find a reasonable schedule as well as an apartment; he sleeps little with many interruptions, makes formula, seeks solutions to infant care when he himself is sick, keeps Mason from annoying his three female roommates, and shapes his study schedule around Mason's needs. Tim's struggle, his uncertainties, and even his failures are inevitable, his strength and determination fluctuating, but nonetheless his bond to Mason grows. A certain doggedness had prompted Tim to take on this huge task, but the rewards keep him from altering his resolve. Through the complications of Tim's life, the realities of emotional and physical difficulty are revealed and implicit themes emerge: Single-parenthood involves sacrifice and is far from easy. As readers see the change in Tim's father, who now is much involved as a grandfather, the reader sees that the experience of committed parenthood changes one's life and one's outlook. A further theme is implied, one rarely explored in today's woman-as-single-parent stories, that a young father also has responsibility for the welfare of his child. Klein wisely notes that Tim is fortunate in having an inheritance and by living simply can manage financially; she avoids a sentimental theme that would say, "Everything always works out." Everything does not always work out for the single parent; regardless of dedication, it is tough, very tough.

The title *Dinky Hocker Shoots Smack!* is Dinky's cry for her parents' attention. M. E. Kerr's story, humorous though it is, deals with the agonizing young adult problem of overeating and overweight. Dinky's mother is a do-gooder who exerts all her energies in her efforts to help drug-dependent people become clean, but in the process she pays no attention to Dinky's food addiction. Dinky, whose name emphasizes the irony of her weight, buries herself in a variety of hobbies, each one an effort to repress her wish for her mother's attention. While Dinky's parents continue to be critical and demanding without really listening to her, Tucker's parents present a contrast; they give him space and responsibility and ask friendly questions, but because they trust his judgment they lay down no edicts about his behavior. Being attentive to young people can help them solve their problems. As Tucker says, "Things [amount] to a lot more than people think they amount to."

Fostering Hope Despite Differences

When in the late sixties "problem novels" first appeared for children and young adults, many were preoccupied with hopelessness, even despair. But everyone, young adults as much as anyone, needs to discover hope. Themes about feeling different also occur in stories for young adults, a theme that cries out for hope and reassurance. Throughout *Words by Heart* by Ouida Sebestyen, Lena must live by the dictates of the white society around her. Lena has won the prize for memorizing the most Bible verses, but no matter how rightfully she wins, since she is black she does not receive a prize for accomplishments. To be a proper black child, Lena must not expect to be rewarded for hard work, to be the brightest in the class, to state her opinions, or to resent having to stay out of school so that others can be comfortable in their mediocrity; in short, Lena must not make waves. Lena's father has other ideas, and says so explicitly: "You have a right to an education and hope and the chance to use your gifts. I pray to God you won't ever have to live your life by somebody else's rules."

Throughout Paterson's *Jacob Have I Loved* runs a hope-fostering, implied theme that one is not denied love but finds it when open to it. Wheeze, for example, has not been sure she wanted Call's love, but resents Caroline's "stealing" it from her, as she has "stolen" her parents' and the community's approval. Wheeze's irrascible grandmother, too, fantasizes that long ago the Captain's love had been stolen from her. Wheeze discovers, however, that love is neither stolen nor earned, but found—when one is ready for it.

Ursula K. Le Guin, writer of high fantasy, successfully helps the reader to understand a strong and hopeful implicit theme in *The Beginning Place*. Hugh and Irena separately find the way to "the ain country," a place of peace and timelessness. Both are troubled about their home lives, Hugh because his options for life are constrained by an unstable mother, and Irena because of her stepfather's unwelcome attentions. Tembreabrezi offers each the opportunity to serve its inhabitants, who are failing to prosper because of an unnamed source of evil. With courage that defies their fear of traveling in the cold and treacherous mountains, where there is no sound and where paths converge or disappear, the two young people confront the evil monster. With the sword given him, Hugh kills the monstrous evil, and brings peace and comfort once again to the Tembreabrezians. Irena and Hugh's sacrifice frees them from the unpleasant restrictions of their lives, and, once they find the gateway to return home, they are "home free" as Hugh says. Together they go on about living. High fantasy focuses on the conflict between good and evil, in this case personified by the two young people and the monster: restrictions are defeated and hope grows when people have the courage to fight and to move on toward a life of autonomy.

Becoming Aware of Interdependence

In addition to the struggle for independence, the young adult faces the need to acknowledge the importance of interdependence. In the unusual story *Wolf of Shadows,* Strieber's explicit theme is stated by the mother wolf: "Each of you is all of you, pack and species. And you know it and take your love of one another from it." Interdependence is the way of survival. The human mother and child survive because they become part of the wolf pack whose members care for each other; she in turn helps them all survive by sharing the canned food she finds, and steering them away from nuclear ground zero. Before the nuclear blast people had become so independent that they "were like leaves in the sea . . . alone." Now the wolves hear flowing water, evidence of a warmer place, and with hope lead the human survivors to discover where and whether they can all survive.

In Norma Fox Mazer's novel *Downtown,* both Pete and Cory face uncertainty, Pete that of the reappearance and arrest of his fugitive parents, and Cory that of hoping to be adopted by her current foster parents. One thematic idea effectively explored is that "Home is where you find love," Cory in this last of many foster homes and Pete with his bachelor uncle, who has raised him while his parents are in flight. "We all have our secrets and can reveal them only to those we totally trust" seems an appropriate statement of an implicit theme, demonstrated when Pete and his girlfriend, Cory, reveal their past lives to each other. "Living with uncertainty is difficult" is also implied.

Dealing with the Sense of Isolation

As Erik Erikson has noted, young adults often experience a sense of isolation. A number of novels confront the issue, either as central focus or one peripheral to other action. Although once a taboo topic for literature for young adults, the lover-mistress relationship is the focus of Janine Boissard's novel *A Matter of Feeling,* set in Paris and its suburbs. The novel is about first love, in this case 17-year-old Pauline's affair with a man more than twice her age, with another mistress and a 12-year-old daughter. The context of the romance is that Pauline comes from what seems to the older Pierre an absolutely ideal family of four sisters and caring, listening parents, a family that meets together in "a priority. A priority is a friend in trouble, an unusual conversation, anything that is a matter of feeling. A roast dinner can wait. The heart can't." The concept of feeling isolated comes into play in the novel as the mother says explicitly, "The main thing is to participate [in life] in one way or another. Don't shut yourself up in nullity." Pauline is maturing both emotionally and sexually in a permissive time and place. The insecurity common to young adults makes her wonder if she will ever be lovable, have a lover, or find a mate, and makes her fall precipitately in love with Pierre, who had grown up without caring family life and who seems more in love with the idea of Pauline than with Pauline herself. Pauline's eldest sister Claire, at 21, is also unhappy in isolation and loneliness and is unable to make a decision about getting out of the house and being on her own. Cecile, at 12, uses an imaginary boyfriend, Nicolas, to camouflage her withdrawal into loneliness; Bernadette, a boyish riding instructor of 19, seems the most integrated, her love life complete with the gentlemanly Stephen. Mother is the idealized homemaker and Papa the wise and caring doctor to whom Pauline can go for birth-control pills. What readers come to realize implicitly is that the idealized family has its own problems, its isolated young people, its internal rivalries and anxieties. Explicitly stated in a broader context is that no family is without pain. Despite a youth-and-middle-age-in-an-affair theme—a topic that even today may seem a doubtful story line for young adult literature—Boissard manages to write a tender love story about early sexual feelings, and yet convey the theme that such vast differences in age and experience do not augur well for a successful marriage. With the help of her sister Bernadette, Pauline discovers that one's own insecurity and feelings of isolation are a poor basis for a lasting relationship, and that marriage is not merely romance, but also responsibility and routine. She has more maturing to do before she is ready for so big a step.

Judging by Appearances

Just as "A book cannot be judged by its cover," "People cannot be judged by appearances" may seem to be a cliché, but it, too, is one of the important discoveries of a young adult. In Rosa Guy's *The Friends,* Phyllisia lacks the courage to keep shabby Edith as her friend, but instead turns to neatly dressed Marian, who personifies the middle-class virtues of cleanliness and family stability, only to discover that Marian is catty and disloyal, and only Edith offers real friendship. The revelation that her values are false occurs when in an explicit statement of theme, Phyl can say to herself, "I had seen things the way I *wanted* them to be. I had wanted to be the unhappy princess living with the cruel king of a father. . . . I had wanted to be rich, to live in luxury, so that I could feel superior to them—to people like Edith. . . . *I* was the fraud."

Other novels suggest explicitly stated themes that also resolve around judging by appearances. M. E. Kerr's *Little Little* is about teenagers who are dwarfs or diminutive people, and who have the same wishes as others—to find someone special and to be liked for themselves. Theme is clearly stated in several places, one of them a direct question: "Can't you ever get past that thing you have about physical appearances?" Restated in declarative form, the question becomes "Physical appearance has little to do with the real self." Little Little states the theme in another way when she says that the town of LaBelle is just like her, only the reverse: "It looks good on the outside but it isn't that way on the inside."

Understanding the Nature of Society

Caught up in the microcosm of school, young adults often wonder about "the real world." In Sleator's *Interstellar Pig* readers may glimpse a larger society, identifying it as concerned with the arms race and nuclear war: Barney, a novice at playing the game named in the title, implies that the game is the international arms race, now with nuclear arms: "I didn't know what happened at the end of the last game. Because this was its first game," and it has gone on for a very long time. In the intense international competition of the game, every greedy country is out for itself, while the threat of annihilation is imminent. That same theme also persists on a more individual and personal basis. The three unrelated aliens who rent the house next door to Barney's seem at first to be friends, but as they live together, exchange verbal snipes, and play the continuous game of Interstellar Pig, each person's total preoccupation with finding the Pig for the sake of self-interest becomes increasingly apparent. Deceiving one another and calling on their own interpretations of the intricate rules, all seek to control or annihilate the others for their own advancement, a behavior pattern parallel to countries' acting in their own self-interest. An implied theme evolves: one who operates only on the principle of self-interest may bring about self-destruction, a truth for both nations and individuals.

Not all themes in novels for young adults are optimistic. In strong contrast to some of the optimistic themes lies Cormier's *After the First Death,* another intricately plotted novel that pits fanatical patriotism against humane and compassionate values. Significant statements about values and motives, and questions about commitment and sacrifice define these themes. Artkin, leader of a terrorist band, doubts that the American commander Marchand will submit his own son to the danger of being an emissary. He asks himself, "Who knows Americans? They may love their children more than service to their country." Subsequent action proves otherwise. Fathers Artkin and Marchand are two of a kind; for both, patriotic motives transcend parental love. Patriotism and blind obedience motivate Artkin, who has trained his son to be an automaton so that he can murder—patriotically. Even the American general is more patriotic than paternally loving. Because Marchand's son Ben cracks under Artkin's torture, Ben kills himself, never knowing that his own father had anticipated his submission and given him false information for the benefit of the American agency. Marchand, alone in Ben's dormitory room, speaks to Ben about patriotism during World War II and today, and says flatly that patriotism is unquestioning:

> We were poorly trained in those days, Ben, but trained superbly in one thing: patriotism. There are all kinds of patriotism; ours was pure and sweet and unquestioning. We were the good guys. Today there is patriotism, of course. But this generation is questioning. This generation looks at itself in a mirror as it performs its duties. And wonders: Who are the good guys? Is it possible we are the bad guys? They should never ask that question, Ben, or even contemplate it.

Theme in *The Chocolate War* goes beyond the personal to comment on psychological and physical violence in society. Smart student Caroni, in order to have his rightfully earned grade accepted by Brother Leon, allows himself to be blackmailed. "If teachers did this kind of thing, what kind of world could it be? . . . And he did see—that life was rotten, that there were no heroes," and that you cannot even trust yourself. This recognition comes to Jerry, too, as he plants a vicious blow on Emile and realizes that he is hitting from a wish for vengeance against all coercive behavior. As his recognition grows, Jerry is "invaded" by "the new sickness of knowing what he had become, another animal, another beast, another violent person in a violent world."

One of the themes explored in *Ratha and Thistle-chaser,* a fantasy by Clare Bell, involves human behavior in groups, behavior based upon a sense of superiority. A group of creatures called the Named regards itself as the most intelligent; they have learned to speak, to herd other, lesser creatures that serve as food, and to plan and execute their plans for survival in time of drought. In moving from the larger group to one-to-one relationships, several themes emerge. "Cooperative effort can enable a beleaguered group to survive." "Groups appraise their own traits and define themselves as superior to others, excluding and deriding those unlike them." A more personal theme also emerges. Ratha, leader of the Named and mother of Newt/Thistle-chaser, rejects her offspring, whom she believes to be less intelligent than the Named. Newt, in her fury aroused by distant memories of rejection and injury, nearly kills her own mother. Although Ratha had first intended to kill an alien nurseling, she cannot, and begins instead to take it to safety, finally nurturing it to health. As Newt watches her mother, Ratha, Newt recognizes her own actions as vengeance that cannot rectify any earlier actions. Maternal feelings can be suppressed or killed, but mutual forgiveness can reawaken them.

Americans have grown up with a romanticized view of the pioneers' motives for exploring and settling the West. *Borderlands* by Peter Carter, a novel much longer than most written for young adults (424 pages), explores a sound theme far less common: the search for a comfortable homesite with space of one's own or the challenge of conquering the wilderness were not what settled the West. The motivation was greed. Carter's story follows a boy of 13 for several years as he lives the life of cowboy, buffalo hunter and skinner, frontier store-owner, and victim of financial chicanery. An innocent carried away by his craving for money and what it can buy, Ben is constantly on the brink of accepting and adopting for himself the frontier lawlessness. Ben, whose dream of money keeps him going, represents on a small scale the overwhelming greed of buffalo hunters who destroy the animals by the millions, taking hides and leaving the flesh to rot, land grabbers who are dishonest and ruthless in their money dealings, amoral opportunists who murder and maim for vengeance or money, soldiers and hunters who ambush and destroy the Indians without regard for their legal right to live on the reservation. When the buffalo are gone and the Indians deprived of their livelihood, and when the settlers who come to farm turn a community into a law-governed town, the greedy opportunists will turn to gold and silver prospecting and other exploitative behavior. The very immensity of the continent is a factor in human disregard for sensible behavior in pursuit of "real money." Human lust for wealth, not a romantic wish for open spaces, fueled the westward movement.

> I don't mean there wasn't none [buffalo] left in the world, nor even in the United States. Just there wasn't none where we was, so if we wanted more hunting, we'd have to move on, and to this day I'm not sure we wouldn't have done so, that being how dollars grab you.

> . . . That was America. There was plenty of it. Plenty to move around in, plenty of it to make a fortune in, to go broke in, too, come to that, and plenty of it to die in.

A universal theme related to human fascination with violence and disaster is clarified by the characters' regular telling and retelling, their hearing again and again of violent actions and incidents, "hanging on . . . every word like kids listening to a fairy tale."

There we was, out on the wild frontier, shooting buffalo and with sav-
age Indians on the loose, but most of life was just plain hard toil, and
most of the fellers you met was the same, having the same thoughts and
saying the same thing, just like folks most anyplace, so they was looking
for romance, I guess you'd call it, in other people's lives."

Acknowledging Contradictions

Life is not as simple as Right and Wrong, Good and Evil. Sometimes a
novel may have contradictory themes, as *The Chocolate War* seems at
times to have: "Dare to disturb the universe" and "It's futile to try." An explicitly stated theme and an additional contradictory one recur in Peter
Dickinson's *Eva*, an unusual story that might be called science fantasy.
Eva's body has been so damaged by an accident that her scientist father, a
researcher of chimpanzees, resorts to keeping her alive in a chimp's
body. Slowly, through the help of neuron memory electronic systems,
Eva becomes a chimp, one who helps in the Institute's research projects.
As she lives with the chimpanzees, she increasingly adopts their ways and
retreats from her human self, her human intelligence improving the
chimps' lives. For example, she teaches them to build litters for the sick
and wounded and to hollow out graves for their dead and cover them
with stones. In an increasingly overpopulated world, it seems that
chimps may be the only survivors, while human beings—who in their
search for answers to all their questions have destroyed the natural
world—die from wars, disease, and mass suicide. Human curiosity is the
basis for experimentation and discovery; explicitly, "Once [the human
mind] found one thing out, it had to move on." People ask questions and
seek answers "out of the endless human longing to know." The story also
has an implicit and somewhat contradictory theme less prominently dis-
played, that this longing may result in experiments that change the nature of all life, and may ultimately destroy human beings.

Multiple and Secondary Themes

Many of the themes discussed above are not primary but secondary in importance. In *Catcher in the Rye* a secondary theme might be drawn from
the school settings, both Holden's many prep schools and Phoebe's elementary school. Idealistic Holden is continuously disillusioned in prep
school after prep school, settings for the transition to adulthood: Growing up is a process of education not only in a school setting but in the
larger imperfect world, here exemplified by the city. Holden wants
Phoebe to remain in her innocent state, and to ensure her continued innocence, he rubs out the bad words so she will never see or know them.
In fact, one of the things he likes about the carousel is that it never ages

but stays the same, always going around at the same pace playing the same songs. He loves the Natural History Museum, where things stay the same, despite the visitor's changing and growing older. He mentions several possible reasons for children being different on their trips to the museum, like having just seen a street puddle with rainbows of gasoline, or heard parents fight, or having a substitute teacher; he then concludes that although he can't explain how, people do not remain the same. As Phoebe's reaching for the gold carousel ring exemplifies, it's useless trying to keep children innocent, to prevent them from growing into adulthood. You cannot keep them from trying to grab the gold ring. Although they may fall, they must be permitted to try.

Bridgers's *All Together Now* is filled with variations of one significant theme, never too obvious to bore us but subtly demonstrated by the many loving relationships between characters. As characters struggle against their inclinations to hide their individual truths, they find that the best way is to admit who they are and how they feel. Casey, who is spending the summer with her grandparents, wants Dwayne, the child-like baseball-pitching adult across the street, to think she is a boy, K. C.; she fears that if he learns she is a girl, he won't love her anymore. Not so. Casey's brother Taylor struggles to admit that he loves Gwen, although she had spurned him when he had in an act of kindness given away her gift to Dwayne. Gwen tries to forget Taylor—until, understanding Taylor's motive as kindness, she admits she loves him. Alva, the town commissioner and Dwayne's brother, struggles to face his embarrassment at Dwayne's childlike behavior and rather than have Dwayne committed, once again resumes their loving relationship. Pansy, who has settled unhappily into middle-aged single life without Hazard, swallows her pride and admits that "different" as Hazard is, she loves him and wants to be married to him. Hazard, on the other hand, defies his timidity and risks the town's laughter when he camps on Pansy's front lawn until she says she will have him. And even Barbara's mother, who has sent Casey to her grandparents for the summer, faces up to her need for her daughter. Obviously, "Loving's got a lot more to it." Casey's grandmother would always love Hazard "simply because he was there and needed her." Casey thinks, "Loving people was hard. It meant always trying to tell the truth." Pansy knows Hazard's idiosyncracies and tells him "you are worth the risk." The need to support others so that they may survive and thrive is expressed by Hazard as he says of Casey's serious illness, "she's got to want to get well, we've got to make sure she wants it bad enough." As Jane ministers to feverish Casey, "Nothing else mattered. Nothing counted but the woman and the child, the precious cooling of one body with the skill of another, the laying on of hands." Casey learns from Dwayne that "having someone to love gave you a chance to be loved yourself." And finally, Casey hugs Dwayne goodby, thinking to herself, "he would survive because what he saw of life was so often good, and because he was willing to forgive what wasn't." These fragments of the text all support a network of optimistic love that supports them all, together.

Young adults frequently insist that everyone measure up to their impossibly high standards, just as Holden Caulfield does. Several secondary themes related to how we come to appreciate people and their differences are explored in *Dixie Storms* by Barbara Hall. Tension, anxiety, and downright fear over the drought threaten to pull Dutch's farming family apart. Her recognition that even people she has little love for are feeling the same about the weather leads her to say, "I suddenly knew what Papa meant when he said that people weren't all good or all bad—the hard part was knowing that we were a little bit of both." The breakup of her brother Flood's marriage has troubled Dutch, but when his wife Becky returns briefly from Norfolk to the tobacco farm and the family who loved her, Dutch realizes that events, hard though they may be, need not destroy one: "And then I knew that the world didn't have to make people worse; sometimes it made them better." Throughout the novel Dutch has been struggling with her anger at Becky for leaving Flood and with her father for his anger at his brother for abandoning the farm. Flood tells them, "You've got to let go of folks. . . . The world has got its own motion." Implicit within these themes is the notion of accepting change, in family fortunes as well as in loving relationships.

Evaluating Theme

Young adult readers seek themes that relate to their interests and concerns, themes that are not preachy, that do not say with false optimism that the world is an easy place and minimize the difficulties of growing into maturity, that do not shake at them the fingers of "you should do this," and "ought not to do that." The moral simplicity of folktales and fairy tales constitutes an ideal world where good is rewarded and evil punished. On the other hand, the search for "reality" sometimes causes writers to write and critics to praise books that stress the sordid or the most fashionable social problems, whether they be incest or sexual abuse. On the contrary, young people, whether "advantaged" or "disadvantaged," need books that will open their minds and imaginations to other ideas, real and yet hopeful. Remembering that such themes are also "real" may justify a mixture of offerings.

Integrated schools are an effort to help one ethnic or societal group become acquainted with another. Ideally, with this acquaintance come acceptance and understanding. A number of such thematic ideas emerge from Mildred Taylor's *Let the Circle Be Unbroken*, as the story addresses one issue after another in the lives of southern black families during the Depression. Sharecroppers and farm laborers, both black and white, unite against pay of $1.50 a day and attempt to form a union that is immediately thwarted by white violence. Jurors are chosen from among registered voters, but blacks are denied their legal right to vote. When the accused is black and all jurors are white, justice becomes impossible. Intermarriage between black and white presents the couple and their children with two worlds that do not always mesh; spurned by both segments, life may be difficult for both black and white in the North and subject to violence from whites in the South. Young black girls are fair prey to white males and must be constantly protected and carefully instructed about what to expect and avoid. As readers follow the Logan family and its struggle to survive during the Depression and the Agricultural Adjustment Act's efforts to raise cotton and other farm prices, Stacey sets out to find work in the cane fields, where he is worked mercilessly without adequate health care or the promised compensation. Like other farm families, the Logans split up as the men seek work elsewhere, and the family fears they may not survive to be reunited. As with Taylor's *Roll of Thunder, Hear My Cry,* the title of the novel comes from a hymn sung in the black churches; the unbroken circle here refers to this fear that the family circle may never again be complete. At first glance the story seems filled with agonizing problems, but Taylor manages to show hopeful signs of change.

As noted earlier, young adults often see conditions and ideas as either right or wrong, as does Holden Caulfield, who at first sees the world as either good or bad. He is not alone in his wish for perfection. Literature can help young adults to recognize gradations and accept some compromise. An implicit theme, "No one can know another's experiences, no matter how hard one tries" is the discovery made by Sam in Bobbie Ann Mason's *In Country.* Sam, who never knew her father—a casualty in the Vietnam War—tries in every way to know what he was like and what his war experiences were, and why her Uncle Emmett returned from Vietnam so drastically changed. She reads voraciously, gets to know other veterans and tries to persuade them to talk, watches M*A*S*H faithfully, and even camps out in Cawoods swamp to try to learn what living in the jungle was like. But she can never know the vicious and futile experience of men who fought in the jungles and returned to uncaring towns.

One implicit theme of Cormier's *Fade* suggests that given opportunity to go undetected, we might permit forces within us to overcome our scruples and to lead us to commit acts of horrendous violence. A literary diet made up exclusively of such pessimistic predictions might be destructive, but this recognition of human flaws can also be useful in the maturing process.

Simplistic Themes

Sometimes a dominant theme may strike the reader at the same time as another theme is subliminally received. That is the situation in *Weetzie*

Bat, the story of teenagers whose lives are intertwined as they entertain themselves without the hated school, going to clubs and matinees, making successful films, and holding their rubber chicken out the car window. The two young men, Dirk and Duck, are homosexual lovers affectionately close to Weetzie. Weetzie's "My Secret Agent Lover Man" thinks her too young for motherhood and the world too filled with babies and troubles, but Weetzie's wish for a baby results in her being impregnated, either by Dirk or Duck. The dominant theme is that people can accept differences, particularly differences in sexual orientation, and live, as they say, "happily ever after." Such a theme needs exposure and development. However, the book's fairy-tale tone falsely conveys another theme, a romantic, implicit theme that all will be well for a baby who is loved, that that's all that's needed. The never-never land of a perfect Los Angeles of "glitter and glitz" will be an ideal setting for child rearing, and no problems will arise for a baby and its drop-out mother as long as they "plug into the love current." Such an implied theme does disservice to young people whose understanding is not awakened, but whose naiveté is reenforced.

Some simple themes recur over and over again. Young love, how quickly it strikes and how total its impact, is explored in any number of stories, including *Tom Loves Anna Loves Tom:* here the circular title implies that the feelings are mutual. There seem to be hundreds of stories with similar themes, including the romantic series novels. Important as the first experiences of love are to young adults, they are not the sole preoccupation of the age group. Other themes infringe upon and even take precedence over the growth of young love, as well as prepare young adults for more complex relationships later. What seems relevant here is that the stronger novels deal with additional themes about additional issues facing the age group. The exclusion of other themes seems to say that the only issue in life—like that in romantic novels—is finding the romantic and sexual bond. Return once again to the touchstone novel, *The Chocolate War,* a novel that acknowledges interest in the other sex, but also has themes about human understanding of self and others, and courageous actions that touch lives in a great variety of ways. Reading the same simplistic theme again and again does little for young readers.

Didacticism

The theme that it is best to be honest with oneself is explicitly stated in several places in *Tiger Eyes;* the theme has merit in itself, but is so frequently emphasized that it becomes **didactic** or preachy. For just three examples, Davey urges Jane, her alcoholic friend, to "face herself" and go to the alcohol abuse clinic. Davey believes she herself has also been dishonest because she has led others to believe her father died rather than tell them that he was murdered. "Isn't it about time you face the facts? Isn't it about time you were honest with yourself?" she asks. Referring to the family's return to Atlantic City, Davey makes a related explicit thematic statement on the final page of the novel. "You have to pick up the pieces and keep moving ahead."

Look closely at other behaviors found in novels for this age group, the casual but illegal use of alcohol, for example. In Kate Gilmore's *Enter Three Witches,* a novel that realistically portrays the uncertainties and the three-steps-forward-two-back of young love, underage Erika and Bren drink illegal beer together, Bren's father buys him a cocktail, and separately Erika and Bren both get drunk. An additional question involves honesty. Bren's mother, the witch Miranda, needs frogs for her brew and suggests, without using the actual word, that Bren steal some from the biology lab. In a scene that seems to condone dishonesty through its use of humor, Bren does just that. In Deaver's *Say Goodnight, Gracie,* Jimmy's and Morgan's mothers, although acknowledging that they "feel funny" doing it, habitually call the school to say the two are sick when actually they are going to Chicago for ballet or theater tryouts. While such actions are by no means unusual among young people or their parents, the question of appropriateness remains.[5]

Summary

Themes may be either explicitly stated in so many words, or implicitly understood from the story itself. Whether implicit or explicit, theme is essential to literature for any age. Stories may have one or more explicit themes, and one or more implicit themes. Although the number does not matter, a principal theme or group of related themes usually emerges. Both objective and optimistic themes like those in *Roll of Thunder, Hear My Cry* and pessimistic themes like those of Robert Cormier in *The Chocolate War, I Am the Cheese,* and *After the First Death* have their place. Although sometimes the latter kinds of themes are thought to lead to despair, they keep the reader intensely interested; perhaps they serve not so much to discourage or disenchant readers as to provoke them to thought and discussion.

Notes

1. Criticism is the process of making judgments about what is good and what is not good, approving and praising or pointing out flaws and failures. All criticism of any kind, of literature, world events, human behavior, or anything else, is value judgment. Moral human beings make value judgments, and should. Those whose responsibility, as teachers or parents, is to ready the young for adulthood

are particularly charged with awakening their recognition of what is good and what is not so good, to making value judgments.

2. Nina Bawden, *Hornbook Magazine,* February, 1980, pp. 25-26.

3. Wayne Booth, *The Rhetoric of Fiction* (Chicago: University of Chicago Press, 1961), p. 136.

4. My first reaction to *The Chocolate War* was strongly negative, as discussed in Rebecca J. Lukens, "From Salinger to Cormier: Disillusionment to Despair in Thirty Years," in *Webs and Wardrobes: Humanist and Religious World Views,* ed. Joseph Milner and Lucy Milner (New York: University Press of America, 1987).

5. Does the writer have a responsibility not to preach values but to avoid the appearance of accepting these behaviors? Is this compromise possible or desirable? Does the answer lie not in censorship so much as in the test of the story's contribution to young adult growth toward responsible maturity? Discussion helps.

Recommended Books Cited in This Chapter

Bell, Clare. *Ratha and Thistle-chaser.* New York: Margaret McElderrry Books, 1990.

Boissard, Janine. *A Matter of Feeling.* New York: Little, Brown, 1988.

Bridgers, Sue Ellen. *All Together Now.* New York: Knopf, 1979.

Brooks, Bruce. *Midnight Hour Encores.* New York: Harper, 1986.

Carter, Peter. *Borderlands.* New York: Farrar, Straus & Giroux, 1990.

Childress, Alice. *Rainbow Jordan.* New York: Coward McCann, 1981.

Cleaver, Vera and Bill Cleaver. *Trial Valley.* New York: Lippincott, 1987.

Cole, Brock. *Celine.* New York: Farrar, Straus & Giroux, 1989.

Cormier, Robert. *After the First Death.* New York: Pantheon, 1979.

———. *The Chocolate War.* New York: Random House, 1974.

———. *Fade.* Delacorte, 1980.

Dickinson, Peter. *Eva.* New York: Delacorte, 1988.

Fox, Paula. *The Moonlight Man.* New York: Bradbury, 1986.

Guy, Rosa. *The Friends.* New York: H. Holt, 1973.

Hall, Barbara. *Dixie Storms.* New York: Harcourt Brace Jovanovich, 1990.

Hamilton, Virginia. *A Little Love.* New York: Philomel, 1984.

———. *Sweet Whispers, Brother Rush.* New York: Philomel, 1982.

Hoover, H. M. *The Dawn Palace: The Story of Medea.* New York: Dutton, 1988.

Hunter, Mollie. *Cat Herself.* New York: Harper & Row, 1985.

Kerr, M. E. *Dinky Hocker Shoots Smack!* New York: Harper, 1972.

———. *I'll Love You When You're More Like Me.* New York: Harper & Row, 1978.

———. *Little Little.* New York: Harper, 1986.

Klein, Norma. *No More Saturday Nights*. New York: Knopf, 1988.

Le Guin, Ursula K. *The Beginning Place*. New York: Harper, 1980.

Lipsyte, Robert. *One Fat Summer*. New York: Harper, 1984.

Mason, Bobbie Ann. *In Country*. New York: Harper, 1986.

Mazer, Norma Fox. *Downtown*. New York: Avon, 1984.

O'Neal, Zibby. *A Formal Feeling*. New York: Viking, 1982.

Paterson, Katherine. *Jacob Have I Loved*. New York: Harper & Row, 1980.

Peck, Richard. *Princess Ashley*. New York: Dell, 1987.

Salinger, J. D. *The Catcher in the Rye*. Boston: Little, Brown, 1951.

Sebestyen, Ouida. *Words by Heart*. Boston: Little, Brown, 1979.

Sleator, William. *Interstellar Pig*. New York: Dutton, 1984.

Strieber, Whitley. *Wolf of Shadows*. New York: Knopf, 1985.

Taylor, Mildred. *Let the Circle Be Unbroken*. New York: Dutton, 1981.

———. *Roll of Thunder, Hear My Cry*. New York: Dutton, 1976.

Voigt, Cynthia. *Sons from Afar*. New York: Atheneum, 1974.

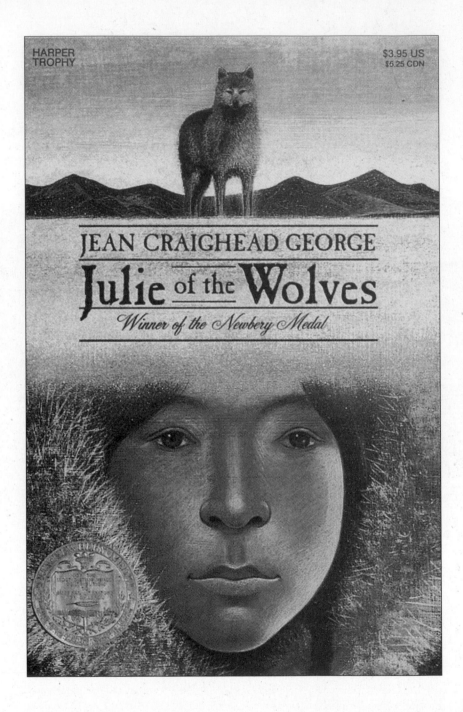

HARPER
TROPHY

$3.95 US
$5.25 CDN

JEAN CRAIGHEAD GEORGE

Julie of the Wolves

Winner of the Newbery Medal

— 5 —

Setting

Depiction of character and description of conflict and plot occur in time and place, elements called **setting.** Unlike setting in literature for children, which is usually concretely described or even pictured for the very young, setting in literature for young adults may occur almost anywhere, including the mind of the protagonist, where it needs no concrete description.

Endless possibilities for setting are available to the writer, from a primordial time of early human development to a future time of outer-space living, in places like caves and cliffs or orbiting capsules. Nothing limits the writer's choice of time and place, nothing but the capacity to imagine and speculate. It all depends upon the story the writer wishes to tell. If the story depends upon our envisioning a particular time and place, the writer makes an appropriate choice and then describes it. If the story could occur anywhere and is not influenced by a particular time and place, the author need not describe setting specifically. In fact, a setting shown too specifically might in some cases minimize a theme, or make the characters or conflict less universal. The writer determines the story and thus determines the setting.

To realize the importance of setting, think back to a recent visit to the theater. The curtains part to present a dark scene: a dim street light, buildings wing to wing, graffiti smeared from one end to the other, beverage cans, paper and plastic wrappers, and liquor bottles littering the stage. Something about the nature of the action to come is revealed. In some stories readers must know details of setting—what it looks like, what buildings or vegetation exist, what sounds and sights and even smells are present—details relevant because they influence character, conflict, and theme. Such details may also be essential to create the atmosphere and mood of the story. Gothic tales, for example, rely heavily on our sensory awareness of setting in order to create in our minds the mystery, fear, and even terror typical of that genre.

The preceding discussions of character, plot, and theme show how interrelated these elements are as they influence and reflect one another; setting, too, may be closely related. *Roll of Thunder, Hear My Cry* needs the rural South, and *The Chocolate War* requires Trinity School. If these novels or *Catcher in the Rye* took place in the Nevada desert, they would be very different stories.

Types of Setting

In evaluating a piece of literature, awareness of the basic kind of setting shows how setting functions in the story. For any piece of imaginative writing the author chooses one of two types: the **backdrop** or relatively unimportant setting, or the **integral** or essential setting.

The determining factor in this choice is the purpose of the story. For example, in a story of internal conflict, the first-person narrator may tell the progress of the plot in narrative, dialogue and action, or in letter or diary form. The reader may not need to know the setting because the conflict about the protagonist's relationship with his parents occurs within the mind of the protagonist; in such a story, a setting described in detail, like a classroom, for example, might distract from the focus of the story. On the other hand, the classroom could serve as a useful setting if it shows the character's difficulty in concentrating on the demands of schoolwork while her mind is totally preoccupied with conflict in the family.

Descriptive language makes the setting clear. *Catcher* takes place primarily in New York City, but everyone has a personal view of the city, none quite right for Salinger's purposes. If the reader's only experience of the big city is Fargo, North Dakota, and only idea of a prep school is Oak Grove Academy, without clear description Salinger's novel would lack its total impact. But since the setting is vital to understanding the story, the reader needs details—concrete and explicit details with sensory pictures and vivid comparisons—to make the setting so clear that the reader understands how this story is related to this place. While reading *The Chocolate War,* the reader may make mental comparisons to his or her own high school, either private or public, but the places bear at least some similarity. Because the differences influence the action, they must be made clear.

In contrast, if the unskilled writer insists the setting is significant and yet creates a setting shallow in concept and superficial in depiction, the reader may reject everything—character, conflict, and theme. A setting made "three-dimensional" by description can make character, conflict, and idea real and acceptable.

Backdrop Setting

Obviously the term **backdrop setting** comes from the theater. Parts of the action in musicals often occur against a two-dimensional painting of a place, a ranch for *Oklahoma!* or a London street for *My Fair Lady.* Some of the action in Shakespeare's plays occurs on the stage apron before a plain curtain serving as backdrop for a conversation or for a soliloquy, an argument or discussion in which the protagonist reveals his thoughts. Or a forest backdrop may suggest a place of evil or of mystery, a busy street the presence of encroaching society. Particulars of who lives where may not be important.

Setting is for the most part a backdrop in Bruce Brooks's action-filled *The Moves Make the Man,* in which the real focus is the black-white friendship between Jerome and Bix. When, however, we need a vivid description like that of the free-food concession truck at the ballpark, Brooks is not at loss for words; colors and shapes, sounds and smells are rampant. The same is true of *Interstellar Pig,* William Sleator's science fiction story that focuses on mysterious cottage neighbors and the frightening, competitive game that totally absorbs them. Barney's interest in the house next door focuses on the game table and the playing pieces, which in turn reflect the strange relationships between the unusually attractive group of players and their obsessive curiosities. In *Someday I'll Laugh About This* Linda Crew needs little description of setting because the story spotlights the relationship between Shelby and her cousin Kirsten, who over the summer has aged vastly more than a year and is now preoccupied with hair and clothes and boys. Although Shelby—who wants to stay a carefree child unconcerned about beauty and boys—is angry that a developer wants to close off the beach path into town, the reader has no need for detailed descriptions of the beach environment or the Oregon coast. The major focus of the story is elsewhere.

Integral Setting

A story has an **integral setting** when the particulars of time and place influence action, character, or theme. Novelist Eudora Welty has said that setting has "the most delicate control over character . . . by confining character, it defines it."[1] These characters in these circumstances in this time and this place behave in this way. Because theme and action are also closely related to character, setting may have strong effect on the whole of the story. In novels written for adults in other times, setting was occasionally described at great length early in the book; perhaps the slower pace of life allowed readers to settle into long passages of description.

Contemporary stories are more likely to weave details of setting into the
action.

Because young adults spend a major part of their lives in school, it is
often the setting for fictional action. Since teachers play a significant part
in the exploration of the theme of *The Chocolate War* and the conflict
stems from the rigidly demanding environment of the rule-bound school
and its authority figures, most of the action occurs in Trinity classrooms
and athletic facilities, the "universe" that Jerry hopes to disturb. In descriptions of the setting within the school, Cormier describes in brief sentence by brief paragraph the microcosm of the world with its hidden bul-
lies who control for no reason other than the pleasure of being in
command. Avoiding lengthy descriptive segments, Cormier weaves in the
setting where necessary as Goober stealthily prepares the classroom for
total chaos, and Jerry is attacked and nearly bludgeoned to death by
Archie and the Vigils.

Integral, too, is setting in *Roll of Thunder.* This is the rural South and
these are the days before the civil rights movement. Because it owns
land, the Logan family is unusual for this time and place; they are more independent and can show strength in defying the white store owners. The
area farmers, and particularly the black families, are sharecroppers, living
for the most part at subsistence level. The poor white members of the Ku
Klux Klan resent the blacks, and are always ready to usurp or threaten
their success, to punish them for real or imagined grievances. When Mr.
Barnett is killed in the burglary, Klansmen blame T. J.; they accuse him of
the burglary and the resulting murder, and attack and beat him till he cannot stand. These events and situations of the story exist because of the
times and the place, the Depression era in the South. All are essential to
readers' understanding of the story.

Settings in *Catcher* are multiple, but each is an educational site of
one kind or another—Holden's prep school and Phoebe's grade school,
the theater, hotel, museum, bars, and "the wicked city" in general.
Schools are sites for assistance in growth from childhood to maturity, for
education, but to Holden each of the several prep schools is disillusioning. Materialism, snobbery, cliquishness, exploitation, dishonesty, cruelty, unreasonable demands, and above all phoniness are traits he sees in
classmates, teachers, alumni, even parents. Phoebe in elementary school
does not yet face these disillusioning experiences. The four-letter words
scratched into the stairwell walls, however, hint that even for Phoebe innocence will not prevail forever. School is the appropriate setting for education, even for discovery of human imperfection.

Museums preserve, maintain, protect, and hold in pristine condition
all that they house. Holden's profound wish for Phoebe is to preserve,
maintain, protect, and hold her innocence in pristine condition. Each
time a child goes to a museum, she may be a bit different for having heard
her parents argue at breakfast, or for having a different partner in line.

But the Indians in the canoe at the museum are always the same Indians in the same canoe. The display is constant, the children different. On the one hand, this split maintains continuity and sameness, and on the other acknowledges change. And that is the conclusion that Holden must come to in his maturing process. The setting has helped to clarify the theme.[2]

Virginia Hamilton has written a story clearly set in reality and yet with a fantastic element. Since readers see clearly the little alcove room used for storage and later for Tree's private world in *Sweet Whispers, Brother Rush,* they are able to accept her visions of Brother Rush. An ordinary place filled with everyday items, it has a round, wide table holding "all kinds of things—a broken television, pieces of things. Magazines from ages ago . . . dusty comic books. There was the television; part of a chair, its soiled canvas seat ripped. Half of a black telephone. A cardboard box of old tired-out shoes. . . ." A disparate list of items, and yet their random ordinariness serves to set in reality the fantastic appearances of Brother Rush. Had Brother Rush appeared to Tree in a dream world, the effect of the story would be quite different; readers might view all of it as fantasy rather than wonder if perhaps it might be possible—and true.

Most of the action in *Permanent Connections* by Sue Ellen Bridgers occurs in the southern Appalachians, a place important to the story. Rob and his father, Davis, fly from urban New Jersey into a "dinky airport" and drive thirty miles to Tayler Mills, stopping to visit Rob's Uncle Fairlee in a one-story hospital, a "concrete-block building with a brick face. Rob . . . could see into the lobby: chrome and vinyl sofas, scraggly overgrown plants tilting out of plastic pots, a television attached to the wall projecting a rolling colored picture." Ellery, Rob's new girlfriend, lives in a home revealing her mother's craft as she tries to make a living from her weaving:

> . . . One big room cluttered with big wooden looms, baskets of yarn hanging from open beams, strange equipment he assumed had something to do with weaving scattered everywhere. Bright colors in abundance but no plan to it, nothing to make the room comfortable. He had to sit in a kitchen chair at a table strewn with thin S-shaped hooks, wooden boats with metal rods through them, a contraption with ribs like an umbrella attached to the table edge with a vise . . . confusion. . . .

Other locales are described with equal vividness: the river where four friends go tubing, the sparsely furnished home of Rob's grandfather, the dense forest where Rob and Ellery run. The social limitations of the tiny town and the natural Appalachian beauty reinforce urban Rob's feelings of isolation and of being a stranger from another world.

Because action in *V for Victor* involves a German submarine's attack on an oil tanker and a yachtsman's effort to save the merchant seamen, the reader must see the wild seacoast where such treachery can occur. In

Mark Childress's story of a boy who lives on the coast of Alabama and yearns for the excitement of soldiering, the time is World War II. Victor, who is taking care of his grandmother, can easily disappear into the rugged coastal wilderness. The island is "a half-mile of marsh grass, a long stretch of thickety woods, a high place of two or three acres well-shaded by live oaks." "The bay was an indistinct line through the trees. . . . Branches swatted his face." Pursued by a suspicious boy of his own age, Victor "made his way down river, walking where he could, swimming for long stretches, flailing and kicking until he reached another shallow place . . . pulling out, stumbling on. . . . He tripped over cypress knees, swatted mosquitoes . . . up to his calves in sucking swamp mud that threatened to drag him on down." In this rugged coastal environment, Victor stumbles on the bloated body of a murdered man, a credible event considering the rugged setting ideal for treachery.

Setting determines story in Berlie Doherty's *White Peak Farm,* in which the quiet action involves daily life for a family of distinct characters and their struggles with breaking out to be themselves. "My home is on a farm in the soft folding hills of Derbyshire. Not far from us the dark peaks of the Pennines rise up into the ridge that is called the spine of England." So the novel opens. Remoteness from the city, the hard work of sheep farming, the demands of a controlling father, and the continual threat of poverty force the family of six to rely upon each other for everything. The break to art school, marriage, and the university are believably difficult for lives shaped by the chores and demands of the farm. When Kathleen slips away from her angry father, she runs to the highlands where the boy she later marries lives, and Jeannie follows; the passage below emphasizes the geographical as well as emotional distance between family members.

> Kathleen turned around, but she didn't come running down to meet
> me like she would have done once, spreading her arms to slow her
> speed, plugging the slope with her toes, and shrieking with laughter.
> She stood, not moving, staring down at me, till all that distance away I
> felt ashamed for . . . prying into things that were no business of mine;
> or anyone else's for that matter.

When the father's tractor accident forces Jeannie's mother to be the farmer in the family, life is even more strenuous. In spring a windstorm tears the roof off the lambing shed, and with her mother Jeannie struggles to save the lambs.

> The door of the shed slammed brutally backward and forward as fright-
> ened ewes tried to stagger through it. . . . With my mother leaning
> down dangerously and heaving from above and me pushing from be-
> low, we managed to pry up the beam that had crashed down across the
> pen where newborn lambs lay in the warm straw. Frightened ewes
> huddled together, terrified. . . .

There can be no doubt that for the reader to understand this story, a clear view of this setting is essential.

Functions of Setting

Setting That Clarifies Conflict

As these examinations of setting reveal, an integral setting plays an important part in the story's conflict. The horror that Jessie of Paula Fox's *The Slave Dancer* feels as he looks into the slaves' quarters in the hold of the ship is essential to our understanding his revulsion toward the ship and its cruel crew; the horror becomes clear with a description of the sounds he hears coming from there. Nothing "could mask the keening of the slaves as they twisted and turned on the water casks, or struggled to find an edge of one of a handful of straw pallets upon which to rest their shackled ankles." Later, dropping down into the hold in search of his fife, Jessie draws a breath "horrible, like a solid substance, like suet, that did not free my lungs but drowned them in the taste of rancid rot. . . . To search the hold meant that I would have to walk upon the blacks." A number of other descriptions of setting are equally vivid, among them his quarters "tween decks" in the slave ship, the "spider webs" of ship rigging, Jessie's modest home, and the wealthy neighborhood that fascinates him. Awareness of the prisonlike life on the slave ship emphasizes Jessie's internal conflict as he courageously defies the captain and refuses to play his fife, and later as he helps the slave boy so that together they escape to the southern mainland.

The Forty-Third War by Louise Moeri is set in the junglelike surroundings of an unnamed Central American country in the midst of revolution. At 12, Uno is forcibly "recruited" to fight for the revolutionaries. Busy scrounging a few cents a day to support his family by loading bananas at the docks, he has paid no attention to the jungle behind the village or to the politics of the loyalists and the revolutionaries. Once he is a soldier, his country's conditions become clearer to him, his patriotism is aroused, and his awareness of the futility of fighting a jungle war grows.

> . . . He slid under the spreading leaves of a low palmetto and watched his footing so he didn't stumble over the springing roots of a strangler fig tree. . . . Where there was open water the trees leaned out so far that even here there was little sunlight. . . . The smells of rotting vegetation were everywhere, as well as the smell of the slick black mud and even of their own sweat.

> . . . Even following a tight line [in the dense jungle] it was hard to keep track of the man ahead and the one behind. Leaves slapped their faces,

vines snagged their feet, flies and mosquitoes rose in blinding clouds
that swarmed around their faces.

All around him the men were so silent they could hear the flies
buzzing as they appeared out of nowhere to circle around the bodies,
drawn by the smell of blood. There was no wind, and the only thing
moving was a vulture, already scenting death, turning in slow circles
above [the murdered villagers].

Descriptions of the swamps and jungles show the impossibility of deci-
sive victory, or of this forty-third war as the last.

Setting That Acts as Antagonist

As noted in the chapter on plot, person-against-nature is one of the major
types of conflict. The protagonist is caught in a struggle to survive in a
harsh and impersonal nature that has become a ruthless force. In *Wolf of
Shadows* Strieber shows the antagonist clearly; nuclear winter is vividly
described as the protagonist experiences the frightening cold, with sleet,
snow, and bitter rain that freezes to deathly ice, covering all that is non-
living, living, or caught to die.

The northern tundra is the setting for another novel, *Julie of the
Wolves* by Jean Craighead George, the story of a young adult who has run
away from home and becomes lost in the frigid and snowy North. As the
novel opens, Miyax (sometimes called Julie) eyes the Arctic sun, "a yellow disk in a lime-green sky."

Her hands trembled and her heartbeat quickened, for she was frightened . . . because of her desperate predicament. Miyax was lost. She
had been lost without food for many days on the North Slope of Alaska.
The barren slope stretches for three hundred miles from the Brooks
Range to the Arctic Ocean, and for more than eight hundred miles from
the Chukchi to the Beaufort Sea. No roads cross it, ponds and lakes
freckle its immensity. Winds scream across it, and the view in every direction is exactly the same. Somewhere in this cosmos was Miyax. . . .

Only by making friends with the wolves, the "natives" of the area,
and sharing in their kill can she survive.

Setting That Illuminates Character

Setting illuminates the characters of Cassie Logan in *Roll of Thunder* and
Jerry in *The Chocolate War*, as is true of other novels as well. In Robb
White's *Deathwatch*, the guide Ben's client Madec has killed a man and
wants to kill Ben so he can't report it; stripped of clothing and shoes, Ben
is hiding among the rocks and cliffs of the desert, trying desperately to
evade the murderer:

> Ben estimated the butte to be about four hundred feet tall and half a
> mile in circumference. In some places enormous, almost flat-surfaced
> slabs had been broken away and lay scattered on the desert below,
> making a rubble of stone . . . around the base. The breaking away of
> these thin slabs had left flat ledges like giant steps up the sides of the
> butte, and other erosive elements . . . had split the surface stone, leav-
> ing long, perpendicular cracks in the sides.

This is the terrain through which Ben flees. The suspenseful story depends upon readers' seeing Ben's desperation as, naked, he not only
fights Madec but struggles for survival in the raw, forbidding landscape.
Ben's determination to turn in Madec the murderer, even at high personal
cost, illuminates the principled human being he is while simultaneously
showing the ruthlessness that controls Madec's character.

Look also at *Bearstone* by Will Hobbs, the story of Cloyd, a Native
American who has never lived with his natural parents and has run away
to search for his dying father, but who now must leave the desert and the
Utah reservation and go on to Colorado to live with a rancher. As he approaches the ranch, Cloyd anxiously watches the changing landscape.

> Cloyd . . . studied the cliffs high on the mountain above the river
> canyon. In reds and whites, the cliffs seemed like a huge chunk of the
> desert hovering over the forests. They reminded him of home. In a mo-
> ment, he realized that the boulder underneath him made a perfect fit
> with a huge notch in the cliffs up above. It must have fallen long ago,
> leaving behind a shallow cave.

Remembering his grandmother's telling him that these mountains are
part of his tribal past, Cloyd climbs eagerly into the rough, mountainous
terrain. When he finds in the mountain cave a carved turquoise bear
buried with the remains of an Indian infant, he feels more than ever that
this is his homeland.

> Their band of Weminuche Utes hadn't always lived at White Mesa.
> Colorado, especially the mountains above Durango, had been their
> home until gold was discovered there and the white men wanted them
> out of the way. Summers the people used to hunt and fish in the high
> mountains, she'd said: they knew every stream, places so out of the
> way that white men still hadn't seen them. "So don't feel bad about go-
> ing to Durango," she told him.

Cloyd finds in the old rancher a new father, and in Colorado not only
terrain he'd heard about, but also a sense of his own heritage. These discoveries help Cloyd to hang on to his Ute Indian heritage and find the
new rootedness he had yearned for.

Through setting the reader sees Carl Staggers of Alden Carter's *Up
Country:* Carl had moved to the basement of the home he shares with his

alcoholic mother, a waitress in a questionable Milwaukee bar. Seeing the whole house enables readers to understand both Carl's feelings toward his mother and his intense wish to save enough money to get out. If he wears his headphones, he can sleep "through the noise of partying and later the squeaking of bedsprings" drifting into the basement from the bedroom above. He's made "more than one breakfast of Coke, peanut butter and stale bread," checking it for mold, washing the sandwich down, and zinging the can in the general direction of the wastebasket to add to the overall mess. On his basement workbench stands a series of car stereos ripped from cars by Steve, his associate in crime, and an assortment of electronic equipment for repairing them. Tucked away behind the furnace is his record of radio repairs, serial numbers, and money made from selling the radios. Carl thinks of himself as a "pale slug," a nerd, but a smart nerd who would some day win a scholarship, become an electrical engineer, and live happily ever after. When Carl's mother goes away for alcoholism treatment, Carl must move to northern Wisconsin to Blind River, his uncle's home, where dense trees hang over the roads, and he anticipates freezing to death or being eaten alive by a bear. Here his home is a frame house and a decrepit barn, a country of trapping, hunting, and fishing. In this environment, Carl's life changes. Among family members who work together but with realistic friction, and who live with little money but have the energy needed to work hard and survive in a cold climate, reluctant Carl finds good times, new friends, and a hearty girlfriend. Although, as has been noted, the city is often used as symbol of evil and the country of good, Carter stereotypes neither his characters nor his setting, but allows readers to see the difference in people's lives as the setting influences it, as well as the effects of the setting upon Carl himself.

Setting That Affects Mood

The mood of high fantasy is frequently engendered by discovery of a kind of utopian world where life is sweet, serene, and inhabited by gentle folk for whom there is no harsh reality. In Ursula K. Le Guin's *The Beginning Place,* Buck and Irena have escaped from a place in the real world to a place where "here is always." The necessity to make the reader believe what seems otherwise unreal dictates that LeGuin, like other writers of high fantasy, describe a strange and unreal place that is simultaneously real. For example, Buck explores his environment as he looks for the gateway clearing, the opening to Tembreabrezi where he spends many hours without time having passed. In the dense trees, walking has no direction and his compass is little help. And yet the description of a fantasy world seems anchored in reality.

> So he explored the paths and thickets, hollows, glades, side valleys, hillside springs, windings and turnings of the forest on both sides of the

creek upstream from the willow place. . . . He had gone several miles now along the creek . . . he followed the faint paths of the deer but never saw one, found sometimes an old bird's nest fallen, but never, in the changeless time and season and the weather without change, heard an animal cry out, or a bird sing.

The mood of a never-never land is created to large extent through setting described as an "evening land" of "eternal twilight." If readers are to believe in the fantastic battle, they must lose themselves in the created world. By contrast, a less successful portrayal of setting appears in the science fiction fantasy *Children of the Storm* from the Planet Builders series; here, almost nothing is known of setting, only that Gaugin has three native creatures that can communicate with human beings: jonahs, theskies, and quufers, creatures from a world unseen and thus unknown to readers.

The realistic setting of *Dixie Storms* influences the mood of Barbara Hall's farm story. The drought has kept the family fearful about survival for some time. As tension mounts between family members, the tobacco crop browns without reaching full growth, the bank presses for payment of both mortgage debts and the loan on the tractor. Flood threatens to leave his father's farm, and Dutch's nephew Bodean becomes a troublesome child. Even Dutch's relationship with her visiting cousin Norma and her love for Ethan Cole seem threatened by worries about survival on the drought-stricken farm.

Setting That Acts as Symbol

A **symbol** has meaning beyond its literal one, is supported throughout the whole story, and is emphasized or repeated. Settings, too, may work as symbols. The obvious symbolic setting is the darkness of an evil world, the bright light of a benign one. Looking back to folk tales from Western society, readers may recall the importance of the "deep dark forest" where lived witches, or the palace where lived the powerful and wealthy sovereign. Variations of the "humble cottage" found in folktales of many cultures are symbolic of the honest simplicity of the main character.

In Madeline L'Engle's *A Wrinkle in Time* Camazotz symbolizes the rational, mechanical, and conforming world where emotion is nonexistent, and where buildings and people operate like machines, without individuality and without feelings:

Then the doors of all the houses opened simultaneously, and out came women like a row of paper dolls. The print of their dresses was different, but they all gave the appearance of being the same. Each woman stood on the steps of her house. Each clapped. Each child with the ball caught the ball. Each child with the skipping rope folded the rope.

Each child turned and walked into the house. The doors clicked shut behind them.

The huge CENTRAL Central Intelligence Building had only one door, but it was an enormous one, at least two stories high and wider than a room, made of a dull, bronzelike material.

. . . [Calvin] raised his hand [to knock], but before he touched the door it slid up from the top and to each side, splitting into three sections that had been completely invisible a moment before . . . [revealing] a great entrance hall of dull, green marble. Marble benches lined three of the walls. People were sitting there like statues. The green of the marble reflecting on their faces made them look bilious. They turned their heads as the door opened, saw the children, looked away again.

Evaluating Setting

The number of possible settings is unlimited. All the reader expects is that if the setting is to be important, it must be revealed through the senses of sight, hearing, or even smell. If the action is threatening to the characters because of where they are, then the reader needs to know how and why it threatens. For example, in *Deathwatch,* is the climate so hot and dry that it may cause Ben to die of exposure? Is the place so isolated, so barren of habitation that he cannot find refuge with protectors? Is Ben so invisible to the helicopter circling above as it scans the desert floor that there is no hope for his rescue? The setting clearly is a significant element in the conflict and the sustained suspense.

Setting may serve as an escape from an imperfect world to another more ideal, as it does in some fantasies or science fiction. In contrast, a science fiction setting in other spaces and future times may also serve as a threatening force that makes improving the real contemporary world an essential challenge. In high fantasy, where conflict pits good and evil against each another, setting may seem vastly moral, benign, and loving or accepting, or, depending upon the story line, may be filled with evil and threat. A realistic story, however, may require a realistic setting; if readers are to believe this conflict occurred in this place, they need to see this setting. Stories like *Wolf of Shadows* with animal protagonists require settings typical of the natural environments in which these animals live.

Backdrop settings need little description, and should remain in the background. Consider the possibility of placing greater emphasis on setting in *A Hero Ain't Nothin' But a Sandwich.* Benjie, who believes he can shake the power of drugs at any time, is unaware that his addiction is growing, and despite the concern of his "father" and mother, is becoming powerless to shake it. As the novel stands, little is seen of Benjie's home, its furnishings, or the apartment house, nothing of streets outside with thriving drug dealers, frightened or drug-ridden adults, or curious and vulnerable children. If the environmental elements of a drug-ridden neighborhood were described more fully, the conflict might shift to a battle between the dealers and Benjie's parents for Benjie's life, rather than remain the contest within Benjie. Realistic stories may require realistic settings, but internal conflicts in realistic stories may not need detailed descriptions. Personal struggles can be exactly the same whether people live in Boston, Massachusetts, or Fielding, Nebraska.

Summary

Setting is of two principal types. It may be a backdrop setting for the plot, like the generalized backdrop of a forest, a street, or a small town, against which the action and conflict occur. Or the setting may be so integral, so essential to understanding characters, conflict, or themes that a convincing and detailed description of setting is essential. Setting may clarify conflict, illuminate character, set the mood, or act as symbol. The many settings of a novel may help the reader to see related themes. Today's writers are likely to weave description of settings into the characters' speech and action so that the reader is aware of their essential nature but does not greet a lengthy descriptive passage with "Oh, here comes the setting."

Notes

1. Eudora Welty, *Place in Fiction* (New York: House of Books, 1957), p. 22.
2. Other settings may be less significant. The train, for example, provides a bridge for Holden from the immaculately beautiful countryside in its virginal white cover to the "wicked" city of drunkenness, prostitution, dishonesty, opulence, phony charity, varied forms of sexuality, and commercialized religious display. The movies and the theater are concrete examples of accepted unreality, legitimized phoniness. Note also the hotel and the bars as setting; both are transitional places, with transient occupants, disparate and unrelated human beings whose actions seem amoral and unrelated to any constant standard. They serve, however, to further disillusion Holden. Two other settings also filled with unrelated people serve as contrasts. The train station may be filled with transients, but there Holden discovers the goodness of human nature through the nuns who acknowledge human imperfection yet remain devoted to service, living as martyrs to a cause. Central Park provides glimpses of serenity and pleasure in the heart of the city. Roller-skating children, playful seals at the zoo, the musical merry-go-round and its excited young patrons constitute an oasis of innocent play; the park reenforces the thematic idea that evil does not entirely prevail. In

the park Holden finally realizes that children cannot be kept from reaching for the brass ring—even if they fall off the carousel horses, fall from complete innocence. Even though the story is essentially Holden's rumination and self-revelation, when the novel is seen in its total complexity, setting is an integral part of *Catcher in the Rye.*

Recommended Books Cited in This Chapter

Bridgers, Sue Ellen. *Permanent Connections.* New York: Harper & Row, 1987.

Brooks, Bruce. *The Moves Make the Man.* New York: Harper & Row, 1984.

Carter, Alden. *Up Country.* Putnam, 1989.

Childress, Alice. *A Hero Ain't Nothin' But a Sandwich.* New York: Avon, 1977.

Childress, Mark. *V for Victor.* New York: Knopf, 1989.

Cormier, Robert. *The Chocolate War.* New York: Random House, 1974.

Crew, Linda. *Someday I'll Laugh About This.* New York: Delacorte, 1990.

Doherty, Berlie. *White Peak Farm.* New York: Orchard Books, 1984.

Fox, Paula. *The Slave Dancer.* Scarsdale, New York: Bradbury, 1973.

George, Jean Craighead. *Julie of the Wolves.* New York: Harper & Row, 1972.

Hall, Barbara. *Dixie Storms.* New York: Harcourt Brace, 1990.

Hamilton, Virginia. *Sweet Whispers, Brother Rush.* New York: Avon, 1983.

Hobbs, Will. *Bearstone.* New York: Atheneum, 1989.

Le Guin, Ursula K. *The Beginning Place.* New York: Harper, 1980.

L'Engle, Madeleine. *A Wrinkle in Time.* New York: Farrar, Straus & Giroux, 1962.

Moeri, Louise. *The Forty-Third War.* Boston: Houghton Mifflin, 1989.

Salinger, J. D. *The Catcher in the Rye.* Boston, Little, Brown, 1951.

Sleator, William. *Interstellar Pig.* New York: Dutton, 1984.

Strieber, Whitley. *Wolf of Shadows.* New York: Knopf, 1985.

Taylor, Midlred D. *Roll of Thunder, Hear My Cry.* New York: Dial, 1976.

White, Robb. *Deathwatch.* New York: Dell, 1973.

THE
PIGMAN

A NOVEL BY **PAUL ZINDEL**

—6—

Point of View

The term "point of view" is in common use. When we hear someone say, "My point of view is. . ." we expect an opinion to be expressed, an opinion about how to discuss a sensitive issue in class, how student government has been successful, or what was fair or unfair about an exam.

In literature, however, point of view has another meaning. As we read a story we may be aware that we are seeing the events and characters through the eyes and mind of a particular character, perhaps a major participant in the action or perhaps an objective observer, one who is outside the central action. The author, of course, always knows everything, but sometimes we realize that the author not only knows everything but is letting us know all that he or she knows. **Point of view** in literature signifies, then, the mind through which we view the story.

Try asking three friends who were all at the same dorm party what happened when an argument broke out. Three stories will result, depending upon where the friend stood in the lounge during the quarrel, the friend's sympathies for either side of the subject, the sympathy or antagonism of the friend to participants in the argument, or upon a number of other factors. The friends' points of view will determine the three reports you hear. Recognizing that your friends have these varying points of view helps you as listener to sort out what actually happened. The same condition occurs in fiction. If *Roll of Thunder, Hear My Cry* were told from the point of view of Uncle Hammer, the reader would see more clearly his anger, his frustration, his very different life up North. If Mama told the story, the reader would know her anxiety about Papa's injured leg, her despair at losing her teaching job, her effort to protect her children. Little Man and Christopher John would have told still other stories as they recounted events, their understanding limited by being less involved and less able to understand the dangers the family has endured. Cassie tells the story, and it is told as she sees it.[1]

Types of Point of View

The writer decides on point of view when she or he chooses who is to be the narrator and how much that narrator can know. The first possibility is the **first-person point of view,** used when the narrator speaks as an "I." In such storytelling, the reader lives, acts, thinks, and feels the experience with the narrator as it happens or is told. Occasionally the first-person narrator is not the protagonist but someone close enough to the narrator to observe.

The second possibility is the **omniscient point of view.** Here the writer tells the story in third person using *he, she,* and *they,* knowing everything there is to know about all of the characters, and revealing whatever is necessary for the reader to know to follow the story and usually to be sympathetic to the protagonist. The writer also knows and can tell hopes and dreams, as well as reveal what characters' lives have been in the past and what their lives will be in the future.

A **limited omniscient point of view** is a third possibility, one in which the writer, again telling the story using third-person pronouns, limits what the writer knows and tells, frequently restricting this knowledge to the principal character or protagonist in the action. In other instances, the writer may choose a few additional characters whose minds the reader is shown. This, too, is called the limited omniscient point of view.

The fourth possibility is the **objective** or **dramatic point of view,** in which the writer, again using third-person pronouns, reports only what can be seen and heard, but does not take on the privilege of knowing and revealing past or future, thoughts or feelings. Stage plays offer an understandable example. Unless the character speaks in soliloquy, spectators do not know what the character thinks, but must draw conclusions from what they see and hear. While the play is a clear example of the dramatic point of view, films can be more subtle; the film director chooses the camera shot the audience sees, thus influencing its view of character and action. However, bear in mind that in each artistic case—novel, play, or film—and in each point of view, the writer or creator determines how reader or observer sees character and action.

First-Person Point of View

Cassie tells the story in *Roll of Thunder, Hear My Cry.* She is the second Logan child, hotheaded and at times defiant, character traits that influence her account of the events. In the store, for example, she resents that Mr. Barnett turns from filling their order to fill those of white people.[2]

I was hot. I had been as nice as I could be to him and here he was talking like this. "We been waiting on you for near an hour," I hissed, "while you 'round here waiting on everybody else. And it ain't fair. You got no right—"

"Whose little nigger is this!" bellowed Mr. Barnett.

Everyone in the store turned and stared at me. "I ain't nobody's little nigger!" I screamed, angry and humiliated. . . .

Shabanu: Daughter of the Wind by Suzanne Fisher Staples offers another example of the first-person point of view. Using a narrator who speaks in present-tense verbs creates a sense of immediacy, and at times of danger; the reader sees the action as it happens.

. . . I am angry to think of Dadi or anyone else telling me what to do. I want to tell [Mama] I spend more time with the camels than Dadi, and sometimes when he asks me to do a thing, I know something else is better. But Mama's dark eyes hold my face so intently. . . . She and Dadi are thinking of how I will behave when Murad and I marry.

. . . On the ridge at eye level stands a band of Bugtis, a breeze filling their voluminous trousers and shirtsleeves. My heart leaps into my mouth. Their chests are crossed with bandoliers. Their eyes are fierce. . . . Several of them lean on long, brass-studded rifles.

Occasionally an adult first-person narrator tells a story from early life and fails to capture the interest of the young adult reader; perhaps it reminds the reader too much of a parent's "When I was a child. . ." or perhaps it fails to convince the reader that the remembered incidents accurately show the reactions of the child protagonist. Paula Fox, however—despite the mature vocabulary of the adult Jessie, who is the narrator in *The Slave Dancer*—makes the first-person point of view seem an accurate "looking back." Jessie is convincing in his straightforward recollection of events and thus convinces the reader of their truth and their effect on him. Dreading daylight's coming when he must play his fife while the sailors force the sick and dying slaves to dance, Jessie listens and wonders:

I wondered if I dared leap overboard and take my chances on reaching the shore. But what could I find there? Other men who might use me worse than I was being used? Or a captain who tortured his own crew? God knows, I had heard of such things!. . .

. . . One night as we lay at anchor . . . I heard a scream of inhuman force, of intolerable misery. I began to weep helplessly myself, covering my mouth with an old cap of Stout's for fear one of the crew would hear me.

When Jessie must go down to retrieve his fife thrown by a crew member into the hold filled with slaves, he recalls his boyhood horror, using the diction of the adult but recalling the emotional reactions of a child:

> I sank down among them as though I had been dropped into the sea. I heard groans, the shifting of shackles, the damp sliding whisper of sweating arms and legs as the slaves tried desperately to curl themselves even tighter. . . . I saw a man's face not a foot from my own. I saw every line, every ridge, a small scar next to one eyebrow, the inflamed lids of his eyes. He was trying to force his knees closer to his chin. . . .

Another story told in first person about a young adult and yet using the more sophisticated wording of maturity is Taylor's *Let the Circle Be Unbroken*. Cassie narrates convincingly, both speaking like the child she was in the past and relating events in mature adult vocabulary:

> Finally, on the day Papa was to return to his search, I was given permission not only to get out of bed for a few hours but to put on my pants and shirt. I felt a little wobbly at first, but as soon as I was dressed I hurried out the front door and down the softness of the lawn to the road, where Wordell had already taken up his morning vigil.

Using the words of Wordell the neighbor boy, Cassie says that his music helped and repeats what he said in appropriate diction.

> "That business of staying in bed all day ain't no fun at all when ya gotta do it day in and day out. And being hot all the time and coughing and feeling sore, that wasn't no fun either. I ain't never really been sick before, but I tell you one thing, I ain't never wanting to be sick again. I guess I was sorta lucky though. . . ."

First-person narration using a written journal occurs in *So Much to Tell You . . .* by the Australian writer John Marsden. Defaced by an accident that has caused her to withdraw and stop talking, Marina gradually begins to open up to her journal, writing daily entries as her boarding school teacher requires. Slowly responding to kindness, little by little she gains confidence to reach out sufficiently to make friends and to write to her imprisoned father. The slow pace of Marina's self-discovery as she confides to the page the feelings typical of her age and yet special because of her experience makes the first-person narrative believable. Notice how Marina over the months begins to face herself and to see her family more clearly. These changes are made credible by the "I" narration.

FEBRUARY 6: . . . When Mr. Lindell gave [the journals] out in class I felt
the fear and promised myself that I would not write in it, that it would
stay a cold and empty book, with no secrets.

MARCH 16: Having me in class inhibits everyone, though. People were
talking quite openly about the things they do to make friends and keep
friends; then a girl . . . started saying how awful it would be not to have
any friends, and in a moment a cool pink breeze blew through the
room and embarrassment brushed every face. They've become so used
to me that . . .

JULY 11: . . . So I don't know what's best. I'd hate to be poor, but look
where we've ended up after all his hard work—a family that's ex-
ploded, a father in prison, a mother's who's married a creep and who
cares only for herself, and a silent daughter with a face like raw . . .

Another convincing first-person narrator speaks in John Donovan's
I'll Get There. It Better Be Worth the Trip. The plot involves two lonely
boys, each living only with a difficult, divorced mother, each zealously
guarding his privacy and yet wishing for the approval of schoolmates. In a
moment of comradeship as they play on the floor with the dog, they exchange a kiss, and Davy speaks honestly of his fear at the implications of
where the relationship might lead. They lash out at each other, but, once
they at least partially understand how their encounter happened, they return to their friendship. Davy Ross is characteristically introspective and
speaks and thinks like a thirteen-year-old boy, with humor, overstatement, and recognition of his own feelings.

> We get up, and we avoid looking at each other. When our eyes
> meet, we laugh, but not like before.
> Fred [the dog] comes back and we horse around with him for ten
> minutes. Altschuler says he has to go home. I tell him he doesn't have
> to go home because of what happened on the floor. He says he knows
> that, and he also says that we're pretty great in the play.
> . . . We mess around for a few seconds, pretending we are two ban-
> tam-weight tough guys. I mean very tough. I mean a couple of guys like
> Altschuler and me don't have to worry. . . .

The first-person character revelation of Marcus Jenkins in A. E. Cannon's *The Shadow Brothers* is essential to our understanding of his internal conflict. Marcus speaks about his jealousy of his Navaho foster
brother Henry, who is successful in his studies, in his running form, and
in attracting beautiful Celia. As Marcus slowly recognizes his own intelligence and running skills, he grows in self-confidence and in appreciation

of Henry. Through the first-person record of self-recognition, Marcus reveals his move from being the shadow of another to seeing his own strengths.

Consistent point of view that convinces the reader of the age of the first-person narrator is a hallmark of Richard Peck's novels for young adults. In *Father Figure,* for example, Jim at fifteen speaks in the diction of his time and age. "The coffee, while good, is a big mistake. It's clearing my mind. I'm thinking at the top of my lungs." Jim, "looking her in the lashes," is attracted to his father's waitress friend Marietta. When he dreams of her, he says, "I arise . . . aroused. . . . My number on the cold-shower roster has come up, and I'm a prime candidate." Speaking of the summer's slow changes in his tense relationship with his father, who had left his mother when brother Byron was an infant, Jim says, "In Florida it's tough staying uptight, but I find ways." Later he says, "We touch up the truce . . . and don't bog down over petty details. We iron out some with a couple of words and walk around the rest. A little goodwill seeps in, depending on the day." On the final page of the story, the relationship has become comfortable. Jim is at the airport for his return to New York.

> . . . In a setting like this, who's to notice if we put our arms around each other? We have no history of hugging, but who's to notice?
>
> Dad puts his arms out. I put my arms out. We grapple a little. Then step together for a moment. . . . We bang each other on the back, make it hearty, make it quick. Then we make a break.

Perhaps Paul Zindel's *The Pigman,* in which narration of chapters alternates between the two protagonists, Lorraine and John, started an innovative trend in first-person narration; the technique is now often used. M. E. Kerr in *Little Little* alternates chapters of first-person narration, first one narrated by Sydney Cinnamon, then one narrated by tiny Little Little. Another novelist, Alice Childress, uses a variation of the first-person point of view in *A Hero Ain't Nothin' But a Sandwich.* Each chapter, titled according to who is speaking, is told by a first-person narrator:

> *Benjie:* This counselor think he slick. He actin cool and maybe talk about baseball or bout how he did jazz; he lookin up in the air or down at the ground, to sneak up on makin me talk bout myself. Is all right with me cause he's a social worker and thass how they taught to do, but it gets me in the gut how he be actin like he really care.

> *Walter:* The pusher, the pusher, that's all you hear! They don't call no other salesman a pusher, but that's what he natural is . . . a pusher, no matter what he's sellin. Your TV set is fulla pushers tellin you to run right out and buy. . . .

The Principal: Walking through these corridors, I remind myself that in three years I'll be ready for retirement. I have done some good in my time and would like to leave with my sanity and pension. I look forward to peaceful moments in which to write this definitive book on better methods of education.

Stepfather: I've seen a lot in my lifetime, but never anything like this. Bein strung out on junk wasn't invented yesterday, no indeed, been goin on a long time, but damn if it ain't gettin worse. This the first time I've seen a child junkie thirteen years of age.

Childress uses the same technique in *Rainbow Jordan,* although the story is primarily told from 14-year-old Rainbow's point of view. Her "interim caretaker" Josephine speaks out about how difficult it is to be both a mother and not-mother, loving and caring about Rainey, and yet lacking the authority to discipline as she feels she ought to. In two chapters Rainbow's mother, Kathie, tells about the difficulty of being so young a mother; at 29 she has a 14-year-old daughter, no husband, and the necessity to take whatever job is offered her, even if it means being gone for weeks at a time on a go-go gig. Childress, who dedicates her book to those who have been reared by people other than natural parents, through Rainey's point of view sympathetically exposes the sexual pressures facing a young adult, as well as the effects of too-young motherhood.

Another writer using this variation of first-person narration is Ernest J. Gaines in *A Gathering of Old Men.* Twelve old black men speak, telling why they have gathered to defend Mathu, who they believe is guilty of murdering a white man. Old injustices spur them to courageous stands supporting Mathu against the sheriff and a lynch mob; with little to lose but the few years of life they have left, each one stands up to the white mob, claims to have fired the lethal shot, and decries his ever having run from white injustice in the past.

Omniscient Point of View

Point of view in *The Chocolate War* is omniscient. As noted in the earlier discussion of character development, Cormier describes and characterizes each of the principal schoolboys in the character's own chapter, each showing the mind of one of them. First the reader meets Jerry at football practice. "His breath went away, like the ball—a terrible stillness pervaded him—and then, at the onset of panic . . . he was grateful for the sweet cool air that filled his lungs." Chapter two opens: "Obie was bored. Worse than bored. He was disgusted. He was also tired." Chapter four is a conversation between Archie and Brother Leon, who surprises Archie by being vulnerable. "Archie whistled in astonishment. . . . Then he saw the mustache of moistness on Brother Leon's upper lip, the watery eyes and the dampness on his forehead. Something clicked. . . ." The first glimpse of Emile catches him siphoning gas, "amused that Archie should have discovered him." Emile has "found that the world was full of willing victims, especially kids his own age." Peace is worth any price, Emile has discovered, and because he knows that people fear embarrassment or humiliation, he can control them. Goober's chapter shows his feelings, too. Running, "he even loved the pain, the hurt of the running, the burning in his lungs and the spasms that sometimes gripped his calves. He loved it because he knew he could endure the pain, and even go beyond it."

In the closing chapters, each of which includes all the principal characters, the author shows their feelings with complete omniscience: Carter "sensed the impatience of the crowd." Looking at the bloodthirsty spectators, Goober feels "they'd become strangers." "Jerry had girded himself for the blow, but it took him by surprise with its savagery and viciousness." "Janza got ready. . . . I'm not a chicken. I'll show them." "Stupid, Archie thought, they're all stupid. He was the only one here with the presence of mind. . . ." Cormier has effectively used the omniscient point of view for characterization and for carrying the suspense of the plot.

In *Beyond the Chocolate War* Cormier uses the same device, each chapter relaying the point of view of one character. On the first page a new character is introduced, one not included in the first *War*—Ray Bannister, who "began to construct the guillotine out of sheer boredom. More than boredom: loneliness, restlessness. . . . He had found Monument to be a dull and ugly mill town." In the next chapter, it's Obie's turn: "Obie was in love. Wildly, improbably, and wonderfully in love. The kind of thing he thought happened only in the movies." An early chapter introduces Goober, the runner who finds that a collie "had taken to running beside him, and he felt a sense of kinship with the animal." Several pages later the reader is in Archie's mind: "He enjoyed what he saw in the eyes of the other students when he directed his attention to them—fear, apprehension, resentment." Because of Cormier's attention to the actions and thoughts of all the characters, in this novel as in the earlier one readers are sympathetic to their simultaneous reluctance and feelings of powerlessness. Try as they might, they cannot avoid the Vigil's assignments nor can Archie shed his leadership role; the reader is pulled into the tension created by their anxiety and apprehension both felt individually and created as a group.

Limited Omniscient Point of View

Limiting the omniscience in a story has an effect upon other elements. Look first at *A Wrinkle in Time,* in which L'Engle limits the omniscience to protagonist Meg. The reader does not learn what other characters think and feel. Flying on the back of Mrs. Whatsit, Meg, Calvin, and Charles Wallace are puzzled by the land they see beneath them:

> Charles Wallace got his look of probing, of listening.
> *I* know that look! Meg thought suddenly. Now I think I know what it means! Because I've had it myself, sometimes, doing math with Father, when a problem is just about to come clear—
> Mrs. Whatsit seemed to be listening to Charles's thoughts. "Well, yes, that's an idea. I can try. . . ."

When the group reaches the CENTRAL Central Intelligence Building, Meg observes Charles and thinks to herself:

> —I wish he wouldn't act so sure of himself, Meg thought, looking anxiously at Charles and holding his hand more and more tightly until he wriggled his fingers in protest. That's what Mrs. Whatsit said he had to watch, being proud. —Don't, please don't, she thought hard at Charles Wallace. She wondered if Calvin realized that a lot of the arrogance was bravado.

Because omniscience is limited to Meg, the reader sees her human uncertainty and her other imperfections, as well as her concern for the others. She is not superhuman, but must overcome her sense of ineffectiveness in order to will her love for her father and for Charles Wallace to conquer the forces of evil. The theme of *Wrinkle* is made clear through the limited omniscient point of view.

Norma Fox Mazer reveals the story in *After the Rain* only through the mind of Rachel, using a limited omniscient point of view and a variety of methods. Writing in her notebook, Rachel tries her hand at a story about her family. As she writes, she asks herself questions about what to include: more opening? more description? names for characters, or "the man," "the woman"? At other times, Rachel reveals her thoughts as she writes a letter that she may or may not mail to her brother Jeremy: "It seems I always write to you when things are bothering me. So here goes again. . . . Ma got right on my case." At still other times she reveals herself in her journal: "*Friday night.* Today, when I got to Grandpa's, I knew right away that he was in a bad mood. He had these little eyes and his eyebrows were going off in every direction. . . ."

Difficult to sustain but convincing in *Wolf of Shadows* is the limited omniscient point of view of an animal, in this case the wolf mother. The wolf mother describes the behavior of the human mother and child in terms of wolves and cubs. Behavior of the human mother and children, plane-crash survivors who follow the wolf pack, seems strange to Wolf, who watches them in their "den," a tent they have taken from the downed Cessna. "Inside the opening of the den the mother could be seen touching her healthy cub with her mouth, then putting water on the raw flesh of the burned one. Strangely, she did not lick the wounds." A group of survivors, hunters, steal the small plane, "the bird-thing," as Wolf watches:

> Moving stealthily, the hunters waded into the lake. Wolf of Shadows heard them approaching the great dark bird-thing, heard it open its craw for them with a scraping growl, then saw them entering it and the craw closing again. The mother and her cub did not notice this. But when the bird-thing began to cough and snarl they both jumped up, running to the shore of the lake, waving their forelegs and shouting.

Observing the human beings, Wolf notes that "they did the thing with their forepaws that made fire leap out onto some bits of wood." The mother's "other long foreleg came around his neck and for an instant she confined him." In the destroyed city, Wolf sees abandoned "rolling things" and not tumbled ruins "but rather the fallen bones of trees, and the scattered shambles of human dens." Because Strieber's point of view is so consistently and convincingly that of Wolf, the reader follows the story with intense interest.

An interesting variation of point of view is used by Norwegian writer Mette Newth in *The Abduction,* the seventeenth-century story of Osuqo, who with her betrothed is kidnapped by sailors and taken from her home in Greenland to Norway. The victim of brutality and rape on shipboard, in Norway she is accused of witchcraft but found innocent, then made the responsibility of Christine, a young servant of her own age whose sailor father lost his life during the return voyage from Greenland. The story is told in alternating chapters from the point of view of the two young women. Osuqo's story is told in limited omniscient point of view; she writhes in pain and despair over her treatment, and the reader sees how desperately she wishes to die. In a different typeface, Christine's first-person chapters tell that she is ashamed of her townspeople's treatment of the Greenlanders, and comes to appreciate Osuqo's humanity, then helps her to escape. Christine also overcomes her wish for revenge over the death of her father on the voyage, death that relegated her to a servant's life. The differing views of the events help the reader to see the struggle that each young woman must confront.

In a similar use of two different points of view in *The Soul of the Silver Dog,* Lynn Hall alternates chapters, first telling the thoughts of Sterling, the blind Bedlington terrier, then those of Cory, his owner. After months of training, Cory has brought Sterling to his first dog show since canine glaucoma blinded him:

> Through the lead, Cory could feel Sterling's tension. The dog was moving on stiffened legs, keeping himself hard against the lead and

moving his head continually. . . . He pulled away, whining and moving his head in scooping motions, trying to dislodge his blindness.

Sterling's reactions are shown in italics:

> *The day had been confusing for him. . . . The dog shows in his memory had been all confinement in his crate except for the exciting time in the ring. Today was different, unsettling. But as long as the girl was close . . . He closed his eyes and drifted.*

The effect of this point of view is to show convincingly Sterling's reliance on Cory for every reassurance, and at the same time to show Cory's dedication to the dog's welfare.

Objective or Dramatic Point of View

When the writer does not enter the mind of any of the characters but lets the behavior, appearance, speeches, and others' opinions about them define that character for the reader, the story is written in the **objective** or **dramatic point of view.** When people try to be objective, difficult as it is, they attempt to recount a story without offering opinion or reaction. In conversations we consistently interpret meaning by close observation, becoming increasingly skillful with experience. As noted earlier, when people attend the theater, they see the action, note appearances, hear the speeches, and see no intrusive writer interpreting what is going on. Drama is played out as the audience listens, observes, and draws its own inferences. Inner thoughts are revealed only by visible means, and the audience figures out for itself what is meant.

Avi's *Nothing But the Truth* is subtitled "a documentary novel," suggesting that the story is objectively told. The reader finds transcripts of conversations, and one-to-one, group, and class discussions, all in the form of dramatic dialogue. Some memos are brief and factually objective in point of view; others are persuasive, expressing the opinion of the principal or superintendent regarding, for example, the school budget. At times Avi includes letters or Philip's diary entries, which naturally express opinions and are therefore in first-person point of view.

With the exception of *Wolf of Shadows,* successful realistic stories with animal characters are usually written in the objective point of view. Sheila Burnford's *The Incredible Journey*, much read by younger children, as well as Allan Eckert's *Incident at Hawks Hill,* offer two examples. Eckert carefully maintains a combination of two points of view. He writes in an omniscient point of view when dealing with the human characters, but his careful observation and thorough research control the objective descriptions of badger behavior. At no point does Eckert tell readers of the badger's terror. Here is his description of the male badger caught in the trap:

> Had he been able to reason over his predicament, even though his front feet were imprisoned he might have been able to dig enough to unearth the stake and hobble away with the trap. Such reason, however, was beyond his capacity; he knew only that he was caught and his instinct drove him to jerk and struggle and bite at the object which held him, the trap itself.

Summary

Point of view is an integral part of story telling; it can determine and limit for the reader the view of events, thoughts, and feelings, or tell of the future and the past. Four major kinds of point of view are available to the writer: first person, limited to what "I" can know; omniscient, in which the writer knows and may tell everything about thoughts and feelings as well as past or future; limited omniscient, in which the writer chooses to reveal thoughts and feelings of one or few characters; and objective or dramatic, in which the reader merely listens, observes, and draws conclusions. Loss of credibility results when a first-person narrator professes to know the thoughts and feelings of other characters, or violates what the narrator can know by predicting future events.

Literature's pleasure comes from many sources, but the view of story and action that readers have available to them is determined by the writer's choice of how the story is to be told, whose eyes and intellect tell the story. Because the same events, when told through different points of view, will yield quite different narratives, point of view is a powerful element in story telling.

Notes

1. If the novel *The Catcher in the Rye* were told by Stradlater instead of Holden, it would be quite different; he would be rationalizing his behavior with the girls he takes out, justifying his asking Holden to write his essay, perhaps bragging about his athletic prowess and his favored status with Ed Bankey, the coach. If Ackley were telling the story, he might be complaining about the way he is treated, yelling at the Pencey Prep games and telling the players what they ought to be doing.

2. In *The Catcher in the Rye* Holden repeats the speeches of other people, but can only speculate about what they are thinking. Speaking with the two nuns, for example, Holden mentions the sexy novel *The Return of the Native* as his personal favorite, but wonders about a nun's reactions to Eustacia's experiences.

When one nun then asks what school Holden goes to, he guesses that she is uncomfortable with the topic. Salinger permits Holden only to speculate about what others are thinking.

Recommended Books Cited in This Chapter

Avi. *Nothing But the Truth.* New York: Orchard, 1991.

Burnford, Sheila. *The Incredible Journey.* Boston: Little, Brown, 1961.

Cannon, A. E. *The Shadow Brothers.* New York: Delacorte, 1990.

Childress, Alice. *A Hero Ain't Nothin But a Sandwich.* New York: Putnam, 1973.

———. *Rainbow Jordan.* New York: Coward McCann, 1981.

Cormier, Robert. *Beyond the Chocolate War.* New York: Knopf, Dell, 1986.

———. *The Chocolate War.* New York: Random House, 1974.

Donovan, John. *I'll Get There. It Better Be Worth the Trip.* New York: Harper & Row, 1969.

Eckert, Allan. *Incident at Hawks Hill.* New York: Bantam, 1973.

Fox, Paula. *The Slave Dancer.* Scarsdale, New York: Bradbury, 1973.

Gaines, Ernest J. *A Gathering of Old Men.* New York: Knopf, 1983.

Hall, Lynn. *The Soul of the Silver Dog.* New York: Harcourt Brace Jovanovich, 1992.

Kerr, M. E. *Little Little.* New York: Harper Keypoint, 1986.

L'Engle, Madeleine. *A Wrinkle in Time.* New York: Farrar, 1962.

Marsden, John. *So Much to Tell You.* Boston: Little, Brown, 1989.

Mazer, Norma Fox. *After the Rain.* New York: Morrow, 1987.

Newth, Mette. *The Abduction.* New York: Farrar, Straus & Giroux, 1987.

Peck, Richard. *Father Figure.* New York: Viking, 1978.

Salinger, J. D. *The Catcher in the Rye.* Boston: Little, Brown, 1951.

Staples, Suzanne Fisher. *Shabanu: Daughter of the Wind.* New York Knopf, 1989.

Strieber, Whitley. *Wolf of Shadows.* New York: Knopf, 1985.

Taylor, Mildred. *Let the Circle be Unbroken.* New York: Dial, 1981.

———. *Roll of Thunder, Hear My Cry.* New York: Dial, 1976.

Zindel, Paul. *Pigman.* New York: Harper, 1968.

— 7 —

Style

As noted in an earlier chapter, one definition of literature is "a significant truth—or theme—expressed in appropriate elements and memorable language," suggesting that memorable language constitutes style. Style is how the story is told. **Style** is words, *how* a writer says something in concert with *what* a writer says. An infinite number of words are available, but the choices that the writer makes and the arrangement or juxtaposition of those words constitutes style.

Writers have their own definitions of style. One might say it is the perfect adaptation of language to ideas; another might call it the best expression of the author's individuality and the idea in mind. To E. B. White, author of the children's favorite *Charlotte's Web* and co-author with William Strunk of *Elements of Style,* "style is the sound words make on the paper. . . . With some writers, style not only reveals the spirit of the man but reveals his identity, as surely as would his fingerprints." White warns, "Young writers often suppose that style is a garnish for the meat of prose, a sauce by which a dull dish is made palatable. Style has no such separate entity; it is nondetachable, unfilterable." He advises writers to turn "resolutely away from all . . . mannerisms, tricks, adornments." White says that his own "approach to style is by way of plainness, simplicity, orderliness, sincerity."

Because readers often choose a story by how it begins, look, for example, at Cormier's style in the opening of *The Chocolate War:*

> They murdered him.
> As he turned to take the ball, a dam burst against the side of his head and a hand grenade shattered his stomach. Engulfed by nausea, he pitched toward the grass. His mouth encountered gravel, and he spat frantically, afraid that some of his teeth had been knocked out. . . .

Here action, violent action, is described in vivid words: "dam burst," "hand grenade shattered," "engulfed by nausea," "pitched," "spat frantically," "knocked out." This is Cormier's style for this book, his choice of words that suggests to us that the story will be filled with action, and perhaps with violence.

Compare this action-packed opening to the quiet, even pensive beginning of Mette Newth's *The Abduction,* her own "adaptation of language to idea."

> The snow retreated reluctantly from the slopes of the mountains.
> Clouds heavy with rain hastened across the sky. Shadows, like long dark fingers, drew somber traces on the glowing colors of the mountainsides. One brief moment and then the clouds drifted on, and the icebergs at the mouth of the fjord were once again bathed in the dazzling light of the spring sun.
> The wind came from the inland ice cap, warm as the breath of an eager young hunter.

Through words we hear, see, perhaps even smell the setting, and thus discover its effect on characters' behavior and thoughts as they are involved in the conflict. Another story, another style.

Roll of Thunder begins with a paragraph of graphic description that tells something of setting and identifies the four children of the story.

> "Little Man, would you come on? You keep it up and you're gonna make us late."
> My youngest brother paid no attention to me. Grasping more firmly his newspaper-wrapped notebook and his tin-can lunch of cornbread and oil sausages, he continued to concentrate on the dusty road. He lagged several feet behind my other brothers, Stacey and Christopher-John, and me, attempting to keep the rusty Mississippi dust from swelling with each step and drifting back upon his shiny black shoes and the cuffs of his corduroy pants by lifting each foot high before setting it gently down again.

Look finally at the stylistic exaggeration that opens Jill Pinkwater's *Buffalo Brenda,* a story told in first person: "It was Sunday morning. I had exactly twenty-four hours left on earth before facing my doom. I was about to become a freshman at Florence Senior High School. Where was Brenda when I needed her most?" A breezy exaggeration of the anxiety that narrator India Ink feels about starting a new school results from Pinkwater's choice of words like "hours left on earth" and "doom."

In each case, the reader is carried into the action and characters are introduced, in some cases their conflicts already gripping the reader because of the chosen words—the style. These people become known through the words they say, words that describe how they look and move, as well as those that reveal attitudes. Clearly, E. B. White is right; style is not something *applied* to story. Style *is* story.

Major Devices of Style

The element of style most easily recognized is the writer's use of certain specific devices, devices that can make the story live. Many of these devices are used in everyday speech. Others, while occurring in prose, are more common to poetic expression and will be further dealt with in the chapter on poetry. Stylistic devices of sound are defined throughout the paragraphs that follow.

Imagery

Imagery, the appeal to any of the senses, is the most essential and frequently used device of style. As we read of a child dressed in pale pastels, a man or woman in rough tweeds, a woman or man in satin and silk, pictures or images are created in our minds, and certain expectations raised. If the writer goes on to describe the man's rough tweeds as "somber gray," and the satin and silk as "brilliant yellow," characters mentally pictured take on even more distinctive qualities. The imagery assists in describing time and place, setting a mood, and picturing character. When a story is set in the Ozarks, for example, we expect the places described for our senses to be right for the time and place, and the images and dialect of the characters' speaking style to be those of mountain people.

Return to *The Chocolate War* and notice how Cormier uses sensory appeals to show Jerry's reactions to the brutal blows of the final raffle-boxing match. Sight, taste, and muscular or kinesthetic senses are described; perhaps even the sound of the blow is suggested to our imaginations.

> Jerry had girded himself for the blow but it took him by surprise with its savagery and viciousness. The entire planet was jarred for a moment, the stadium swaying, the lights dancing. The pain in his neck was excruciating—his head had snapped back from the impact of Janza's fist. Sent reeling backward, he fought to stay on his feet and he somehow managed not to fall. His jaw was on fire, he tasted acid. Blood, maybe. He shook his head, quick vision-clearing shakings and established himself in the world once more.

One of the most suspenseful segments of *Shabanu, Daughter of the Wind* is the battle between two male camels for mating rights; Suzanne Fisher Staples uses vivid nouns, adjectives, and verb forms to create visual and aural images that hold Shabanu and the reader breathless. Tipu "trots up to the female, his teeth squeaking as they grind together. A rumbling starts in his belly, emerging through the pink bladder in a slobbering, foamy belch. Tipu shakes his head, and the foam flicks out, sticking to the ears and necks of the other camels. . . ." The younger Kalu, "puffed up and full of himself," challenges Tipu, who "roars again, lowers his head, and charges. Kalu is ready with a deft feint. Tipu bumps him with his chest, but Kalu lowers his huge black head, ducks it under Tipu's chest, and clamps his powerful jaws around Tipu's foreleg." Here Dadi and Shabanu must intervene lest one or even two valuable camels be killed. Dadi jams his stave between Tipu's jaws, but the camel "backs away and lowers his head, knocking the stick aside with a toss of his neck. His fierce eyes fix on Dadi's face." Shabanu screams and raises her stick, but the camel lunges while her stick "glances off his ribs." Appeals to the readers' senses make the incident vivid.

Other styles are needed for other stories. Myths, for example, are the record of cultures past, told and retold by one generation to the next. Language used in retelling such literature should give the reader a glimpse and flavor of the times and the place, as well as the sense of oral tradition. H. M. Hoover in *The Dawn Palace: The Story of Medea* addresses this task successfully; the details she chooses record images of time and place, and retain the long cadences of the oral tradition. The following segment appeals to the reader's senses of sight, hearing, and touch as it describes the mysterious room changes, as well as the dignity and elegance of a home fit for the goddess Circe:

> In the center of the island, almost hidden by the great trees, Circe's palace was a warren of chambers, passageways, and secret rooms . . . opened onto a terrace overlooking the sea. Their walls glowed with murals that altered themselves daily, and the floors were carpeted with what felt like warm moss. Her wicker couch was soft with furs; her bed a net of woven gold suspended from four cone-shaped stands of carved ebony. A pool cut into the living rock served as her bath and was sluiced by the artesian spring flowing up from under the building.

Imagery creates a mystical and eerie mood here and in the description of an unearthly battle fought by Jason:

> A mist was rising up from the field, and in the mist, forms moved. Smokelike, they drifted up from the furrows and billowed into beings, fearsome warriors, their bodies faintly blue with swamp light and decay. . . . When fully formed, they swayed, as though awakened from a long sleep, and then, one by one, moved. . . .

Figurative Language

Another device of style often used is **figurative language,** in which the writer uses words not as literal representations but with meanings other than common definitions, making comparisons to like or unlike objects or people and thus giving added dimension to meaning. Figurative language also relies upon appeals to our senses; in showing how one thing is like or unlike another, the comparison may mention visual, auditory, tactile, olfactory, or other sensory qualities. Among the most commonly used kinds of figurative language are simile, metaphor, and personification.

A **simile** states a comparison by saying that one thing is *like* or *as,* or, through the contrasting term *than,* is unlike something else; "round like a ball," and "hot as fire" are common but clichéd comparisons. In the above selection, "forms" are "smokelike"; there are carpets "like warm moss," and "shadows like long dark fingers." The wind is "warm as the breath of an eager young hunter."

A **metaphor** is an implied comparison rather than a stated one. We may comment that a problem is "a tough nut to crack," or that she "walks the fence" on a political issue. In *Buffalo Brenda,* India Ink faces the first day of high school, her "doom," implying that it is both scary and threatening. In *The Chocolate War,* Jerry Renault's face is "on fire," implying that he is in severe pain. In a chapter about Goober, Cormier uses related water metaphors to describe Goober's beautiful running form. He "poured himself liquid through the sunrise," neighbors "see him waterfalling" down the streets, as Goober "floats" and "flows" in graceful form. Using both metaphor and simile, Cormier describes Jerry leaving the cemetery with his father: a "fiery knot of anger had come undone, unraveled . . . leaving a yawning cavity like a hole in his chest."

Sometimes a book title may be a metaphor. *Rumble Fish,* the title of a novel by S. E. Hinton's, is a clear metaphor for the action and theme of the story. The fish that Rusty-James and the Motorcycle Boy stare at in the pet store are Siamese fighting fish, who must be isolated or they will kill each other, even if the "other" is just the fish's own image seen in the mirror. The fish must live solitary lives to avoid destroying others and themselves in the battling process. Since the story's focus on teen violence explores the self-destruction that accompanies the destruction of others, the metaphorical title is apt. The title *The Catcher in the Rye* is also metaphorical; it comes from the song "If a body meet a body, coming through the rye," the song that the child sings incorrectly as Holden watches him walking the Sunday streets with his parents. As Holden pictures children playing ball in a field of rye, oblivious to the danger of falling over the cliff, he sees himself not meeting but catching them before it's too late, a metaphor for his wish to keep children innocent.

Personification is the giving of human traits to animals or other nonhumans. In the selection above from *The Dawn Palace,* the mist seems alive, "fearsome," with "bodies" resembling "warriors." In the selection from *The Abduction,* like human beings, snow "retreats" and clouds "hasten" rather than melting as does snow, or being blown as clouds are blown, while dazzling sun "bathes" the mouths of fjords.

Roll of Thunder is rich in imagery and figurative language. The description of the school bus as it approaches the trench in the road during the heavy rain uses imagery and several figurative devices, including personification, metaphor, and simile:

> The bus rattled up the road. . . . It rolled cautiously through a wide
> puddle . . . then, seeming to grow bolder as it approached our man-
> made lake, it speeded up, spraying the water in high sheets of back-
> ward waterfalls into the forest. . . . The bus emitted a tremendous crack
> and careened drunkenly into our trap. . . . Then it sputtered a last mur-
> muring protest and died, its left front wheel in our ditch, its right wheel
> in the gully, like a lopsided billy goat on its knees.

Symbol

A **symbol** operates on two levels of meaning, the literal and the suggestive or figurative. The flag that flies above the county courthouse or the
town post office is the symbol for a public building. The hammer and
sickle is the symbol of communism, the swastika the symbol of Nazi Germany. The dove and the olive branch are universal symbols for peace.
Within a work of literature, particular objects may be particular symbols
suggesting abstract ideas or principles. For example, the long yellow con-
vertible of the slick villain may become a symbol for villainy; whenever
the car appears in the story, the same feelings or premonitions of deceit
are aroused in an observing character as well as in the reader.

The novels here serving as touchstones use symbol effectively. In *The
Chocolate War,* the chocolate sale serves literally and also as symbol for
defiance of the status quo, daring Jerry to act on principle rather than under coercion. The black box with its one black and five white marbles is a
symbol of the risk Archie takes whenever he makes a Vigil assignment; if
he draws the black marble, he must take the assignment himself. Just before the raffle-fight, Obie brings out the box. Without further explanation, readers are caught in momentary suspense, knowing that Archie,
who hates all physical activity, risks having to be the fighter who attacks
Jerry and perhaps being beaten himself. The land owned by two genera-
tions of the Logan family in *Roll of Thunder* is both important in the plot
and a symbol of the family's freedom and independence. In *A Wrinkle in
Time,* IT, on a literal level, is revolting and terrifying, a disembodied brain
that controls all of Camazotz. On a symbolic level, IT represents control
by the mind and intellect without any influence whatsoever from human
feelings or emotions. *Catcher* also uses a symbol, Allie's baseball mitt. Literally the mitt is associated with Allie's activities, but references to it also
have a suggestive or symbolic meaning; the mitt represents innocence
like Allie's, perfect and unsullied. In *Blue Heron* Avi uses the heron both
as an important element in the plot and as a symbol for the timidity of the
boy who has grown up in a home isolated by wilderness.

Connotation

Figurative devices not only supply information, but also create mood and effect tone. Added to their literal meaning is a wealth of **connotation,** the associative or emotional meaning of a word that varies from denotation or factual meaning. Look, for example, at a variety of terms for a male parent: Daddy, Dad, Pop, Father, or even Colonel-Father. The first suggests the loving, trusting relationship of a small child to the parent; the second, the somewhat increased distance almost inevitable between parent and young adult, particularly a son; "Pop" implies a humorous or easy friendship, and "Father" suggests a more distant or respectful relationship, or perhaps an absent parent, "my father." The last term, "Colonel-Father," by mentioning status beyond family, suggests power or a strict disciplinary relationship between parent and child. The connotations of the terms make the difference. Many of the fictional examples cited in this chapter are filled with connotative language; for example, the "snow retreated reluctantly" not only personifies snow but also connotes the slow arrival of spring.

Richly connotative words used in Mollie Hunter's *Cat, Herself* in the scene in which Cat delivers her baby brother in the travelers' trailer demonstrate how vivid and vigorous verbs engage and convince the reader of Cat's empathic response to her mother's labor.

> Hands clenched, nails biting into her palms, Cat shuddered back from the sound, and then, in an agony of sympathy for her mother, she was bending over the bed, clutching Ilsa's writhing hands tight in her own, weeping, crying out to her in a wordless love that begged to share the pain. Ilsa's body fused with her own. For a moment, they were poised together on the same high point of endurance.

"Clenched," "biting," "shuddered," "agony of sympathy," "clutching," "writhing," "weeping," "crying," "begged," "body fused" are strong and even painful in their connotations. Cat cares so much about her mother that she seems to suffer with her.

Hyperbole

Exaggeration, commonly used in conversation, is also called **hyperbole.** We are so accustomed to hyperbole that we scarcely pay attention to it: "I just died" with embarrassment. "It's an oven in here." The title *The Chocolate War* is not a literal war, but hyperbole. Nor—although the force and the pain of Jerry's being tackled is clear—did they "murder" him on the football field.

Understatement

The reverse of hyperbole, minimizing rather than exaggerating, is **understatement.** Neither *Roll of Thunder* nor *The Chocolate War* uses much understatement, but Salinger's protagonist uses it extensively. Holden spends a long paragraph describing a revolting picture of Ackley, an unpleasant-looking boy with green teeth who shows masticated food when he talks with his mouth full; Holden then concludes with an understatement about how little he likes Ackley and how no hearts were broken when Ackley retreated to his own room.

Allusion

The mature reader is able to catch an **allusion** or reference to something generally known in our common past, our understanding, or our literature. For example, biblical and mythological allusions occur in fiction but are more often used in poetry; understanding some poems may, in fact, depend upon our recognition of the origins of the allusions. In ordinary speech, we might say that the chemistry exam was "Waterloo," referring to the general knowledge that Waterloo was the final defeat of mighty Napoleon. Or we might call a particular book "my bible," referring to the Bible as a book of guiding principles for life and theology. News writers mention a situation as "another Watergate," meaning an illegal political mess. A much-used stylistic device, allusion relies upon a common knowledge, but is lost on those who lack experience or background.

The touchstones use allusions that enrich meaning. In the setting for *The Chocolate War,* a Catholic school named Trinity, a biblical allusion seems appropriate. Jerry, naming himself a coward, a betrayer who believes one thing and says another, feels as if "he had been Peter a thousand times and a thousand cocks had crowed in his lifetime"; the reference is to the disciple Peter, who, at the time of the trial and crucifixion, before the cock crowed had denied three times that he knew Jesus. "Do I dare disturb the universe?" is a line from T. S. Eliot's "The Love Song of J. Alfred Prufrock." *A Wrinkle in Time* is filled with allusions, perhaps disconcertingly so to many readers. The many quotations allude to wisdom found in world literature. Specifically, the Dark Thing clouding the time and space travelers' vision of the earth, as Mrs. Whatsit says, has been fought by Jesus, Schweitzer, da Vinci and Michelangelo, Bach and Beethoven, Gandhi and Buddha, and others who represent intellect combined with emotion, wisdom with compassion.

Dialect

Dialect or diction that by its style gives the flavor of a country, a region, or a social segment is an effective means of showing character as well as a place and time. Ernest Gaines uses the language of the South spoken by the black men in his *A Gathering of Old Men,* each one different from the others but each speaking in credible local dialect. Here Mat explains to his wife the origin of the anger that sends him out to defy the sheriff and a lynch mob intent on hanging another black man. Mat had spent years struggling

> in George Medlow's field, making him richer and richer and us getting poorer and poorer. . . . The years I done stood out in the back yard and cussed at God, the years I done stood out on that front garry and cussed the world, the times I done come home drunk and beat you for no reason at all—and, woman, you still don't know what's the matter with me? Oliver, woman! . . . Oliver. How they let him die in the hospital just 'cause he black. No doctor to serve him, let him bleed to death, 'cause he was black. And you ask me what's the matter with me?

Similarly, distinctive dialect and convincing language depends upon words characteristic of people and place in Mollie Hunter's *Cat, Herself,* where characters speak in the vernacular of their Scottish locale. At one point, Cat and her mother, Ilsa, have been picking raspberries, and Ilsa says: "Tell you what, Cat. We've picked enough for a wage today, both of us. I'll away and make a cup of tea. You take a dander up the river where it's cool and see if your daddy's had any luck at the pearling, and I'll just sit in the shade till you both come back. Eh, now?"

When a writer assumes the diction of a region, consistency is essential. Olive Ann Burns uses the vernacular of rural Georgia in *Cold Sassy Tree,* the town name. Will Tweedy, age 14, tells of Granny's death and funeral. "What happened, while Granny was on her deathbed, Mama got up a black outfit for Mary Toy to wear to the funeral—black taffeta dress, black stockings, black slippers, and a little black bonnet. 'It'll give her something to wear on trips later,' said Mama. 'If everything is black already, the train sut won't show.' Aunt Carrie, who thinks Mary Toy's fiery red hair will look out of place at the funeral, dyes it black. "'Just for today, sugarfoot,' she said when my sister had a conniption fit."

One of the pleasures of the novel *A Day No Pigs Would Die* is its vigorous and earthy language, dialect filled with comparisons often unexpected and fanciful. Robert Newton Peck's story is set in Vermont among Shakers, plain people who believe in living their faith without show or pretense. Rob, who has helped in the birthing of twin calves, is given a baby pig; his father warns him that "Care taking of a pig can keep a body as nervous as a longtail cat in a room full of rocking chairs." The cow has mauled Rob during the battle to help in the calves' birth, and Rob's mother has stitched up his cuts with a needle and thread. Dreading the pain of stitch removal, Rob guesses the stitches will "be there until Hell froze and got hauled to the ice house." When Rob protests that they are not rich, his father lists the family wealth, using a lyrical diction that is nonetheless compatible with Shaker simplicity and appreciation of nature: "We can look at sundown and see it all, so that it wets the eye and hastens the heart. We hear all the music that's in the wind, so much music that it itches my foot to start tapping. Just like a fiddle."

Evaluating Style

The pleasure of reading is increased by the appropriateness and vitality of language. On the other hand, flat or drab language is ineffective as a means to describe unusual activities or actions, or as a way of making a significant point about human beings.

Effective Style

Readers enjoy literary work that gives them the sense of a personal or particular voice or person. Fortunately, a great many writers for young adults are very much aware of the necessity for stylistic excellence.

Notice first the effective style of the writers of the touchstones. In *The Chocolate War* Cormier's figurative and connotative language are filled with unusual but plausible comparisons in the form of similes and metaphors. The ellipsoid football "squirts" away from Jerry's grasp. His body "mutinied against movement." He bobs "like one of those toy novelties dangling from car windows." The coach looks "like an old gangster: broken nose, a scar on his cheek like a stitched shoestring . . . his stubble like slivers of ice." Jerry's conflict makes him toss in bed while the sheet twists around his body "like a shroud, suffocatingly." Brother Leon looks "like a mad scientist plotting revenge in an underground laboratory." Jerry lies awake wrestling with his memory of defying the Vigils, refusing to sell the chocolates. "It was like the third degree, only he was both interrogator and suspect, both tough cop and wounded prisoner, a cruel spotlight pinning him in a blinding circle of light."

Other stylistic devices are evident. Imagery, or appeal to the senses, occurs on every page. For example, Archie, initiator of all Vigil assignments, hates sports, "he hated the secretions of the human body, pee or perspiration. . . . He couldn't stand the sight of greasy, oozing athletes drenched in their own body fluids . . . bulging with muscles, every pore oozing sweat." Cormier also uses symbol, as he describes Jerry's poster on the back wall of his locker; in addition to showing a literal picture, the poster acts as reminder of Jerry's conflict: A stretch of beach, a broad sky, a single star, a tiny figure of a man, and beneath it all the question "Do I dare disturb the universe?"

Watch Cassie of *Roll of Thunder* as morning light makes visible the burned cotton fields.

> When the dawn came peeping yellow-gray and sooted over the horizon, the fire was out and the thunderstorm had shifted eastward after an hour of heavy rain. I stood up stiffly, my eyes tearing from the acrid smoke, and looked out across the cotton to the slope, barely visible in the smoggish dawn. Near the slope where once cotton stalks had stood, their brown bolls popping with tiny puffs of cotton, the land was charred, desolate, black, still steaming from the night.

Examining other fiction with highly effective style will serve to contrast it with ineffective style. In *Are You in the House Alone?* Richard Peck uses explicit, concrete detail to describe, for example, Sonia Slanek's clothing to show her as a nonconforming outsider who is "still back there" in New York City. No jeans for her, but slacks of "velvet printed in art deco pyramids and rainbows, all colors, and enormously belled at the bottom. The cuffs swished around a pair of lemon yellow shoes with three-inch platforms."

Stylistically, Bruce Brooks's novel *The Moves Make the Man* is noteworthy for the authenticity of its first-person language. The narrator uses typical oral sentence structures, from terse to long and meandering, to produce a convincing vernacular: "This is nothing hard to figure." The moonlight "came in slanty through the window." "Bix was gone and worse the Bix I used to dig was gone even before he went and I didn't know where either of them was but he left his glove behind, which he must be unhappy without regardless of being the old Bix or the new." Imagery and unusual metaphors make Brooks's pictures vivid: The black baseball teams play on the field in Catalpa Park, which has "a big outfield where there isn't a fence but a creek running the border. . . . It is a nice place to play, with all those huge catalpa trees wearing long bean earrings on their flappy-ear leaves." Describing the refreshments offered after the black vs. white baseball game, narrator Jerome uses metaphor and imagery to describe the many colors of the soft drinks "through this chunky blanket of ice that caught the sparkles from the sun which was just getting down there where everything it hits looks better than usual and brighter."

Onomatopoeic words, those that sound like their meanings, also help make language vivid, as "bammatta, bammatta" describes the sound of the basketball being dribbled in Brooks's novel. The writer manages in still other stylistic ways to convince readers that the story is truly being told by a young boy. Speaking of his cooking, Jerome says, "Things burn when you think you have hardly put any heat to them at all, and other things lie cold and wet in the pan all the while." On discovering that although he is the only black in the school, he will not be the only boy in the cooking class, Jerome says that he feels his "onlyness broken." Going

off in the dark to play basketball in lantern light, he says "I felt like a secret as I stopped through the town . . . [and] used the shade like some
slinky superdude in a comic."

Another novel, Chris Crutcher's *The Crazy Horse Electric Game*—a
title arising from a high point in Willie's 16 years, a day when he was a
hero—also uses the vernacular of sports effectively:

> Petey Shropshire flips a ball into the air with one hand and whacks a
> high pop fly over the hurricane fence on the right foul line and down
> the highway toward them. . . . Willie turns his back, catching it over his
> shoulder, basket style . . . flips it to Johnny, who fires it back over the
> fence.

> . . . He throws a high, inside, medium fastball to back the batter off the
> plate some, but instead of backing down, the batter edges into it and
> takes the ball on his elbow, then walks to first. Willie curses himself for
> not throwing it harder, making the hitter pay for a freebee.

Despite some improbabilities in the plot line, the story successfully grips
the reader's interest, much of its hold due to Crutcher's successful style
as Willie's thoughts and feelings are expressed in the language of his age
and experience.

In *The Goats,* Brock Cole uses short sentences with subject-predicate
order whenever he narrates the boy's thoughts; rather than creating monotony, the staccato form maintains suspense, especially by its use of
specifics. The novel concerns a boy and a girl whose clothes have been
stolen, and who are left on an island by other campers. The two "goats,"
apparently the nerds of the camp, take charge of their own lives and, by
imagination and determination that lead to self-confidence, manage to
elude the authorities and find their way back to her mother. "Once outside, he forgot about keeping himself covered up. It was dark and not important anymore. It was the others he cared about. They weren't going to
see him if he could help it. He grabbed a corner of her blanket and led the
way down the path. She held on as if he was trying to take it away from
her."

The fresh style of M. E. Kerr in *Dinky Hocker Shoots Smack!* is full of
vivid imagery and figurative language. "To ask someone like [overweight]
Dinky to go into Woerner's Restaurant just to pick up pies for her mother
was to ask a wino to drop in at a vineyard just to watch the bottling
process." Tucker's 15-year-old anxiety about going to his first dance is apparent in this vivid statement: "Tucker was also trying to dance without
moving his arms very much. He had smelled his armpits in the john and
he was perspiring all right, worse than a Rose Bowl tackle on New Year's
Day." Tucker, thinking over his failures during the evening of the dance,
fears he will end up like the man sitting next to him on the subway, who is

following the words in an encyclopedia with a gnarled finger and whis-
pering them as he read. He had a grease-stained brown paper bag next
to a red cap with ear muffs attached to it, and he smelled of salami and
looked like the type who lived in one of those single rooms you could
look up and see him walking around in, under a naked light bulb dangling from the ceiling, with milk cartons on the window sill.

Vivid figures of speech are often used by Bridgers in *Permanent Connections:* here a metaphor helps the reader see Rob's sense of being
caught in his own sullen rejection of all his parents try to do for him: "He
was caught. He had snagged his foot in his own trap. It was a round trap,
one that would keep him running in circles, always coming back to the
truth of it." His friend Ellery, too, has left a different life; she thinks of her
mother's new life-style as that of a sixties dropout: "So she had chucked it
all, husband, house, furniture, banker's-wife image; watched it sail out
the window like dust kitties off a rag."

Kathryn Lasky uses a variety of stylistic devices in *Beyond the Divide,*
her story of an Amish father and daughter trekking west during the Gold
Rush days. In this example her use of imagery and metaphor enables the
reader to sit with Meribah in the mountains of Cheyenne country and
look out upon the world.

Pressing her cheek against the rock, she moved carefully along the
edge. A perfect rock hollow with a smooth surface for sitting faced due
west. There was an overhang for shade and even a small stone with a
footstool of ledge that cropped out beneath. . . . The flat valley, blue
and placid, spilled before her. Through it the north fork of the Platte,
neither wet nor dry from Meribah's vantage, wound in lazy elegance—
if rivers can be elegant, Meribah thought.

At other times Lasky makes the reader see the rugged terrain and the
covered wagons struggling through, occasionally breaking an axle on the
boulders. Meribah is observed changing the bandages on her father's gan-
grenous arm; cutting in two a damaged wagon; and with the help of
empty water buckets, enticing the parched and exhausted oxen to keep
pulling. Because of Lasky's ability to make the action visual through imagery, the experiences are vividly real.

The vocabulary of classical music is essential to the style of Bruce
Brooks's *Midnight Hour Encores.* In fact, were it not for the clear characterization of Sibilance, the musician-music talk might put off the nonmusi-
cal reader. Sib may be an international prize winner among cellists, but
she talks like a credible young adult. For example, Sib, who as a newborn
was abandoned by her mother, questions her father, Taxi, about whether
it is really a "big deal" to parent a baby:

"Oh, come on. How long does it take to change a diaper? Twenty seconds? How many times a day do you do it? Six? That's two minutes.

How long to give a baby a plate of your dinner mashed up—an extra fifteen seconds? Three times a day, that's almost another minute. . . . what
are we talking about here? A couple of hours a day?"

Stylistically, Janine Boissard's *A Matter of Feeling* is a pleasure to
read for its richly connotative language. In describing the home of this
family of four girls, Boissard pictures its warmth and acceptance:

It was seven o'clock. Warm and floating. I slid into the living room.
Mother was there. In her place near the hearth, her mending basket
within easy reach. Darning, hems, leather patches on knees or elbows—these are done in the evening by the fire. Done for us. It is
never easier to talk than with someone who is sewing.

Because her imagery paints a picture and the cadence of the lines is musical, Boissard's short sentences do not lull us to boredom but show the
quiet hominess that Paula's older lover admires. When Paula describes
her attic room, she says:

Whenever I come into my room, I always have the feeling someone's waiting for me. Someone who looks like me, who watches me
get up, leave, perhaps go through the garden. I sat down on my bed
and stayed there a few minutes with my eyes shut to allow my other
self to find me again. The Pauline of stillness and silence, calm and
dream, rejoined the Pauline who is all mad rush and work.

In order that the reader is willing to believe, to suspend disbelief, a
clear picture and an understanding of the setting are important to high
fantasy, as they are to Le Guin's *The Beginning Place*. Using concrete and
specific details, the author shows the sterile routine of Hugh's work at
Sam's Thrift-E-Market. His barren life, source of the panic attack that
sends him looking for a quiet place free of tension, is suggested through a
description of his neighborhood:

Now in summer the treeless streets were still bright and hot at
seven. Planes gaining altitude from the airport ten miles south cut the
thick, glaring sky, dragging their sound and shadow; broken swings of
painted play-gyms screeched beside the driveways. The development
was named Kensington Heights. . . . There were no heights, no val-
leys . . . [but] two-story six-unit apartment houses painted brown and
white . . . patches of lawn . . . gum wrappers, soft-drink cans, plastic
lids, the indestructible shells and skeletons of the perishables he handled at the . . . grocery . . . lay among the white rocks and dark plants.

Metaphors and similes that seem true to the thinking of the wild animal whose point of view the reader follows are striking in Whitley

Strieber's *Wolf of Shadows*. The black wolf, a big loner, and his pack are
survivors of a nuclear explosion and experience the starvation and nuclear winter following such an event. Describing the mushroom cloud
boiling "in fury," Streiber uses highly visual and connotative language:

> . . . hate unbound—not the struggling rage of an animal trapped by the
> human hunters' angry jaws, nor the anguish of a mouse wriggling on a
> hungry tongue, but something else, a steaming, clotted malevolence
> that killed indifferently, humbling everything from mayfly to man.

> In his heart he also heard the streaks hissing like the icy wind that slips
> winter beneath the warmest coat. . . . The streaks began to fade, be-
> coming as faint as spiderwebs shot with dawn, then disappeared over
> the horizon.

> "Wolf of Shadows heard on the next lake the human hunters who came
> every summer muttering nervously in their camp. Their voices were as
> tight as vines twisting in air."

Without overloading his language with devices of sound so that melliflu-
ence transcends meaning, Strieber also effectively uses **alliteration** or repeated initial sounds to create a smoothly flowing line, "*h*uman *h*unter,"
and "*m*ayfly to *m*an," for example. Imagery describes the natural world
and the appurtenances of man in terms that show the wolf protagonist as
nonhuman observer. "Through the cracks in the storm Wolf of Shadows
heard the hunters coming closer and closer. He smelled their death-sticks
and instinctively faded back into the protection of the trees." During the
rainstorms, "the lake began to crawl up its banks." At the end of the
storm, "the sky lifted from the land."

The sense of an intimate time in a benign setting comes to the reader
through quiet description in Sue Ellen Bridgers's *All Together Now*. Casey
Flanagan is spending the summer with her father's family while he is a pi-
lot in the Korean war. As she fishes with her uncle Taylor and her friend
Dwayne, her enjoyment is enlarged by her memories of fishing with her
father:

> . . . They would spend the day moving up the inlet, their lines dropping
> with no more than a single delicate splash, the only sound the deep
> chug of the outboard when they moved on and the steady click of their
> reels when they were still. They had caught pinfish, their chartreuse
> sides flicking between the dark water and the bucket in the bow of the
> boat. She could hear them flipping against the metal sides, shuddering
> life although their gills fluttered. She had loved to fish . . . liked the
> swell of moving water under the boat, the buoyancy that made her feel
> light herself, able to float, to swim, to dip deep below her world and lift

out a treasure from another time, a primeval beauty welcomed with a spontaneous gasp of delight and a father's praise.

Formal diction in literature for young adults can also be highly effective. Gary Paulsen records the thoughts and actions of Russel Susskit in his realistic story of the Alaskan far north, *Dogsong*. The serious language, which sounds as though it might be a literal translation from Russel's native language, is without colloquialism, uses no contractions, and describes convincingly the spiritual alliance as it develops between the team of five sled dogs and Russel. Russel goes back to the old ways of his people, using the dogsled instead of the diesel-fueled snowmobile, killing caribou, ptarmigan, and even a huge polar bear to share the raw meat with the dogs on their trek from ocean to ocean, across the tundra, ice floes, and mountains. The dogs, well fed and rippling with hard muscle, "had seen and done much and now they knew the man on the sled, knew that he was a part of them, knew that no matter what happened he would be there and that made them stronger still. The strength in them came back to Russel and he fed on it and returned it as more strength still."

Restrained and dignified language characterizes descriptions of Russel's killing the polar bear, for example, descriptions that a less skillful writer might make either sensational or sentimental. As Russel beds down for the night in the fierce cold, Paulsen says with simplicity, "It was a home and he let his mind circle and go down, the same way a dog will circle before taking the right bed." Describing the otherworldly beauty of the northern lights, Russel thinks of them in the terms of his people as they move "across the sky in great pulses of joy, rippling the heavens, pushing the stars back. . . . Many people believed they were the souls of dead-born children dancing in heaven and playing with balls of grass and leather." With such verbal restraint in the adventure story, Paulsen gives great dignity to a people whose way of life is vastly different from that of the majority of readers.

Robin McKinley in her fantasy *Beauty* uses language that sensitively reminds the reader of the story's origins in the fairy tale "Beauty and the Beast." Using richly connotative language and the long lines and cadences of the oral tale, McKinley conveys the sense of "once upon a time, long ago" so much a part of folk and fairy tale. For example, Beauty tells of disliking Ferdy's sudden kiss, and of Ferdy's reaction to her dislike: "I forgave him to make him stop apologizing; but I also began to avoid him, and when I did come to the shop when he was there, or when he ate the noon meal with us, he followed me with his eyes as if I wore a black hood and carried an axe, and he was next in line." In the description of the family's new home, the personification of the stream helps to evoke the landscape of a fantasy land: "There was a well on the small hill we'd come over following the road from the town, but a lovely bright stream jingled its way down from the forest and took a generous bend to be convenient to the forge before it disappeared behind another small hill, heading away from the town." And a tinge of mystery glows through the description of the Beast's castle gardens:

> At the castle, the gardens remained perfect and undisturbed—by seasonal change, animal depredations, or anything else. Not only was there no sign of gardeners, visible or invisible, but there was never any sign of any need for gardeners; hedges never seemed to need trimming, nor flower beds weeding, nor trees pruning; nor did the little streams in their mosaic stone beds swell with spring floods.

Ineffective Style

Examining a group of less effective novels may not only make evaluating style clearer and more understandable, but also help to show that style is important. Look closely now at works that are disappointing for various stylistic reasons.

Unlike the style of *The Moves Make the Man,* the limited jargon of baseball seems the only language known to the writer of *Squeeze Play,* the second in the Rookies series. Three high school teammates are drafted into the major leagues, each playing a different position on different farm teams and each highly successful. Not only are the three characters nearly interchangeable, but the language relies almost entirely upon **clichés,** or hackneyed and trite phrases. Some paragraphs, for example, are almost entirely clichés, which are italicized here: "David stood *frozen in time* as he slowly turned and *soaked in every detail* of his surroundings. *In some strange way, it was everything he'd ever though it might be.*" True, sports lingo may be a part of telling about any game, but lest it seem impossible to tell a story well without vast numbers of sports clichés, think back to *The Moves Make the Man:* The shortstop "whizzed into the picture. He was stretched out full, two feet off the ground, flying like he was shot from a bow and arrow, moving as fast as the ball. WHISH! He snapped his mitt out and snagged the ball. . . ."

Clichéd language can be found in any kind of story. Note the language in, for example, *Hostage!* a novel in the Sweet Valley High series. In a single paragraph on a typical page are three clichés: Mr. Morrow "hung his head." Regina's getting hurt "just tears me up inside." "Well, keep your spirits up!" The overuse of exclamation points, furthermore, is reminiscent of the notes passed between children in elementary school. Here they further emphasize the drabness of language, which should rely for emphasis upon freshness and vigor rather than upon exclamatory punctuation.

A mixture of speaking styles puzzles the reader when at one moment the speaker seems educated and mature but at another the same speaker seems primitive or juvenile. One of the puzzling things about Forrest Carter's *The Education of Little Tree* is the way in which the first-person narrator uses mature, understated, and occasionally lyrical language, and the same narrator speaking of and in the same time period uses the language of a backwoods settler or of an Indian who seems childlike. Look first at the narrator's halting description of the march of the Cherokees to the Indian Lands, misplaced semicolon included:

> The husband carried his dead wife. The son carried his dead mother, his father. The mother carried her dead baby. They carried them in their arms. And walked. And they did not turn their heads to look at the soldiers, nor to look at the people who lined the sides of the Trail to watch them pass. Some of the people cried. But the Cherokee would not cry. Not on the outside, for the Cherokee would not let them see his soul; as he would not ride in the wagons.

A few pages later, the same youthful narrator speaks quite differently:

> Me and Granpa usually run across hickor' nuts, or chinkapins and chestnuts; sometimes black walnuts. It wasn't that we special *looked* for them, it just seemed to happen. Between our eating and gathering nuts and roots, and seeing a 'coon or watching a peckerwood, our leaf carrying would get down to practical nothing. . . .

> I could tell right off that Granpa and Granma liked Pine Billy a lot. . . . She made them [sweet 'taters] into a pie right then, and Pine Billy et three pieces of it.

Spoken language differs from that of fiction, but occasionally a writer assumes that duplication of spoken dialogue is convincing when printed on the page. However, as a simple experiment will demonstrate, spoken and printed language are different. Tape record a casual conversation and play it back. Notice how slowly the spoken dialogue moves, how many unnecessary words we use, how often we repeat ourselves, or pause and then lurch along. Reading such slow-moving and convoluted dialogue quickly bores the reader, a trap that the writer has fallen into in *A Band of Angels.* Two girls are talking:

> "You can see how much I've changed," [Lisa] said to Riley, and she laughed again. "I even carry my own locks around now. Like a modern chastity belt, right? But what happened is, ever since I've been away, I've felt I . . . *I* don't know, I *matter* more. To me and—*you* know— just in general." She paused. "Do *I* sound like the baby now?" She batted her eyes. "Like, wow, kids—look at me! Can you believe it?" She shook her head. "I never said this stuff out loud before. Maybe it's one of those things a person ought to just shut up about."
> . . . "I think I know exactly what you mean. At home, sometimes, going to school and all that stuff," [Riley said]. "[Y]ou sort of feel you're

not anything, just by yourself. . . . You're just a good little, special little
girl who's meant to more or less blend in—like disappear. . ."

"What does it all mean?" the reader asks. "Get to the point."

Awkward and unidiomatic phrasing may occur in any kind of writing.
It is frequent in the high fantasy *The Crystal Shard:* "He walked out
around the bluff, his steady stride unnervingly holding the unswerving
promise of death," is a halting statement made heavy by the complex verbal forms, "unnervingly," "holding," and "unswerving." And words are
sometimes used incorrectly: "Special power Bruenor had imbued upon
the weapon"; the weapon should be "imbued with." "The lavender eyes
burned with a luster . . . never witnessed before." The terms "burned"
and "luster" are contradictory; the first suggests fire and the second a
glow of reflected light. "Wulfgar was truly awe-stricken" bumps along because we expect the more common term "awestruck." "The two adven-
turers . . . tensed reflexively" is difficult to imagine because one action is
voluntary and the other involuntary, and "he was able to catch glimpses
of the battle to his side" prompts a strange picture of people attacking the
character's side.

Repetitive fragment form and choppy simple sentences of drab subject and predicate are characteristic of Harry Mazer's *The Last Mission,* a
novel with a potentially interesting plot about a 15-year-old who enlists
and is terribly lonely: "They were given ten days to get to Lincoln.
Enough time for all of them to get home, though not for long. But everyone was going. Jack, too, back to New York City. He couldn't hang
around the base alone. There would be too many questions raised. Why
wasn't he going home like the others?"

And yet, when Mazer uses the same sentence form in another of his
books, *The Island Keeper,* his action verbs effectively create suspense.
Cleo, overweight and feeling unloved, flees to an island in Lake Michigan
where she lives off the land for seven months and finally crosses the ice
to return to the mainland:

> Cleo stared at the smashed canoe. She would never get off the island
> now. For a moment her mind blurred; she couldn't think of anything,
> except that winter was coming and she would die. She ran toward the
> highest point of the island, vainly hoping to see her rescue coming over
> the water. She faced the island. Dundee was there, in that direction.
> She tried to calm herself by following a gull. . . . How easy it was for a
> bird.

And finally, Judy Blume has once again found a topic of interest to
young adults in her novel *Tiger Eyes,* but in this novel, as in others, her
style is flat and unimaginative. First, the title is intriguing, but the reader
searches in vain for its significance; there is none. Wolf tells the protagonist that she has "sad eyes, Tiger," and hence the book title. Furthermore,
because Blume rarely uses imagery or figurative language or varies word

order in her sentences and fragments, monotony results: "I think about Linaya and Hugh. Will they know how much I've changed this year? Will they have changed too? I'll wait until tomorrow to find out. And then it's possible I won't find out after all. Because some changes happen deep down inside of you. And the truth is, only you know about them."

Summary

A good story is words, lots of words, chosen and arranged so as best to create characters, and involve readers in the plot till they reach the climax and then cool down with the denouement. Words create a tone, show the setting essential to the story, and gather all elements together for a thematic point. The best possible words arranged in the best possible way for this particular story about these particular people in their particular situation constitute the style of the story. The words are more than the style of the story. They *are* the story.

Recommended Books Cited in This Chapter

Avi. *Blue Heron.* New York: Bradbury, 1992.

Boissard, Janine. *A Matter of Feeling.* New York: Little, Brown, 1988.

Bridgers, Sue Ellen. *Permanent Connections.* New York: Harper & Row, 1987.

Brooks, Bruce. *Midnight Hour Encores.* New York: Harper, 1986.

———. *The Moves Make the Man.* New York: Harper, 1984.

Burns, Olive Ann. *Cold Sassy Tree.* New York: Delacorte, 1992.

Cole, Brock. *The Goats.* New York: Farrar, Straus & Giroux, 1990.

Cormier, Robert. *The Chocolate War.* New York: Random House, 1974.

Crutcher, Chris. *The Crazy Horse Electric Game.* New York: Greenwillow, 1987.

Gaines, Ernest J. *A Gathering of Old Men.* New York: Knopf, 1983.

Hinton, S. E. *Rumble Fish.* New York: Dell, 1989.

Hoover, H. M. *The Dawn Palace: The Story of Medea.* New York: Dutton, 1988.

Hunter, Mollie. *Cat, Herself.* New York: Harper & Row, 1985.

Kerr, M. E. *Dinky Hocker Shoots Smack!* New York: Laurel Leaf, 1982.

Le Guin, Ursula K. *The Beginning Place.* New York: Harper, 1980.

L'Engle, Madeleine. *A Wrinkle in Time.* New York: Farrar, Straus & Giroux, 1962.

Levitin, Sonia. *Silver Days.* New York: Atheneum, 1989.

Mazer, Harry. *The Island Keeper.* New York: Delacorte Press, 1981.

McKinley, Robin. *Beauty*. New York: Harper, 1978.

Newth, Mette. *The Abduction*. New York: Farrar, Straus & Giroux, 1989.

Paulsen, Gary. *Dogsong*. New York: Macmillan, 1985.

Peck, Richard. *Are You in the House Alone?* New York: Viking, 1976.

Peck, Robert Newton. *A Day No Pigs Would Die*. New York: Knopf, 1989.

Salinger, J. D. *The Catcher in the Rye*. Boston: Little, Brown, 1951.

Staples, Suzanne Fisher. *Shabanu, Daughter of the Wind*. New York: Knopf, 1989.

Strieber, Whitley. *Wolf of Shadows*. New York: Knopf, 1985.

Taylor, Mildred. *Roll of Thunder, Hear My Cry*. New York: Dial, 1976.

— 8 —

Tone

When we misunderstand one another in conversation, it is frequently because of inattentiveness to tone. Suppose you have worked with other students on an assignment and been the one to deliver orally your joint report. You hear praise from your closest friend, "You did a wonderful job," and it is meant most sincerely. But suppose you then hear the same words, but this time your friend says, "*You* did a wonderful job." Now the tone suggests that the others in the group did not. Then you hear another comment, this time from one in your group who thinks you really let them down. Sneering, he says, "You did a *won*derful job." In each case the speaker's inflection or vocal tone is different, and in each case the meaning changes.

Just as the speaker uses vocal tone in these examples, the writer uses tone to tell the reader how the author feels about his or her subject. Because in reading literature readers cannot interpret meaning through a speaker's vocal inflections, they rely only on the words themselves, words that express the author's attitude toward the story, the subject and theme, and the readers. This means, of course, that without the help of audible inflection, the writer must choose words with extreme care.

Tone cannot be isolated from the words of a story. Words and their sounds and connotations show tone, and tone influences meaning. In the literary sense, point of view is the mind through which we view the story, the voice telling the story, whether a character or an omniscient writer. **Tone**, however, is different. It is the author's general attitude toward story and readers.

It is often easier to identify tone as it is revealed in specific characters than to identify the author's attitude toward the whole work. Notice, for example, how in *The Chocolate War* the tyrannical Brother Leon speaks to Bailey, one of the boys in his class, accusing him of dishonesty because his work is without error. Then suddenly, with no warning, he strikes Bailey on the cheek with the pointer, saying:

> "'Bailey, I'm sorry," Leon said, but his voice lacked apology. Had it been an accident? Or another of Leon's little cruelties?

> . . . Now it seemed that Bailey had been at fault all along, that Bailey had committed an error, had stood in the wrong place at the wrong time and had caused his own misfortune.

The reader is now prepared for Brother Leon's later sarcastic tone when speaking, and for his cruelty to the students. Unless told otherwise, whenever Leon speaks, the reader will be prepared for this or similar tone.

But what is Cormier's own tone, *his* attitude toward his characters and his story? Cormier's tone might be called sympathetic or understanding, perhaps a surprising term considering the ruthlessness in the novel. But, as noted earlier in considering point of view, Cormier shows not only protagonist Jerry's wish to stand up against coercion and his courage as he defies the way things are, but also the pressure Archie continually feels as he seeks to retain his leadership position while devising innovative assignments and facing the possibility of drawing the black marble that will make him the doer of the deeds. In contrast to Jerry with his courageous defiance, Goober may seem at times to be cowardly, but Cormier also understands Goober's way of "getting along" by dropping out and staying away. Emile Janza is surely an unsympathetic character who never plays by the rules, but Cormier makes us understand that even the bully has feelings, can be humiliated, and wishes he might have a close friend in whom he could confide. Character after character—boys as well as Brothers—is shown as having feelings the reader comes to understand and perhaps even respect. Except for Jerry, no one dares to disturb the universe controlled by the Vigils at Trinity school. Because Jerry is the protagonist, Cormier is most sympathetic to him, but the novelist's generally sympathetic tone is his acknowledgement that life is difficult for most people.

Readers may respond differently, of course, to a piece of fiction. It behooves the reader, however, to find the words and phrases that support the reader's choice of a word describing tone. It is more than "a feeling"; it comes through because the writer chooses words that convey that tone. The writer may choose one predominant, overall tone for a work, like, for example a humorous tone in *Buffalo Brenda,* a mysterious tone in *Interstellar Pig,* a serious tone in *The Abduction,* a suspenseful tone in *Deathwatch;* at times, however, tone may be varied, but in general one may seem most prevalent in a particular novel.[1]

Humor

Humor is an important tone in literature for young adults. Younger children laugh at situation humor, but as they mature and their vocabularies grow and experiences increase, they find increasing pleasure in the moods and incongruities that language can create. In fact, young adults may find that significant ideas can be examined and understood without their being stated in solemn or preachy tones, and even that humor may be the most comfortable way of addressing realities. And of course, they find that laughter is its own reward.

Humor may originate almost anywhere, in character, situation, or language. For example, the character Brenda in *Buffalo Brenda* by Jill Pinkwater is humorous; she wears outlandish costumes to school, from a sarong to outfits that seem a compilation from pictures scrounged from *National Geographic.* Brenda remains an outrageous character with few traits other than her inventiveness. Situations also produce laughter. A reporter on the underground school newspaper, the *Florence Free Press,* finds that the cafeteria food is inferior in quality, and that although the school budget indicates students should be getting gourmet fare, they are actually eating horsemeat. The *Press* story arouses the principal's anger and student demonstrations, which end in situation humor—a funeral service for the horses who gave their lives, a grave on the school lawn, and a bronze plaque. The humor of language, however, requires a more careful use of words. Slick, the leather-jacketed hoodlum discovered in detention by *Press* reporters also being punished, recruits a distribution staff for the Free Press, and introduces them: "My men. The Boys." An entertaining novel, it has minimal characterization and relies almost entirely on humor of several kinds.

The same can be said of *The Snarkout Boys & the Avocado of Death* by Daniel Pinkwater, whose invented situations are humorous, but who also plays with words throughout. Walter and Winston's midnight meanderings, or Snarkouts, take them to a park where stump-speaking thrives. They hear:

> "So if The Man says 'Blow!' and us little cats don't dig the riff, all we
> have to say is 'Nowhere!' 'Later!' and that, cats and kitties, would be
> HEA-VY! So if we don't dig the flip, or the number, or the place his wig
> is at, we just take time until The Man cools it."

Translation follows:

> [The trade unionist] is discussing the possibility of a strike at the
> Wanamopo Banjo Pick Factory. . . . What he has been saying, roughly, is
> this: Listen. . . . My intellect may be limited, but . . . employers are im-

posing on the workers, but the workers are very important. If we don't cooperate, then the fctory can't produce anything. If the employers tell us to work, and we refuse, that will constitute a great disadvantage for the employers. . . .

Ron Koertge writes of serious issues, like the growth of self-confidence, the spread of AIDS, and reactions to homosexuality, but his humorous touch manages to make his serious point palatable. For example, in *Arizona Kid,* Billy's Uncle Wes introduces him to his friend Luke, then tells Billy that the two of them have been at a healing service:

> "Luke? What's the matter with Luke?"
> "He has AIDS."
> "You're kidding. He looks like an ad for vitamins."

When Wes hears that to fit in at the racetrack Billy wants a cowboy hat and boots, and that Billy likes Cara, the horse exerciser, Wes firmly presses condoms on Billy.

> "Well, let me give you some condoms."
> "Pardon me?"
> "Condoms. Rubbers. What do they call them in the Midwest?"
> "We call them condoms or rubbers, but how'd we get from boots
> to . . . "

When Billy is about to return home after his Arizona summer, Wes acknowledges Billy's growth in confidence, and makes a final reference to the serious issue: "'By the way, do you have any condoms?' I stared at him. 'For the train?'"

The first pages of *The Boy in the Moon* are filled with Koertge's appreciation of young adult language as he seems to thrive on the pleasures of saying outrageous things; humor seems the dominant tone. Frieda is reading *The Bicameral Brain,* and Nick says, "I didn't read that, but I saw the movie. Robin Williams played the occipital lobe and Tom Hanks was the medulla oblongata." When students hear their assigned essay isn't due till December, "A collective sigh of relief vast enough to mist a florist shop rose from the class." Sometimes Kevin feels "like day-old cake with a lot of fresh icing." But underlying the story with its apparently glib repartee is a serious theme about finding out who you are, what defines you, and what your expectations are, another serious theme made attractive by humorous tone.

Like Koertge, Katherine Paterson makes a solemn point with the help of occasional humor. Although not the overall tone, humor often flashes throughout the serious story *Jacob Have I Loved.* The section in which the confused grandmother expresses anger at her daughter-in-law for stealing her husband is sad and yet humorous; referring to her daughter-in-law as a "viperish adulteress," she reads from the Bible about the ways in which a woman gains power over a man to make him go "as an ox to the slaughter." Although the general subject matter of John Donovan's *I'll*

Get There. It Better Be Worth the Trip is serious, the tone is often gently humorous. In fact, it is the touch of quiet humor that keep the story from becoming tense and self-conscious. For example, as Davy Ross tells of his visits with his dachshund, Fred, to his grandmother's grave, he recounts his one-sided conversation with her, talking to her about the family's move to New York, worrying about how she will survive the cold, and saying that despite his being unable to visit her grave in the future, he still loves her. He concludes the serious chapter with humor: "Fred always lifts his leg on the gravestone." As Davy admits that he doesn't yet have the whiskers to shave, he thinks "he's getting some." "L. T. Murray had hair under his arms as long ago as the fifth grade. He showed it to me a lot and told me that if I would rub spit in this area, hair would come very fast. L. T. didn't know what he was talking about of course, as I discovered." Commenting on his new room in his mother's apartment in New York, Davy says, "Both of [the bunks] are so narrow though that I'm not sure I'd want to sleep in the top bunk. That will be for the people I invite, I guess." Davy's mother jazzes up the scrambled eggs. "The first day she did that I let Fred lick the plate, but she said that was obscene. When I looked up the word in the dictionary, I decided I wouldn't let Fred do that any more."

A comic tone pervades all of T. R. Pearson's novel *A Short History of a Small Place.* The narrator, Louis Benfield, meanders through the events and nonevents of Neely, North Carolina, talking in long compound-complex sentences about the citizens of the tiny town. Much of the humor is created by unexpected comparisons: Mr. Newbery talks so fast he "sounded like both sides of an argument in Portuguese." The fire truck comes clanging down the street with "a full complement of slickered but hatless firefighters who clung all around the perimeter like so many cockleburs." Louis's father uses an **oxymoron,** a term that combines opposites, to describe the Reverend Shelton as having a manner of "flamboyant tediousness"; **synaesthesia,** the simultaneous stimulation of two or more senses, occurs in Reverend Shelton's having "had a way of making [lunch] taste sleepy." Mrs. Philip J. King has a voice "that bypasses the mouth and exits through the noseholes." Mr. Bridger is "not the sort of man to revel in working up a sweat," but occasionally has a "burst of industriousness . . . just to the verge of perspiration." Understatement is also funny: Coley Britt says he knew West Virginia license plates when he saw them because "he'd been reading since he was nine [late for beginning to read] and said he ought to know." The crowd watched as "the front view of the Buick was becoming the side view of the Buick," an understatement about movement. The commander—who is the funeral director—is proud of his caskets, which "provide the deceased with ample room to sit up on their elbows or play the violin," an unlikely possibility.

Creating humorous situations for a novel is not easy, but sustaining a humorous tone throughout a novel is even more difficult. Pearson manages, however, as does Olive Ann Burns, author of *Cold Sassy Tree.* When

Aunt Carrie dyes Mary Toy's red hair a decent black for her granny's funeral, the change is far from permanent.

> Halfway through the service Mary Toy got to sweating. Trickles of black liquid started running down her face. Seeing it, the preacher could hardly keep his mind on how good Granny had been or how it was God's will and all. Mama kept glancing at Mary Toy and finally dabbed at her face with a lace handkerchief.
>
> About then, Mary Toy noticed the black that was smearing off her hair onto her sweaty arms. Thinking it was black blood, she went to wailing. . . .
>
> Soon as we got to Grandpa's from the cemetery, Mama took Mary Toy's taffeta dress off and stuck her head in the wash basin on the back porch. The black leached right out. . . . Only thing, her hair wasn't red anymore. It was purple. Soon as she looked in the mirror, Mary Toy went into mourning for her hair.

Sentimentality

The difference has been noted between sentiment, the awakening of honest emotion, and **sentimentality,** the emphasis on situations that make the reader feel used, or falsely tricked into emotional overreaction.

Telling without sentimentality the story of an injured young athlete who becomes a quadriplegic is not an easy task, but Robin Brancato manages it in the novel *Winning.* The tone might best be described as compassionate and honest. These things happen; they are no one's fault, and although some of life's victims go under, others go on living as fully as they are able. A young man who is an achiever athletically as well as academically is injured in football, and must face being permanently crippled, a quadriplegic. With wry humor, Gary faces his friends and hospital mates, dreams of his girlfriend Diane, and of being the good sport about the football wins and losses at his high school. "Superquad" is the name given him by others in the rehabilitation hospital. Gary struggles to maintain his spirits, to be part of the group, and not to be defeated by the many defeats he sees around him. The story has no false optimism about "all's well," but faces the limitations of life in a wheelchair, the prospect of college with a great deal of needed help, the potential loss of his girlfriend, the possibility that he will not experience sex. Patients around him suffer: the wheelchair-bound psychologist finds his wife has left him, a withdrawn roommate kills himself, and Gary faces recurrent infections and setbacks. Gary, however, does not ignore his own anguish; he is not always up and optimistic, but suffers with fears about how his losses will determine his limited life. His spirits do not always live up to his nickname, but he manages to survive and by his example even to help his teacher-tutor to endure her own grief at the death of her husband. Although the story needs the hand of an editor to cut its length and to tighten sections of slow-moving dialogue, readers are carried along by the believable ups and downs of Gary's emotional struggle, and by the realistic reactions to his accident on the part of family and friends. Gary's emotional winning is over his handicap.

Stories about single parenting can also be very sentimental, suggesting that love for the infant will solve everything. Child rearing is not only a big responsibility, but also a difficult task, even for two parents working at it together. The novel that sentimentally suggests "Don't worry, it will all work out" does a great disservice to the reader who may see an acquaintance struggling with single parenthood, and wonder, "What's the big deal! In this book, it's easy." Further disservice is done to the struggling single parent who has found no solutions and needs the understanding and compassion of others. Norma Klein's *No More Saturday Nights,* the story of a college student who takes on the care of his infant, avoids sentimentality when it honestly shows single parenthood filled with problems, difficulties that sometimes may be surmounted through commitment and occasional assistance, but at other times may necessitate drastic life changes.

Nor is suicide an easy topic to write about for young adults. The shock that someone with all of a promising life ahead has terminated that promise and that life almost invites a sentimental tone. Stella Pevsner has managed to avoid sentimentality in favor of a questioning tone in her first-person story *How Could You Do It, Diane?* The theme of the novel is that no matter how hard we may look for answers to the question raised by the title about motives for suicide, we may never know. As protagonist Bethany searches for answers to the title's question, talking with Diane's boyfriends and friends, Pevsner avoids dramatic revelations or speculations about Diane's motives, like drugs, abuse, pregnancy, or academic and personal failures, and shows instead the sense of failure that parents often feel, the emotional impact of suicide on younger siblings, the slow pace of family healing, and the difficulty of the surviving family and friends to "get on with life."

Tone and Subject Matter

The kinds of tone available to the writer are almost infinite. Any word that describes attitude—friendly, caustic, affectionate, angry, despairing, or loving, for example—may be the tone for any kind of work.

Lois Duncan in her Gothic novel about a double, *Stranger with My Face,* shows the mystery of intangible evil surrounding Laurie's island home, Cliff House; Duncan successfuly maintains the tone of anxiety and fear throughout. The first chapter begins innocently enough: Flu virus has kept Laurie from the party the night before. But before the chapter is over something eerie has happened; several people insist they saw Laurie and a boy on the beach during the time she was sick. She cannot convince her friends that she was not on the beach but at home in bed. In the second chapter, the ominous feeling grows that there is indeed someone around who looks exactly like Laurie. When she returns from school, her brother is surprised, saying that he just saw her go upstairs to her room. Laurie enters her room cautiously but is certain that someone has just been there. This mysterious shadow reappears, each time with evil consequences, like the strange illness of her friend Helen, or the accident on the rocky cliff that threatens Jeff's life. The eerie tone is sustained throughout.

The subject of *Z for Zachariah* is survival after nuclear explosion, and the objective tone is a strong source of the story's credibility. The action is highly suspenseful, but Robert O'Brien never lapses into exclamatory language or sensational tone, which would wear thin. Anne, who at first had thought herself the only survivor, knows that another survivor, Mr. Loomis, is using her dog, Faro, to track her down, but tells the story without sentimentality or sensational suspense:

> They went only a few yards up the road together, perhaps fifty.
> Then they turned and went back to the house, Mr. Loomis once again
> limping slightly. But in that few yards I began to see even more clearly
> the mistake I had made, and also why Mr. Loomis had tied Faro up. If
> he could teach him to track on a leash, he could find me whenever he
> wanted to. Not yet, perhaps, but when he could walk farther.
> Suddenly I had a feeling he knew I was watching. Or worse, that he
> hoped I was. I felt slightly sick; I was in a game of move-countermove,
> like a chess game, a game I did not want to be in at all. Only Mr. Loomis
> wanted to be in it, and only he could win it.

Very early in a novel of the occult, *The Changeover,* tone becomes mysterious. By using foreshadowing effectively, Margaret Mahy intrigues the readers, forcing them to anticipate problems of a supernatural kind. It all begins quietly enough with Laura's morning feeling that something about the day is frightening, then a look at her beautiful little brother and the feeling that he is "in some way her own baby, a baby she would have one day, both born and unborn at the same time." As Laura walks with Jacko, they stop at Brique And Braque novelty shop, where a strange-looking Mr. Braque who seems to be "rotting," pounces "with great agility like an elderly mantis on an innocent fly," "triumphantly" imprinting Jacko's hand "as if he had been working towards that moment for a long time." The burning stamp resembles Mr. Braque, and terrifies Jacko, who rubs it anxiously. In a few hours, "the stamp was part of him now, more than a tattoo—a sort of parasite picture tunneling its way deeper and deeper, feeding itself as it went." Later, when Jacko is sick and Laura stays as a guest in Sorry's strange home, she has no memory of having eaten a piece of bread topped with a salted tomato, but her partaking of bread and salt in Sorry's home ensures that she must return. Page after page hints at a supernatural occurrence, and the necessity for Laura to be capable of supernatural behavior in order to counteract it. Chapter cliff-hangers further sharpen the tone of eerie mystery.

Readers of the same novel may describe its tone in different ways, as they might in the case of *Haroun and the Sea of Stories* by Salman Rushdie. One reader may call it whimsical or playful in tone, while another may say the tone is precious, sentimental, or affected. Haroun asks his father Rashid the storyteller where his stories come from.

> But whenever he asked his father this most important of questions, the Shah of Blah would narrow his (to tell the truth) slightly bulging eyes, and pat his wobbly stomach, and stick his thumb between his lips while he made ridiculous drinking noises, *glug glug glug*. Haroun hated it when his father acted this way. . . . Rashid would wiggle his eyebrows mysteriously and make witchy fingers in the air.

When Rashid loses his storytelling gift, Haroun seeks the reason. Water Genie Iff tells Haroun that Rashid "has discontinued narrative activities, thrown in the towel, packed it in. He has cancelled his subscription. Hence my presence, for purposes of Disconnection. . . ."

> "I don't believe you," [said Haroun]. "How did he send the message? I've been right with him almost all the time."
> "He sent it by the usual means," Iff shrugged. "A P2C2E."
> "And what is that?"
> "Obvious," said the Water Genie with a wicked grin. "It's a Process Too Complicated To Explain. . . ."
> "Advanced or not," Haroun retorted, "you've made a mistake this time, you're up the spout, you've got the wrong end of the stick. . . . My father has definitely not given up. You can't cut off his Story Water supply."

A tone rather infrequently used is **satire,** with its intent to point out society's imperfections and the need for reform; it is best represented by George Orwell's *Animal Farm,* a short novel known to most young adults. By means of humor and exaggeration—in this case using pigs to personify negative human traits—Orwell makes his point about the failures of a communist society and the need for change. More common for young adults, however, is the use of **irony,** an expression of contradictions, with the actual intent expressed in words that carry the opposite meaning. Frequently used by novelists, irony relies significantly upon incongruity.[2] William Wharton's novel *A Midnight Clear* is a World War II story told by a 19-year-old soldier in an intelligence and reconnaisance squad in Europe, stationed where Luxemburg, Germany, and France meet. The soldiers are cold and wet, sick with diarrhea, and so dirty their clothes are stiff. Concealing the discomfort in humor, Wharton leads the reader to see war's reality—quite different from fun and games. "Everything in the army is run by the clock 0-five-hundred and all, but they don't issue watches." "All our towels are army OD, so you can never tell if they're filthy or clean, except by the smell. . . ." The soldiers tear their one novel into sections and circulate the pieces so that all can read them. Mundy, who may have been skipped in the circulating of some of the pages, doesn't see that the characters of their war novel are Germans, but is hungry for story. "We usually leave [Mundy] until last; he reads each word as if he's licking it." When their division is ready to be shipped overseas, "Shutzer insisted this was proof that, despite all the propaganda, we were losing the war. Sending *this* outfit to fight *anybody* must be a desperate last resort." Holed up in a stripped chateau, the group fears making a fire: "there'd be regular clouds of smoke. The Germans will think we've got Indians out here making signals." Commenting on their appearances as "van Gogh potato eaters," the narrator says, "We look as if we're holding things in, at the same time keeping things out; a permanent state of negative expectation."

Commenting on her retelling of Irish folklore and legends in *The High Deeds of Finn Mac Cool,* author Rosemary Sutcliff says that she has retold them in the spirit of delight in story making, "adding a flicker or a flourish of my own, as everyone who has retold them in the past thousand years or so has done before me." As she does in the story of the British hero Cuchulain in *The Hound of Ulster* and in her historical fiction, Sutcliff here writes in the appropriately serious tone of the great, far-off days when, led by their Captain Finn Mac Cool, the Brotherhood of Fianna guarded the shores of Erin. The story begins this way:

> In the proud and far back days, though not so far back nor yet so proud
> as the days of the Red Branch Heroes, there rose another mighty broth-
> erhood in Erin, and they were called the Fianna. They were a war-host
> whose task was to hold the shores of Erin safe from invaders, and they
> were a peace-host, for it was their task also to keep down raids and har-
> ryings and blood feuds between the five lesser kingdoms into which
> Erin was divided.

Ian Serraillier in his retelling of *Beowulf the Warrior* uses the language of today and yet retains the dignified and elevated tone as well as other qualities of the epic as it was first recorded 1000 years ago. The intent of the folk epic is serious or even instructive, since the long narrative centers on a national hero and makes clear the values of a people. Serraillier has respected this intent by maintaining a consistently appropriate tone. He keeps the elevated language, the compound synonyms or kennings, the imagery, alliteration, and extended metaphors. Beowulf and his band set sail for King Hrothgar's land, which is beset by the horrible monster Grendel. The voyage across the sea is no happy, lighthearted sail across the bay; Beowulf and his valiant warriors face a sea worthy of their courage. Beowulf's hand-to-hand battle with the monster has dignity heightened by long, rhythmic lines, richly connotative terms, and alliterative descriptions with long vowels and hard consonants. To understand the source of the serious tone, read the selection aloud, noting the sounds of the language itself.

> Spilling the benches,
> They tugged and heaved, from wall to wall they hurtled.
> And the roof rang to their shouting, the huge hall
> Rocked, the strong foundations groaned and trembled.

The long sounds (extended a's and oo sounds and slowly moving consonants—l's, g's, and r's, for example) make the poetic lines move slowly to create a sense of awe and dignity that accompanies the awesome struggle. After Beowulf defeats Grendel, Hrothgar praises Beowulf, and thereby shows his own generous and humble nature. But here shorter vowel and consonant sounds quicken the pace and so lighten the tone:

> . . . the grateful King,
> All glooming gone, his countenance clear and cloudless
> As the sky in open radiance of the climbing sun,
> Gave thanks to God for deliverance. "Beowulf," he said,
> "Bravest of men, I shall love you now as my son.
> All I have is yours for the asking."

Again in the early lines of Part Three, the reader experiences wonder and admiration for the old man whose life has been a "journey" of heroic deeds, suggesting that Beowulf has been in constant movement and progress, one brave deed following another:

> From youth of fighting and heroic deeds
> Quietly he journeyed toward the tomb, until,
> Old at last—like a mighty oak in winter,
> Flaunting no longer her green midsummer glory,
> But stripped and bare, yet splended still—he hoped
> To die in peace.

The simile comparing Beowulf to a mighty oak whose summer glory is gone but whose strength remains contribute still more to the tone. Beowulf, although he is several times described simply by the statement "mightiest yet mildest," is not merely an average man doing minor deeds of courage. His character is noble and selfless; he leads and he is victorious. His life exemplifies valor and sacrifice. The actions of such a character are grand and elevated; the tone of such a tale must be equally grand and elevated.

The literature mentioned here treats a variety of subjects and uses a variety of tones, some serious, some lighthearted. No matter how serious the issue, *The Chocolate War*'s Jerry standing up for what he believes or *Beowulf*'s willingness to sacrifice his life for the lives of others in a kingdom not his own, or how lighthearted the situation that produces only laughter in *Buffalo Brenda* or *The Snarkout Boys,* any tone can be effective in novels for young adults. Serious actions like those showing the exploitation of one human being by another in *Deathwatch* or *Z for Zachariah,* or the search for a way out in *No More Saturday Nights* and for courage to accept and to live on in *Winning* hold readers' interest and awaken understanding by means of an effective use of appropriate tone.

Summary

Tone, the author's attitude toward subject and readers, is an integral part of story created by the author's choice of tone-describing words. Tone may not seem to be a single and deliberate choice made by the author, but it nonetheless derives from the multitude of choices of words for their connotative meaning. Depending upon the tone, the same story may be either sentimental or compassionate, sensational or suspenseful. Tone can fill us with despair over an imperfect world or with optimistic acceptance of human imperfection.

Notes

1. It may be that in *Catcher in the Rye* Salinger's creation of a young narrator speaking in candid tone is more than adult censors can accept. The written and readable revelation of what goes on in the mind and emotions of a young adult shows the world for what it is, and censors are shocked that young adults like Holden might influence his loyal readers to see life's realities so clearly.

Such censors may be unaware of their similarity to Holden himself. Just as Holden at first wants to keep Phoebe innocent, the censors wish to keep young adults innocent. Holden, among other issues, is sensitive to phoniness of any kind shown by any person—but censors may prefer a rosier picture to prevail, one that shows a perfect world and either ignores or pretties up the imperfections of human behavior and institutions. Those censoring the story might find the novel's dedication noteworthy: Salinger's dedication to his mother suggests that he wants his mother to know that he has made his peace with human imperfection, and, as the end of the novel demonstrates, has come out of his youthful disillusionment on the adult side of recognition and rueful acceptance.

2. **Irony** is often tongue-in-cheek, and is more easily recognized in oral language, less easily in written. It has been said that ability to recognize irony is one of the surest tests of intelligence and sophistication. Dealing with opposites, say-

ing one thing and meaning another, is also the substance of **sarcasm;** the difference lies in intentions. The intent of sarcasm is to wound, but that of irony is usually less harsh, lighter, although it, too, may wound. **Satire,** on the other hand, blends social criticism with wit and humor, its intention being to improve human beings or their institutions, or, as the eighteenth-century British essayist Addison said in imposing a rule upon his own satire, "to pass over a single foe to charge whole armies."

Recommended Books Cited in This Chapter

Brancato, Robin. *Winning.* New York: Knopf, 1977.

Burns, Alive Ann. *Cold Sassy Tree.* New York: Delacorte, 1992.

Cormier, Robert. *The Chocolate War.* New York: Random House, 1974.

Donovan, John. *I'll Get There. It Better Be Worth the Trip.* New York: Harper & Row, 1969.

Duncan, Lois. *Stranger with My Face.* New York: Dell, 1990.

Garner, Alan. *The Owl Service.* New York: Doubleday, 1967.

Keaney, Brian. *No Need for Heroes.* London: Oxford University Press, 1989.

Klein, Norma. *No More Saturday Nights.* New York: Knopf, 1988.

Koertge, Ron. *The Arizona Kid.* Boston: Little, Brown, 1988.

———. *The Boy in the Moon.* Boston: Little, Brown, 1990.

Mahy, Margaret. *The Changeover.* New York: Macmillan, 1984.

O'Brien, Robert. *Z for Zachariah.* Boston: Houghton Mifflin, 1960.

Orwell, George. *Animal Farm.* New York: Harcourt Brace, 1946.

Paterson, Katherine. *Jacob Have I Loved.* New York: Harper & Row, 1980.

Pearson, T. R. *A Short History of a Small Place.* New York: Ballantine, 1986.

Pevsner, Stella. *How Could You Do It, Diane?* Boston: Houghton Mifflin, 1989.

Pinkwater, Daniel. *The Snarkwater Boys & the Avocado of Death.* New York: Dutton, 1983.

Pinkwater, Jill. *Buffalo Brenda.* New York: Macmillan, 1989.

Rushdie, Salman. *Haroun of the Sea of Stories.* New York: Viking, 1990.

Salinger, J. D. *The Catcher in the Rye.* Boston: Little, Brown, 1951.

Serraillier, Ian. *Beowulf the Warrior.* London: Oxford University Press, 1954.

Sleator, William. *Interstellar Pig.* New York: Dutton, 1984.

Sutcliff, Rosemary. *The High Deeds of Finn Mac Cool.* New York: Dutton, 1967.

———. *The Hound of Ulster.* New York: Dutton, 1963.

Wharton, William. *A Midnight Clear.* New York: Knopf, 1982.

White, Robb. *Deathwatch.* New York: Dell, 1973.

Going Over to Your Place

POEMS FOR EACH OTHER

Selected by PAUL B. JANECZKO

— 9 —

Poetry and Verse

"Now, class, we begin the poetry unit."

Groans from some, snickers from others, but (be grateful), genuine interest from still others. What is it about poetry that turns some away? Posing this question to the groaners and snickerers in a class of young adults may result in a variety of answers.

"It's too hard."

"It looks funny on the page."

"It's too concentrated; each word is supposed to have lots of different meanings."

"I read it according to the punctuation, and that's wrong, I guess."

"It always has to be the teacher's interpretation."

Something about the spacing on a page seems forbidding to many readers; the wide left margin and irregular line length mystify. But the same words read in paragraph form give no trouble as readers assume that meaning is straightforward and clear, and make no particular effort to examine the wording carefully. If meaning is not quickly apparent, readers lose interest. "It's hard work," says one protester asked to search for meaning.

But poetry and prose are not as different as at first they may seem, and poetry need not be hard work. In reading a poem, we are attentive to line length as the poet's way of pausing at line's end to emphasize an image or device before going on to complete the thought.[1] One way of approaching a poem is to remind young adults about the scientific method: Set up a hypothesis about the poem's meaning, test it by checking each image and figure of speech to see if each one adds meaning to this hypothesis; finally, verify the accuracy of the hypothesis. Then, if it all refuses to fit together under this theory of meaning, change the hypothesis and test again.

151

Many of the qualities of poetry are those examined under "style." Rhythm in poetry is very like the flow of words and cadences of prose. Poetry is written to be read aloud, to be heard. It follows then that other sound patterns like alliteration, assonance, consonance, and ono- matopoeia occur in poetry just as they do in prose, although probably more often. Just as figurative language enlivens prose, enabling us to see unexpected comparisons and associative meanings, it occurs in and is even more central to poetry, contributing to compactness and emotional intensity. Finally, connotation, which broadens meaning in prose, is even more important in poetry. We already know, then, the elements that con- stitute poetry.

The most significant characteristic of poetry is its **compactness,** the reliance upon few words to say what more might be required to say in prose. This trait is served by the poet's reliance upon connotation, figura- tive language, rhythm, and other sound patterns; these devices in turn re- sult not only in compactness, but also in a second significant characteris- tic of poetry—**emotional intensity.** The source of these traits will be examined more carefully in the following paragraphs.

Here we might turn aside for a moment to ask what are the subjects of poetry for young adults. Logically, the answer is "Whatever interests them." Not surprisingly, old age seems far away and might interest a few, but to young adults in today's society where violence on the streets and highways must seem imminent, even death is a concern. These same top- ics interest mature adults, of course; the difference perhaps lies in the greater breadth of topics that may interest older people, like, for example the transience of time, the inevitability of aging, or the experience of par- enting. If we think about the concerns of young adults as psychologists see them, we find a great variety of topics for young adult poetry. Ideals, honesty, relationships, crisis, goals, identity, both spiritual and erotic love—all concern young adults. To these concerns we can add poetry about their activities.

Poetry and Verse Compared

Is it poetry or verse? And who cares?

Look first at a few of the definitions of poetry, definitions selected from abundant choice. Perhaps it is a secretion, as A. E. Housman tells us, either a "natural secretion, like turpentine in the fir, or a morbid secretion like the pearl in the oyster." Maybe others would agree with Robert Frost who, putting it simply, called poetry "a performance in words." Most de- finers of poetry, however, seem to agree that poetry, a word derived from the Greek word meaning "to make," is made. Poets or makers make po- ems. Such a definition defies the often spoken illusion that poetry is the result of creation or inspiration, a mystical process in which a muse sits upon the poet's shoulder and whispers in the poet's ear; the inspired words then travel down the poet's arm to the page in perfect formation of a poem.

But thinking of writing poetry as *making* suggests a very different process. When we "make" something, we gather materials and work at putting them together. True, sometimes what we had envisioned as the end product may differ from the end product itself, but the process is neither simple nor mystical. Like the seamstress or the sculptor, the poet thinks in terms of a concept or pattern for development, and follows with effort, technical discipline, attention to detail, refinement, and polishing—none of these the products of inspiration. In all probability the poet writes and rewrites, abandons phrases and restores them, leaves places open while searching for a more precise word or a properly connotative one, and at times puts the work aside, wanting to return to it with a fresh mind. Far from being "tossed off," poetry results from patience, skill, and the intellectual process that requires critical judgment with attention to each term, its nuances of connotative meaning and feeling, its capacity to create pictures in the reader's mind and to surprise with fresh and unusual comparisons. Notice how Christine Hemp describes writing a poem, speaking not of making but of building, a similar process.

To Build a Poem

Building a poem is like building a house
where raw material, pointed word and nail,
are laid out—in piles, and mixed without a rule,
two-by-fours stacked in readiness for the saw,
and words anticipate order, in order to beam
the page as nails await the hammer.

Then I hear the sounds start to form and the hammer
whangs and bangs the sill down to ground the house
in a form which will hold every rafter and beam
in place. And the poem takes shape as I nail my
thoughts and stud the page with images I saw
while framing a closet, not in the book of rules.

In my house I rule
out all excess lines, and simplify as I hammer
on the plate with sixteen-penny nails, and saw
the rafters, one by one, careful not to cut too much as I house
possibility with walls and roof. A fingernail
of a moon shines on the skeleton of frame and beams
light on a poem in my mind and I beam
to think of a couplet or a slant rhyme that will fit the rule
of a sonnet or sestina just like the beveled banisters I nail
to the stairs. I hear the singing of those hammer

sounds, like words that leap to dance as they house
the music of the poem, an up-down cadence like the song of the
saw. . . .

The poet goes on to compare the finishing work of house with the polishing of poem, mentioning both an extra foot or a bad rhyme that must
be "chiseled away," and her "hammering heart" as she lets the poem out.
Double meanings for terms like "beam," and "rule" as well as such devices as the implied linking of rhythm in saw movement to the rhythm of
the poem tie together the act of building and that of writing.

The content of poetry is emotion, and when skillfully written, the
poem contributes to our understanding. The Romantic poets speak of poetry in related ways, Coleridge naming its purpose as "the communication of pleasure," and Wordsworth defining it as "the spontaneous over-
flow of powerful feelings recollected in tranquility." Shelley calls it "the
record of the best and happiest moments of the best and happiest
minds." Edgar Allan Poe says poetry is a "rhythmical creation of beauty";
Gerard Manley Hopkins reminds us that poetry is read to be heard, the
"speech framed . . . for its own sake and interest even over and above its
interest [in] meaning." Dylan Thomas says that the stuff of poetry is to be
seen, whether in reality or as a vision: It is "the rhythmic, inevitably narrative, movement from an overclothed blindness to a naked vision." Such
definitions focus not upon the work of writing poetry, the process of
making, but upon its pleasures—joy, intensity, and serenity. Babette
Deutsch, another twentieth-century poet, in a definition calling attention
to both the expression of feelings and the critical mind of the poet,
claims that poetry is "the art which uses words as both speech and song
to reveal the realities that the senses record, the feelings salute, the mind
perceives, and the shaping imagination orders." Finally, we might say that
Emily Dickinson describes poetry as a "mind-blowing" experience; she
describes her feelings about poetry as causing the top of her head to be
"taken off," making her "body so cold no fire can ever warm" her.

Some may believe contrasting poetry and verse is unimportant, or
may believe that any lyric a popular song is poetry. Rod McKuen says of
his song lyrics that "none should be confused with or thought of as poems. I know of few song lyrics that qualify as poetry, certainly none of my
own." T. S. Eliot, who wrote both verse and poetry, believes the distinction is important. He says of poetry that it is an end in itself, work of feeling, and imaginative power, but verse, on the other hand, is merely work
focusing on structure, metrical regularity, and rhyme pattern, a definition
that implies verse, apparently even his own, has little merit in its composition. Verse is often written for commercials; it also occurs in the
proverbs or adages of folk wisdom: "A friend in need/Is a friend indeed,"
and "Man proposes,/God disposes." Greeting cards are filled with verses,
some of them brief and witty and others overflowing with sentimental

abstractions, commonplace images, trite phrasing, rigid rhythms, and throwaway words. Mnemonic verses are useful, their rigid structures helping us to remember their facts: "I keep six honest serving men./They taught me all I know./Their names are What and Where and When/And How and Why and Who."

Wit at its best is fun to read, as this newspaper submission allows: "Of a deep deep love it's a certain sign/When your sweetheart's kisses taste like wine./The best you can get from a casual date/Is monosodium glutamate." Or "Ten fingers, ten toes—that was/Lord God's Creation/Was he preparing for decimalization?" Failed wit evokes groans. The best of poets often write verse; like their poetry, some of it is witty or wise and some quite ordinary.

Does it all matter? That the skillful versifier often gives us the pleasure of laughter and neatly constructed lines of verse should not be denied. Verse is its own excuse for being. The availability of both verse and poetry matters, however, if we want young adults to experience the best, and to discover the pleasures of how words can affect us through distilled language that intensifies feeling. Exposed only to verses with their regular end rhymes and their often predictable figures of speech, young adults are deprived of the opportunity to discover language at its most artful and moving.

Poetry

We may distinguish between kinds of poetry as either **narrative,** called story poetry by some, or **lyric,** once called song poetry but often thought of simply as expressing personal emotion. Narrative poetry might most easily be exemplified by Robert Frost's story-telling in "The Death of the Hired Man," which not only describes events and tells a story, but conveys the couple's deeply felt emotion. Not all narrative poems deal with death, of course, but poems often combine story with strong emotion, as does "Mid-Term Break" by Seamus Heaney. The second line hints that this will be a poem about death: college classes begin and end with bells that ring, but the bells of funerals sound a "knell." The age of the dead child is unknown until it is subtly conveyed by the last lines comparing coffin size to years of life. The emotional intensity of the experience is amplified by compactness that prose description of the event would lack.

I sat all morning in the college sick bay
Counting bells knelling classes to a close.
At two o'clock our neighbours drove me home.

In the porch I met my father crying—
He had always taken funerals in his stride—
And Big Jim Evans saying it was a hard blow.

The baby cooed and laughed and rocked the pram
When I came in, and I was embarrassed
By old men standing up to shake my hand

And tell me they were "sorry for my trouble,"
Whispers informed strangers I was the eldest,
Away at school, as my mother held my hand

In hers and coughed out angry tearless sighs.
At ten o'clock the ambulance arrived
With the corpse, stanched and bandaged by the nurses.

Next morning I went up into the room. Snowdrops
And candles soothed the bedside; I saw him
For the first time in six weeks. Paler now,

Wearing a poppy bruise on his left temple,
He lay in his four foot box as in his cot.
No gaudy scars, the bumper knocked him clear.

A four foot box, a foot for every year.

Like "Mid-Term Break," at first reading "Fifteen" by William Stafford
may seem a simple story, but it is more. It is a compact, economical expression of a highly emotional experience for a 15-year-old, one showing
the allure of a beautiful machine, the promised excitement of mechanical
power, the challenge of speed, the confidence and willingness of the
"ready and friendly" machine added to its invitation to explore, and the
temptation to take a ride, feelings that last until he suddenly thinks of the
absent rider.

South of the Bridge on Seventeenth
I found back of the willows one summer
day a motorcycle with engine running
as it lay on its side, ticking over
slowly in the high grass. I was fifteen.

I admired all that pulsing gleam, the
shiny flanks, the demure headlights
fringed where it lay; I led it gently
to the road and stood with that
companion, ready and friendly. I was fifteen.

We could find the end of a road, meet
the sky on out Seventeenth. I thought about
hills, and patting the handle got back
a confident opinion. On the bridge we indulged
a forward feeling, a tremble. I was fifteen.

Thinking, back farther in the grass I found
the owner, just coming to, where he had flipped
over the rail. He had blood on his hand, was pale—

I helped him walk to his machine. He ran his hand
over it, called me good man, roared away.

I stood there, fifteen.

No longer fifteen, the speaker now recalls the motorcycle driver's
temporary unconsciousness, his bloody hand, his need for help in walking, as well as his flip over a bridge railing; distance from the event has
given him greater awareness of danger. The poet may seem only to recall
his early feelings, but in its compact form, the poem says far more than
can be said in equivalent words of prose.

Often words written in short phrases with consistent left margins appear to be poems, but possess no compactness nor emotional intensity.
Brief narratives arranged on the page to resemble poetry, like the selec-
tions in *My Friend's Got This Problem, Mr. Candler,* for example, treat issues significant to young adults, but like the novels of Judy Blume, which
also treat relevant topics, the "poems" disappoint; they read like prose
written in short lines.

A **ballad,** thought to be one of the earliest forms of literature, is a
kind of verse characterized by its presentation of an exciting or dramatic
episode. In general, ballads from most cultures have common characteristics: an element of the supernatural, themes of courage and love, incidents from the lives of common people, often of domestic nature, little
characterization or description, action developed through dialogue,
tragic episodes narrated with simplicity, repetition with additions, refrains, and often summary stanzas appearing at the end.[2]

The old Scottish ballad "Sir Patrick Spence" follows the description of
the ballad, and exemplifies how the folk, or unattributed and orally repeated, narrative uses dialogue and repetition not only to tell a story but
also to create an atmosphere or feeling.

The king sits in Dumferling toune,
    Drinking the blude-reid wine:
"O whar will I get guid sailor,
    To sail this schip of mine?"

Up and spak an eldern knicht,
    Sat at the kings richt kne:
"Sir Patrick Spence is the best sailor,
    That sails upon the se."

The king has written a braid letter,   [broad]
    And signd it wi his hand,
And sent it to Sir Patrick Spence,
    Was walking on the sand.

The first line that Sir Patrick red,
    A loud lauch lauche'd he;   [laugh]

The next line that Sir Patrick red,
   The teir blinded his ee.

"O wha is this has don this deid,
   This ill deid don to me,
To send me out this time o' the yeir,
   To sail upon the se!

"Mak hast, mak haste, my mirry men all
   Our guid schip sails the morne:"
O say na sae, my master deir,
   For I feir a deadlie storme.

"Laste, late yestreen I saw the new moone,
   Wi the auld moone in hir arme,   [old]
And I feir, I feir, my deir master,
   That we will cum to harme."

O our Scots nobles wer richt laith   [loathe]
   To weet their cork-heild schoone;   [shoes]
Bot lang owre a' the play wer playd,   [ere]
   Their hats they swam aboone.

O lang, lang may their ladies sit,
   Wi thair fans into their hand,
Or eir they se Sir Patrick Spence
   Cum sailing to the land.

O lang, lang may the ladies stand,
   Wi their gold kems in their hair
Waiting for thar ain deir lords,
   For they'll se thame na mair.

Haf owre, haf owre to Aberdour,   [over]
   It's fiftie fadom deip,
And thair lies guid Sir Patrick Spence,
   Wi the Scots lords at his feit.

In another folk ballad, "The Demon Lover," the lover returns to his promised love only to find her wed to another. His promises entice her to leave husband and babes and follow him; suspense builds as she notices first that her former lover has lied and has no eight ships with 24 mariners, then that his feet are cloven, and that ahead are the mountains of hell. The gradual revelation that the lover is the devil holds interest as awareness of the demon's duplicity and the woman's values increases. Ballads of known authorship with the cadence of song also follow traditional forms, using dialogue, abrupt transitions, little characterization, and frequent refrains. Throughout narrative poems and particularly ballads the facts of a story are accompanied by the feelings they evoke.

Lyric, or songlike poems, are distinguished by imagination, emotion, and, by some definitions, a sense of melody. They may be descriptive, but rather than giving only realistic detail, they convey a feeling or an emotional impression of the subject. Look, for example, at the sense of the eagle's power in Tennyson's brief poem "The Eagle" (mentioned later too).

> He clasps the crag with crooked hands;
> Close to the sun in lonely lands,
> Ringed with the azure world, he stands.
>
> The wrinkled sea beneath him crawls;
> He watches from his mountain walls,
> And like a thunderbolt he falls.

Not only are a few "facts" of the eagle's habitat and food hunt mentioned, but the lines give a fresh look at the eagle's very essence; it is a confident, majestic creature with imperial power.

Rhythm

The recurrence of stress is called **rhythm.**[3] Of the characteristics of poetry, rhythm is one everyone has experienced since birth through pulse, heartbeat, and breathing. Oral rhythm is also known from early childhood through the experience of nursery rhymes and counting-out, ball-bouncing, and rope-jumping verses. In anger, children may lapse into spoken rhythmic form: "I *hate* you, I *hate* you, I *hate* you." Or they may sing out, "I *love* it, *love* it, *love* it!" with stress or emphasis on the most significant words.

The function of spoken or written words is communication; the function of poetry is also communication. In prose there is cadence or flow of words; in poetry rhythm may fall into more regular patterns. In either event, rhythm helps to communicate and strengthen meaning. When we are happy, we speak quickly; when the poet wishes to convey a light-hearted feeling, the poet, too, uses quickly moving lines with many unaccented syllables and short vowels, as does Dudley Randall in "Blackberry Sweet," a poem of admiration:

> Black girl black girl
> lips as curved as cherries
> full as grape bunches
> sweet as blackberries.
>
> Black girl black girl
> when you walk you are
> magic as a rising bird
> or a falling star

Black girl black girl
what's your spell to make
the heart in my breast
jump start shake

Limericks, nonsensical and quick-paced, are perfect examples of how fast moving rhythm suits the subject, as it does in this verse:

A flea and a fly in a flue
Were imprisoned, so what could they do?
    Said the fly, "Let us flee."
    Said the flea, "Let us fly."
So they flew through a flaw in the flue.

When we are sad or are speaking of a serious issue, we speak more slowly; when the poet wishes to express serious thoughts, the words move slowly with many accented syllables, slower consonants, and longer vowels. Sometimes even within a line rhythm may vary, to intensify happiness here or solemnity there.

Notice, for example, the solemn tone created by the rhythm of these lines from William Cullen Bryant's "Thanatopsis," a poem about living in preparation for death.

So live that when thy summons comes to join	∪/∪/∪/∪/∪/
The innumerable caravan which moves	∪∪/∪∪/∪/∪/
To that mysterious realm where each shall take	∪/∪/∪/∪/∪/
His chamber in the silent halls of death,	∪/∪/∪/∪/∪/
Thou go not, like the quarry slave at night,	∪∪/∪∪/∪/∪/
Scourged to his dungeon, but, sustained and soothed	/∪∪/∪/∪/∪/
By an unfaltering trust, approach thy grave	∪∪∪/∪/∪/∪/
Like one who wraps the drapery of his couch	∪/∪/∪/∪/∪/
About him and lies down to pleasant dreams.	∪/∪/∪/∪/∪/

It is not possible to read these lines quickly; the slowly moving rhythm created by long vowels and frequent stressed syllables prevents turning them into a lighthearted stanza. But try being solemn while reading aloud lines from Lewis Carroll's "Father William."

"You are old, Father William," the young man said,	∪∪/∪∪/∪∪/∪/
"And your hair has become very white.	∪∪/∪∪/∪∪/
And yet you incessantly stand on your head—	∪/∪∪/∪∪/∪∪/
Do you think at your age it is right?"	∪∪/∪∪/∪∪/
"In my youth," Father William replied to his son,	∪∪/∪∪/∪∪/∪∪/
"I feared it might injure the brain.	∪/∪∪/∪∪/
But now that I'm perfectly sure I have none,	∪/∪∪/∪∪/∪∪/
Why, I do it again and again."	∪∪/∪∪/∪∪/

Here solemnity is impossible. Even more than the nonsense of the words themselves, the rapid rhythm caused by many unstressed syllables and short vowels and consonants adds to the ridiculousness of the story.

In a poorly written poem, rhythm is sometimes the problem. These brief lines in a children's poem use words that in themselves convey the idea of lightness, softness, silence; because the rhythm, however, is ponderous and solemn, the total effect is incongruous.

See the pretty snowflakes	/U/U/U
Falling from the sky;	/U/U/
On the walk and housetop	/U/U/U
Soft and thick they lie.	/U/U/

The choice of heavy and regular **meter**—the pattern of accented and unaccented beats—fails to create the soft, light experience of snow, because the marching, slow-moving rhythm is so dominant that it seems to take over the meaning.

The ironic point of "The Angry Man," by Phyllis McGinley is a good one, but caught up in the regularity of its marching rhythm and regular rhyme, readers may lose sight of its irony.

The other day I chanced to meet
An angry man upon the street—
A man of wrath, a man of war,
A man who truculently bore
Over his shoulder, like a lance,
A banner labeled "Tolerance."

And when I asked him why he strode
Thus scowling down the human road,
Scowling, he answered, "I am he
Who champions total liberty—
Intolerance being, ma'am, a state
No tolerant man can tolerate.

"When I meet rogues," he cried, "who choose
To cherish oppositional views,
Lady, like this, and in this manner,
I lay about me with my banner
Till they cry mercy, ma'am." His blows
Rained proudly on prospective foes.
Fearful, I turned and left him there
Still muttering as he thrashed the air,
"Let the intolerant beware!"

But no pounding beat obscures the irony in John Hall Wheelock's forceful stanza "Earth."

"A planet doesn't explode of itself," said drily
The Martian astronomer, gazing off into the air—
"That they were able to do it is proof that highly
Intelligent beings must have been living there."

Sound Patterns

The sounds that words make as a poem is read aloud—and poems are meant to be read aloud—affect meaning. We may search a long time for a poem that more effectively demonstrates the use of sound patterns to amplify meaning than does Carl Sandburg's "Lost." The poet personifies the fogbound boat as a child and the harbor as the mother.

Desolate and lone
All night on the lake
Where fog trails and mist creeps,
The whistle of a boat
Calls and cries unendingly,
Like some lost child
In tears and trouble
Hunting the harbor's breast
And the harbor's eyes.

The alliterative and child-related phrases "calls and cries" and "tears and trouble" with their long vowels create feelings of loneliness and desolation. Add to the phrases the long vowels of such words as "fog," "trails," and "creeps," as well as the slow-moving consonants in "some lost," "desolate and lone," "unendingly," and the effect is sad, perhaps even despairing. Sandburg's use of "boat" with its long "o" is more effective in evoking loneliness than the alternative "ship" with its clipped sound. Consonants are largely liquid l's and r's or nasal m's, n's, and ng's held together with sibilant s's. The long duration of the vowels and consonants, called **phonetic intensives,** pull and stretch the lines to create the slow groping of the fogbound boat. Note, however, the difference in sounds Sandburg uses in the final two lines; now the vowels and consonants are of briefer duration, and the lines move more quickly to create a reassuring tone. As for rhythm, the unstressed syllables are as frequent as the stressed ones, and the effect is greater security. The scene is vividly visual and audible; the boat is seen and heard partly because of imagery and figurative language but also because of Sandburg's effective use of sound patterns.

Figurativeness

The earlier discussion of style noted that the writer makes comparisons to add meaning and to strengthen and freshen language. Describing one thing in terms of another is **figurative language:** objects otherwise dissimilar are juxtaposed and compared as being alike or unlike in this singular way. Figurative language is perhaps the most effective means of saying a great deal in very few words, thus creating the compactness characteristic of poetry. In fact, poet E. A. Robinson claims that poetry tries to tell us "something that cannot be said," an impossible task made possible through figurative language. Shelley commented that poetry adds "beauty to that which is most deformed," stripping "the veil of familiarity from the world." Using comparisons of unlike things is a significant way of accomplishing these tasks.

The devices of figurative language that say one thing in terms of another make fresh comparisons. Turn back to Tennyson's "The Eagle." Notice how the poet compares the eagle to an old man by using *personification.* The eagle has "hands" not claws, and he "stands" rather than perches. Instead of mentioning the waves, the poet says the sea "crawls" as might a powerless animal or human being before great majesty. Relying on *metaphor,* he calls the mountains "walls," as though they are the battlements of a ruler's castle. In a *simile* he finally compares the eagle's dive to a thunderbolt.

Figurative devices make vividly visual the difficulties encountered and described in Langston Hughes's "Mother to Son" as he makes a fresh comparison of movement through life to climbing stairs. If an explanation of the figurative devices is set up in a this-equals-that form, the poem may be more easily understood.

Well, Son, I'll tell you	
Life for me ain't been no crystal stair.	= easy time
It's had tacks in it,	= difficulties
And splinters,	= pain
And boards torn up,	= crises
And places with no carpets on the floor.	= barrenness and cold
Bare.	
But all the time	
I'se been climbin' on	= keeps moving on
And reachin' landin's	= resting places
And turning corners	= facing changes
And sometimes goin' in the dark	= the unknown
Where there ain't been no light.	
So, Boy, don't you turn back.	= regress to easier things
Don't you set down on the steps	= give up
'Cause you find it's kinder hard.	
Don't you fall now—	= let problems get you down
For I'se still goin', Honey,	
I'se still climbin'	= pushing on
And life for me ain't been no crystal stair.	= no easy fairy tale

A crystal stair implies elegance, but each of the contrasting images of stairs—dark, angled, splintered, torn up, bare of carpet, rough with tacks and the unknown—makes visible the difficulties of life, but acknowledges the occasional rest on a landing. The metaphor is consistent, making the picture real, and the poet's point clear.

Emotional Intensity

Figurative language is one way of evoking emotional intensity, but there are others that also make the poem tight and compact. Look now at Tennyson's use of richly *connotative terms* in the visual *imagery* that paints pictures of the eagle's majesty. To "clasp" with "hands" suggests an easy, comfortable hold, rather than a clawed animal's grip of great strength. As the eagle "stands," he is comfortably poised above the world and in his majesty "close to the sun" itself, an assured position connoting sovereignty. Further connotations of royalty occur in the image of the eagle surveying his kingdom spread out below and "ringed" about him in "azure," the color of heraldry. The powerful, raging sea below the crags of the shore is to the eagle harmlessly "wrinkled," innocently "crawling"; rather than tensely surveying or guarding his kingdom, he "watches" with ease. Each of these words connotes security, dignity, and poise. In the final line the poet refers not to a rumbling, rolling thunder but refers instead to a "bolt" of power that accompanies the eagle's plunge or "fall," not as though fear or weakness had caused the eagle's fall, but that it is a deliberate plunge. Nor does he tumble from his post because his grip has failed, but swoops with strength and purpose to capture prey. Connotative words add greatly to the poem's meaning and emotional intensity.

Look back at "Fifteen" to consider how connotation intensifies meaning and emotional intensity. The engine lying on its side "ticking over slowly" suggests that in the eyes of the boy it is harmless and appealing, even seductive, with its "pulsing gleam," "shiny flanks," and "demure headlights/fringed." His "leading" the machine, "that/companion, ready and friendly," and being answered with a "confident opinion" suggest that they could enjoy a safe and happy ride together—finding "the end of a road," meeting "the sky," finding "hills," anticipating joyful riding with a "forward feeling." The final stanza is filled with a different kind of terminology, all of it connoting the dangers of such riding: "just coming to," "flipped/over the rail," "blood on his hand," "pale," "helped him walk" suggest that as he looks back, he sees things differently. The break that precedes "I stood there, fifteen," suggests an older and wiser person than the one to whom the experience had happened. Connotation has contributed to emotional intensity.

"Newborn Neurological Exam" by Mary Baron depicts intense emotion as someone, perhaps the new mother, watches while the newborn fails to respond to pain that would show the baby to be alive and healthy. Each brief stanza relates another test, another failure, until paradoxically the loving mother prays for the infant to feel pain.

no motion and
no sound
but you willing
to breathe

a Q-tip pressed
on open eyes—
nothing

ice water forced
into your ears
nothing

I stand beside you
leash myself to quiet
pray
for pain

Words such as "pressed," and "forced," followed by the mother's need to bind herself to quiet lest she cry out herself, awaken the reader to the mother's—not the infant's—pain. It is hard to imagine that the situation narrated in prose could evoke a more intense response.

Negative Qualities in Poetry

Poetry has often in the past had a message about behavior and ethical or moral precepts that was clear and self-conscious. Such poetry can be called didactic if its purpose is to communicate a moral, religious, or ethical message rather than to be an artistic expression with emotional intensity. To state it in another way, the poem is didactic if its ultimate effect is outside itself, subverting literature for preaching or teaching purposes. Rudyard Kipling's verses called "If," for example, were once the popular list of abstractions framed for a child's bedroom wall. Not only do the lines lack imagery, figurativeness, and connotative language, but they contain several clichés more commonly found in prose. The poem is didactic:

If you can keep your head when all about you
    Are losing theirs and blaming it on you;
If you can trust yourself when all men doubt you,
    But make allowance for their doubting too:
If you can wait and not be tired by waiting,
    Or being lied about, don't deal in lies,
Or being hated don't give way to hating,
    And yet don't look too good, nor talk too wise;

. . .

Yours is the Earth and everything that's in it,
   And—which is more—you'll be a Man, my son!

Didactic poetry, teaching or preaching poetry, is difficult to define, however, because it often lies in the perception of the reader. Readers may disagree, for example, about William Ernest Henley's "Invictus"; one may say that the lesson is not paramount and thus does not harm any intrinsic artistry. Another may find the message so overwhelming that the poem has become self-righteous. In many instances, however, readers can agree that the poem has a meaning or effect that goes beyond the poem itself. More obvious didacticism can be found in the brief verses of Nathalia Crane, who wrote in the early twentieth century:

For every evil under the sun
There is a remedy or there is none.
If there is one, seek till you find it;
If there be none, never mind it.

You cannot choose your battlefields,
   The Gods do that for you.
But you can plant your standard
   Where a standard never flew.

Walter Gibson in "Advice to Travelers," however, makes a thematic point by using one clear image plus a didactic two-line command.

A burro once, sent by express,
His shipping ticket on his bridle,
Ate up his name and his address,
And in some warehouse, standing idle,
He waited till he like to died.
The moral hardly needs the showing:
Don't keep things locked up deep inside—
Say who you are and where you're going.

Didacticism is sometimes called "guidance," or "inspiration." Under these descriptive terms, one reader might commend the verses; another would object to the writer's effort to convert readers to a way of thinking rather than to evoke an emotional response.

Like sentimentality in prose, *sentimentality* in poetry is an attempt to induce an emotional response in disproportion to the cause or situation. Fainting heroines in melodramatic fiction or the tear-jerking situations of soap opera are easily identified as sentimental, but political oratory, too, may include efforts to arouse emotion disproportionate to the situation with the hope of producing heightened or thoughtless feeling that banishes logical or thoughtful opinion. Here the writer invites the fly to drink from his cup while making the most of life—sentimentality merged with didacticism.

> Busy, curious, thirsty fly,
> Drink with me, and drink as I.
> Freely welcome to my cup
> Couldst thou sip, and sip it up;
> Make the most of life you may,
> Life is short and wears away.

The best poetry is made, made with care and artistry. Sometimes poetry can be found in paragraph form; the writer has chosen each word or term for its capacity to evoke images and grip readers and listeners with its connotative power and emotional intensity. Readers are invited to awaken their imaginations and sharpen their senses to uncover meaning. Conversely, by using irregular line length and stanza form, prose is sometimes placed upon the page to look like poetry. But failure to use richly connotative language, to make figurative comparisons, to use rhythm to enhance meaning, or to paint pictures or images in readers' minds causes the selection simply to stand as prose. Appearance on the page does not make poetry.

Care and skill go into the making of poetry as they do into the writing of fiction. The difference lies in the compactness and emotional intensity of the expression. The conclusion is that ultimately there is no definitive line to be drawn between the two; the difference lies simply in degree. As comparisons become more vivid, imagery more pervasive, rhythm more useful to meaning, and compactness and emotional intensity more central, we are aware that we are approaching poetic expression.

Summary

Poetry is an experience in itself. Increased appreciation of language and of the intense emotion that its skillful use can provide is a profoundly significant movement toward maturity. Rhythm, sound patterns, figurativeness, connotation, and imagery heighten our sensory awareness and tempt our imaginations. The distillation of emotion and experience brought about through poetry permits readers to participate in sensations otherwise unavailable. Such vicarious experience enhances the pleasures of ordinary life. Since both verse and poetry are easily available, it seems reasonable that young adults should taste them both without being confined in any way to one or the other.

The number of poems and verses for young adults is voluminous, and yet we often push upon young people poems that we have been told are "classics" but which have little to say to this age group. At other times we may think that only poems with "lessons" or "guidance" are appealing, forgetting that our own pleasure rarely blooms from preachments. Or we may think only the poems that stayed in our memories are the "good ones." Forcing young adults to memorize our choices of poetry rather than their own may stifle any incipient or growing interest. By keeping in mind, however, that the body of literature is constantly growing, and that it gives pleasure and leads to greater understanding of ourselves, others, and the society around us, we are far more accepting of the great variety that may interest the young and open to them a whole new kind of art.

Notes

1. Reading poetry aloud is different from reading prose aloud. Listening to a poet read his or her own poems on a recording is a useful exercise. Perhaps the greatest surprise is how the poet-maker may pause—a tiny pause—at the end of each line, but pause more fully at punctuation marks. Such end-of-line pauses suggest that the poet wants the listener-reader to realize that the line stops here for some good reason. That intentional pause sets the line apart from those that follow because it is an image to look at and consider, a comparison to think about, a connotation that needs to sink in; it stands apart from the next line at least long enough for the reader to see it more completely.

2. In form, most ballads are similar. The ballad usually has four-line verses, rhyming *abcb*, with first and third lines having four accented syllables and the second and fourth having three. The rhyme is often approximate, and consonance and assonance frequently occur.

3. We will not examine meter or scansion. Rather than the identification of particular kinds of metric structure, what seems more important here is understanding the significance of rhythm to convey meaning.

Recommended Poems Cited in This Chapter

Anonymous. "Sir Patrick Spence." In *Oxford Book of Ballads.* Edited by James Kinsley. New York: Oxford University Press, 1969.

Baron, Mary. "Newborn Neurological Exam." In *The Music of What Happens.* Edited by Paul B. Janeczko. New York: Orchard, 1988.

Gibson, Walker W. "Advice to Travelers." In *Norton Book of Light Verse.* Edited by Russell Baker. New York: Norton, 1986.

Heaney, Seamus. "Mid-Term Break." In *New Coasts and Strange Harbors.* Edited by Helen Hill and Agnes Perkins. New York: Merrill, 1974.

Hemp, Christine E. "To Build a Poem." In *Going Over to Your Place: Poems for Each Other.* Edited by Paul B. Janeczko. New York: Bradbury, 1987.

Hughes, Langston. "Mother to Son." In *American Negro Poetry*. Edited by Anna Bontemps. New York: Hill & Wang, 1974.

McGinley, Phyllis. "The Angry Man." In *Sounds and Silences: Poetry for Now*. Edited by Richard Peck. New York: Dell, 1970.

Randall, Dudley. "Blackberry Sweet." In *The Harper Anthology of Poetry*. Edited by John Frederick Nims. New York: Harper, 1981.

Sandburg, Carl. "Lost." In *American Poetry and Prose*. Edited by Norman Foerster et al. Boston: Houghton Mifflin, 1970.

Stafford, William. "Fifteen." In *City in All Directions: An Anthology of Modern Poems*. Edited by Arnold Adoff. New York: Macmillan, 1969.

Tennyson, Alfred Lord. "The Eagle." In *Favorite Poems Old and New*. Edited by Helen Ferris. New York: Doubleday, 1957.

The Catcher in the Rye and the Nature of Young Adulthood

Young adults in the process of developing more mature and realistic views of the world, its population, and its problems often speak cynically. They grapple with their wish for an ideal world even as they begin to recognize that, given the imperfect nature of human behavior, the advent of such a world is impossible. A number of novels written for this age group address these issues in tones that vary from irony to satire, and yet none so completely confronts these issues—nor has any other been so castigated—as J. D. Salinger's *The Catcher in the Rye,* first published in 1951.

Public Response: Censorship

Look first at public response to the novel. Even as young readers read and shared the novel that struck them with its courage to say what was on their minds, censors castigated and banned it. The statements of some censors demonstrate that they may have read the book without understanding the complex elements in the struggle of the youthful protagonist. There seem to be several reasons among adults for censorious disapproval of the novel. Many have misread it, calling it reprehensible, rebellious against parents, school, family, and society. As noted in the chapter on tone, perhaps the honest or candid tone of *Catcher* is the source of much of the criticism. Holden's quick judgments of people he meets are often similar to thoughts people have but do not express, except perhaps to an intimate. Holden's language is often held up for disapproval, yet television, movies, and conversing adults often use this same language. Some have even counted the four-letter words—undeniably there—but forget that Holden wants to rub them all out. The language, furthermore, is less "offensive" than much of that in more recent

171

literature for young adults. Holden's doubts about society's mores are also unsettling, but many adults feel the same way. Certainly these judgments are rarely printed in a book for everyone—and especially young adults—to read.

Most frightening to those who censor the novel are the protagonist's statements about two forbidden topics—sex and religion. Holden's preoccupation with sex, however, is surely the same preoccupation visible on our living room screens, as well as in film and advertising. Holden says that he isn't oversexed but that he does think about it a lot, so perhaps mentally he is sexually preoccupied. This is a shocking bit of news for some adults who may have forgotten their youth or, impossible though it seems, may be unaware of sexual preoccupation in advertising, television, and film. Holden also addresses another topic many young adults struggle with: they cannot feel as religious or prayerful as their adult advisors would like them to be. Some adults refuse to admit that there are parts of the Bible they have difficulty with; others refuse even to read sensual and clearly sexual books like, for example, the Song of Solomon. But they don't publish their doubts. The Christmas show at Radio City annoys Holden, who thinks it artificial and sensational. Carrying a crucifix around on the commercial stage seems incongruous to Holden; he thinks the actors might really be thinking about a cigarette break. And as for prayer, Holden, like many young people, has been told about prayer, but like many, has difficulty praying. Such observations and admissions make some adults uncomfortable.

Still other critics dislike what they read as Holden's attitudes toward his parents and the rest of his family. Holden knows why he is being expelled from school, but he also knows how deeply disappointed his parents will be and wishes he could spare them their disappointment. His own grief about his brother Allie's death from leukemia is deep and profound, and he worries a great deal about his mother's lasting grief. But, knowing that mothers love to hear good things about their children, Holden satisfies that need for the mother of a fellow student on the train, although he must lie about that student to do it. Holden loves his sister Phoebe, he claims that there never was a little kid so smart and attractive—not a statement about a younger sibling that is often made aloud. His motives for wanting to be the catcher in the rye arise from his wish to keep his wonderful sister Phoebe and all other children innocent and unaware of human imperfections, a wish common to loving parents. He also appreciates adults other than his parents. He values Mr. Antolini for compassionately covering with his own coat the bloody body of a boy who jumped from the dormitory window. He admires the nuns for their selflessness, their vows of poverty, and their love of literature. He pities old Mr. Spencer for his aged fragility and illness. When Holden orders a drink, something he admits he shouldn't do, the nightclub waiter refuses to sell him alcohol, and Holden says honestly that he isn't angry at the waiter because he knows he might lose his job if he served a minor. Notice, too, Holden's honesty and kindness, traits that adults can approve and even praise. Holden is compassionate, kind to Ackley, who he admits is a personal slob and offensive in appearance and behavior. In speech class Holden wants his classmate to be allowed to speak of what interests him, like love for his uncle, without the cruel cries of the class about digressing. But Holden worries, too, about others. He is angry at Stradlater's treatment of his dates, fearful that he is too sexy and persuasive, particularly with Jane. When special privileges are given to athletes in defiance of school rules, Holden finds it unfair and dishonest. Even when Holden is cynical in his judgments, a humorous tone often softens them. In these and many more situations, his attitudes are admirable, as he speaks partly from disillusionment, but also in a gently amused and tolerant way. His view of human foibles and failures is not so much cynicism as disappointment, and accompanying this disappointment is an honest appreciation for what is good, even in the smallest measure.

Psychological Theory: Erik Erikson on Youth

The Catcher in the Rye merits strong defense for still other reasons, defense that identifies causes for the continued popularity of the novel among young adults despite censorship. Although censorship has chased the novel from classrooms and some school libraries, the book has an underground reading public—because it addresses the concerns of young adults.

Erik H. Erikson, one of the leading figures in the field of psychoanalysis and human development, won both the Pulitzer Prize and the National Book Award. In his seminal work, *Identity: Youth and Crisis,* he describes what he sees as the nature of the young adult years. Technology has "put more and more time between early school life and the young person's final access to specialized work"; adolescence (his term) has become almost a way of life, a period with its own mores, rebellions, and struggles prolonged in today's society by material dependence upon parents during the time of normal stretching for independence and maturity.

Erikson goes on to describe a number of issues and conflicts most young adults face. In psychological terms, they are "beset with the physiological revolution of their genital maturation"; in ordinary terms, their changing bodies force them into preoccupation with sex. They are also "preoccupied with what they appear to be in the eyes of others as compared with what they feel they are"; simplified, this means they are self-conscious about their appearances and the impressions they are giving. Furthermore, some adolescents must "come to grips again with crises of earlier years before they can install lasting idols and ideals as guardians of a final identity." The crises of this age are many, including pregnancy—their own or that of others important to them; drugs—their own involvement or that of significant friends or family members; violence threatened or done to themselves or those around them; and issues of poverty, health, and nutrition—their own or those of friends and family.

Ideally, children learn to trust themselves and others during childhood, but this development of trust is far from universal. During the period of young adulthood they look "fervently for men and ideas to have faith in," and in which they can prove themselves worthy. What models are offered to them from the worlds of athletics, entertainment, politics, education? Fearful of misplacing trust, understandably they may be cynical and untrusting. As youth nears adulthood, the necessity of finding an "avenue of duty and service" looms, but once again they see in society around them little reward for those who teach or serve. As they look toward parents for inspiration and guidance, their new awareness shows them that parents are far from the perfection they might have imagined in childhood. They must then fear simultaneously that adults may force them into roles they feel themselves unsuited for, and that their choices may arouse ridicule. Self-doubt seems inevitable.

According to Erikson, many young people, unable to conform to the requirements of adults who expect standardized or even idealized behavior, may "toy with danger," choosing some self-destructive behavior like drugs, alcohol, irresponsible driving, running away, dropping out of school, quitting jobs, falling into remoteness or unaccountable moods, or experimenting with sex. Parents are often concerned about adolescent choices of girl- and boyfriends. Erikson suggests that to young adults love is also a way of experimenting, not only with sex, but with "trying on" different ways of being or behaving, to "see if this is who I am." This experimentation may lead to cliquishness as the person tries on this or that group. Sometimes movement from group to group results in the cruel exclusion of former friends, behavior that Erikson sees as defense against "identity loss." Too-complete merging is frightening. Furthermore, the youth of America, coming from a greater and greater variety of ethnic and cultural backgrounds, face an additional conflict as they try to fit into the youth culture of this country in these times. The need to try on a group, to be approved and accepted by it, may conflict with another pressure, that arising from a Western cultural emphasis on independence and autonomy as part of maturity. Such internal conflicts may result in a pervasive sense of isolation, isolation that makes them seek their own rooms—if they have them—or drive them to artificial gregariousness in an effort to deny their sense of "onlyness." Finally, in their struggles to make the right choices, young people are keenly aware that adults—including, sad to say, their own parents—are not what they appear to be, and may in fact be "phony." Within this awareness lies fear that in the future they themselves may be phony.

The Catcher in the Rye: Its Youthful Readers

Some young people annually read *The Catcher in the Rye*. If we seriously consider the novel's continuous popularity since 1951—underground though it may be—we cannot evade the question "Why?" Surely the answer must be that Holden Caulfield's thinking, his accusations, his behavior, his uncertainties, his idealism, and his guilt are qualities common to young adults.[1] It seems most sensible that Holden's struggles with accepting the imperfections of individuals and society must speak to youthful readers, help them to recognize themselves and their peers, and describe their efforts to make peace with the flawed world around them.

Youth we here define as the period between childhood and adulthood, but because of individual differences, it is undefined in actual years. Holden is clearly just that age, between child and adult. He fools around like a child, teases his roommate Stradlater while he shaves, pretends to be a boxer and a tapdancer, wears his red cap with peak to front, back, or side, flaps up or down, assumes different names and personalities depending upon whom he is talking to, packs a snowball but doesn't want to disturb the world's white perfection by throwing it. And yet, man-about-town, he checks into a hotel, orders drinks, takes cabs to nightclubs, tries to be suave when he meets his older brother's old friends, even talks with a prostitute and considers discovering what sex is all about—because he'll need to know about it when he gets married. While Holden behaves in this child-adult way, he speaks of his hair as strangely half gray, sure evidence to him that he is old, but metaphorically descriptive of his age—half child and half adult, neither one and yet both. He claims sometimes to act like he's about twelve or thirteen, calls his behavior ironical because he's well over six feet tall and has gray hair. Holden is clearly both child and adult, behavior characteristic of the young adult.

Catcher must often be read by young adults with a sense that they are reading the forbidden and must hide the book. Even the briefest look at its long and successful publishing history suggests that Salinger and Holden Caulfield must be speaking to readers about what is on their minds. In fact, had Erik Erikson written a novel instead of a psychological description of adolescence, he might have written *Catcher*. Erikson and Salinger speak the same language: They both know youth and its internal conflicts. Mr. Antolini, Holden's favorite teacher, tells a despairing Holden that others have felt the same disappointment, confusion, and fear, have even felt sickened by human behavior. Holden is not alone; many have experienced the same moral and spiritual disillusionment. The commonality of that experience of fear and confusion may well be the source of the novel's popularity.

Erikson notes that idealism, although it comes and goes, is often characteristic of this age. Holden is uncertain of his career goals; at the same time his idealism makes him uncomfortable with his father's financial success in corporate law. Talking with Sally Hayes about going off to live in the woods, Holden decries empty affluence and adult preoccupation with it. He mentions people being clothed at the finest and most expensive men's stores, being obsessed with cars and trading them frequently for newer and more expensive models, living in luxury apartments and having the best leather luggage. Holden thinks adults have sold out for trivia. If Holden and Sally don't escape now to the simple life in the woods, they will end up living in the high-rise apartments of the wealthy, traveling constantly from foreign hotel to hotel, riding to work in taxis from the housing districts of the wealthy, and spending their leisure time in the trivial pursuits characteristic of affluent society. In literature, the woods or wilderness often represent the natural and unspoiled; the city represents evil and wickedness. Holden proposes to Sally Hayes that they live not in the city but in the wilderness. Living in the woods, in an idealized and innocent world without the corruption of materialistic neighbors, would keep Holden and Sally from living shallow and egocentric lives.

While dreaming of an ideal world, Holden wishes that everyone behaved in a perfect manner. When his little sister, Phoebe, asks him why he has flunked out of prep school once again, he lapses into a description of the imperfections of Pencey Prep students who search for the group in which they are comfortable, and simultaneously practice Erikson's "cruel exclusion" of others. He describes his schoolmates as phony and unkind, refusing to let others into their conversations if they aren't perfect duplicates of themselves. They have secret exclusive organizations, and refuse admission to those they consider boring or unattractive—like Ackley. Holden is ashamed that he was too cowardly not to join such a group.

Holden's idealism covers how he wants to live his own life, and how everything ought to operate. Speaking of religion, he dislikes the Catholic proselytizer not for his faith but for his deception and circuitousness in recruiting others. He deplores the artificial splendor of the Radio City Christmas show while the actors really can't wait to get off into the wings for a break. And at the same time he sincerely admires the teaching nuns, whom he meets in Grand Central Station, for their dedication, their love of literature, their acceptance of simple lives of poverty, and their commitment to helping others. In conversation with Phoebe, Holden has a sudden inspiration about what he'd like to be, an inspiration of idealistic proportions. He pictures innocent children playing a game in a field of rye at the edge of a cliff; oblivious of the danger, they don't look where they're going. And Holden must catch them, coming out from somewhere to save them, save them in their innocence. Holden wants to maintain the innocent purity of the world's children. One of the discoveries of youth is that all is not what it seems. After Sunny, the childlike prostitute, leaves, Holden recalls Allie's innocence and is saddened by a number of things: Sunny's loss of innocence, her youth and her spotlessly clean dress so carefully hung up in the hotel closet, her days spent in the movies, her tiny, girlish voice. No one would have guessed her to be a prostitute, so young and innocent looking is she. No one has "caught" her before she fell off the edge of the cliff of childhood innocence and discovered the imperfections of society.

Like many young adults, Holden toys with danger, indulging in self-destructive behavior, but even here runs a thread of idealism. He says ruefully that if there's another war, a crazy piece of human behavior, he's going to sit right on top of an atomic bomb; he swears he will volunteer for it, thus saving the world. Holden refuses to blame his history teacher for flunking him, and refuses to hurt his feelings; even Holden's answer to the exam question protects Mr. Spencer and yet is characteristically honest. He admits he knows little about the Egyptians, but nonetheless calls Mr. Spencer's lectures very interesting, and forgives him in advance for the failing grade.

Young adults seem addicted to trying out new places and to movement, whether it be dancing or "cruising." Holden's craving for motion is apparent in his restless exit from the dormitory in the middle of the night, followed by his train trip to New York City. During his hours in the city, he takes a cab from here to there and back again, walks the streets, goes home to his parents' apartment in the night, searches the stores for the Shirley Beans record, accompanies Sally Hayes to the theater and then to the Rockefeller Center ice rink, goes on to Central Park looking for Phoebe, moves to the museum, to the school, to the zoo, and throughout much of this actual wandering about town, he fantasizes about going to the woods of Vermont to live in the wilderness at subsistence level, then to the West to live on a ranch, a silent mute. As restless in the city as he has been in his several prep schools, Holden, as Biff says in *Death of a Salesman*, "just can't take hold . . . can't take hold of some kind of life," even in his imagination.

Suicide is distressingly frequent among adolescents. Young adults often experience a sense of depression and isolation brought on partly by feeling different from everyone else; the possibility of suicide hangs over young adults just as it does over Holden. After his fight with his roommate Stradlater about his behavior with Holden's special friend Jane, Holden does an unexpected thing. Feeling so alone that he almost wishes for death, he goes next door to visit Ackley, whom he despises and pities. Feeling inexplicably lonesome, Holden even asks to sleep in Ackley's room. In New York, after his night of wandering from bar to bar, Holden goes back to the hotel, again so depressed he almost wishes he were dead. Holden's experience with the nuns as he is eating breakfast in Grand Central Station impresses on him their simplicity and the courage of their vows of poverty. Sorry that he had given them only ten dollars for their charity basket, he is again depressed, bemoaning money as an agent of depression. When Holden is attacked by the bellman who tries to cheat him, he fantasizes movie-fashion, dripping blood, about having been shot. He stays in the bathtub for an hour, then goes to bed but cannot sleep for thinking about suicide by jumping out the window. What deters him is the thought of his broken body lying uncovered on the sidewalk. Holden's frequent attempts to break his isolation are momentarily satisfying, but his depression and isolation return again and again. Feeling like an outsider during his walk toward Broadway, Holden notices a family walking contentedly together while the little boy sings to himself, and Holden feels better. An admirer of family closeness, he says that the sight of the family lightens his depression. In a moment, however, he is once again saddened by all the people hurrying or standing in long lines, intent upon getting to the movies, the ultimate in fraud and phoniness.

Holden telephones a friend, a phony, and asks him to meet him; his conversation, aggressive and provocative, irritates Luce, who leaves lonesome Holden, despite his being begged to stay. A short time later, Holden is sitting on the radiator in the men's room, shivering, and counting the white squares of tile on the rest room floor. During his nighttime visit to Phoebe's room, Holden bursts into inexplicable tears. A profound sense of isolation and depression is often evident in Holden's thoughts and actions, just as it is for many young people of his age. Once again, Salinger has shown what Erikson describes.

Young adult readers find in *Catcher* verification of preoccupation with old crises as common to their age group, in Holden's case the death of his younger brother Allie. When Stradlater asks Holden to write him a descriptive composition for English class, Holden spends an hour describing Allie's baseball mitt, covered all over with poems. Holden goes on to reminisce about Allie, who, red hair and all, had been perfect, intelligent, funny, never angry. Holden recalls how in his grief, anger, and frustration at Allie's death, he broke all the windows in the garage, but was unable to break those in the station wagon because his hand hurt so much. He didn't even realize he was committing these self-destructive acts. Alone at another time, Holden lapses into another one-sided conversation with innocent Allie, this time trying to make up for the times he had excluded him. Allie, perfect and innocent, had wanted to go with big brother Holden and friend Bobby. At first, Holden hadn't let him, but Allie never complained, and now Holden's guilt surfaces. This old crisis—the loss of his brother who did not live long enough to lose his innocence—surfaces frequently. Allie, a child at his death, was uncorrupted, but Holden, who had behaved like a normal older brother, now feels guilty. As he sits on a bench in Central Park, his wet hair freezing into icicles, Holden remembers the family trips to Allie's grave. When it rained, the visit was awful, traumatic, because it rained on Allie's tombstone, and on the grass growing above Allie's body. Phoebe challenges Holden to name just one thing he likes, and Holden can name only his dead brother, who did not live

long enough to become a phony. When Phoebe expostulates, insisting
that Holden recognize Allie's death, Holden is emphatic. Death has nothing to do with liking someone. He can like Allie just the same.

Holden, like the young adults who read his story, is "beset with the
physiological changes" of his youthful body, changes that result in preoccupation with sex and sexuality. His concern that before marriage he
must know about sex causes him to agree to a visit from the prostitute,
but he cannot go through with it. He is afraid of Stradlater's behavior
with Jane, and admits that unless he is watchful he himself can easily be
carried away on a date. He avidly watches the behavior of the transvestite
and of the couple in the hotel room across the way; he worries about the
nuns' reaction to the sexuality of Tess and of Romeo and Juliet. He is curious about homosexuality, but simultaneously scorns Luce, the prep
school acquaintance who talks incessantly about it. Mr. Antolini's fatherly
and sympathetic touch frightens Holden, whose concern about his own
sexuality causes him to misinterpret kindness.

Erikson mentions youth's search for truth and reality, a search that
prompts young people to rally around idealistic causes, hoping that there
lies truth. Most pervasive of all words in *Catcher,* and most significant, is
the word *phony,* the explicit denial of truth. In his search for what constitutes honesty, Holden decries phoniness in Stradlater and his classmates, his teachers, the headmaster, the alumni, the school food, the
money-earning populace, Sally Hayes and her mother, the dating process,
actors of both stage and screen, the audience, and on and on. His parents,
the nuns, Allie, Phoebe, Jane, Mr. Antolini, and old Spencer escape the accusation of phoniness, but even his grown brother D. B., who prostitutes
himself by writing phony stuff for the phony world of the movies, is a
phony. Even words can be phony, words like *grand,* for example. The silence in the bar when the pianist Ernie sits down at the piano is phony;
his trills and ripples are phony. People who meet in the bar lie when they
say they're glad to meet each other; ministers speak in phony Holy Joe
voices, and Sally Hayes with her stories about the boys at Harvard and
West Point who call her up day and night is a phony; her mother is a
phony because if she stood around collecting money for a cause, she'd
then hand in her basket and take off for some plush place for lunch. The
movies are truly phony, but stage plays are a close second; it follows that
anyone who acts or writes for stage or films—like D. B.—is a phony. On
and on.

True to those of Holden's age, he too is a phony as he tries on various
selves, hoping to discover what he really is. When he calls Ackley a gen-
tleman and a scholar, he lies about his regard for Ackley; he lies to Ernest
Morrow's mother on the train about how popular Ernest is; he lies to the
principal at Phoebe's school, and to the girls dancing at the Lavender
Room. He grips his stomach, faking a fatal bullet, fakes his age in the bars,
lies when he tells Sally Hayes he loves her. Not satisfied with who he is,

Holden "tries on" one more manner or one more role, gives a different name, and, although conscious of his own fraudulence does not connect it to the phoniness of the rest of society; he lacks the awareness, the will, or the courage to be totally honest in his own behavior. At this point in his life, he may not in fact know what behavior would be totally within character, but instead tries on one kind and then another, each of them a pretense.

Readers have always taken pleasure in reading about those who question and seek answers to the same issues that we do, and who thus increase our understanding. Just as this wish to understand is true of adults, it is true of young adults. The issues that adults and young adults face are similar; the differences are based upon the less extensive experience of the young, and upon their social and physiological stage in maturity. As we read with pleasure and vicariously experience all this, we come to understand ourselves, other people, and society.

Erik Erikson and J. D. Salinger know young adults. Although they serve different professions and write in differing formats, they arrive at the same definition of youth. Erikson has received credit for his analyses of human development. J. D. Salinger deserves praise for the wisdom of *The Catcher in the Rye*.

1. While teaching veterans of the Vietnam War, I found in my classes young men who had never in their lives read a novel in its entirety. They were, however, universally absorbed in *Catcher*. "Is there another book like this?" they asked. Such a group must surely have seen reality and phoniness, experienced idealism and loss of innocence, and have discovered through *The Catcher in the Rye* that they were not alone in their struggle with society's imperfections.

Understanding Adolescents and Their Reading

Ruth K. J. Cline

Knowledge of literary elements is one essential part of the equation for successful reading experiences with young adults. The other essential ingredient is an understanding of *who* these young adults are: What are their interests? Their abilities? Their expectations? Their concerns? The answers to these questions should guide the teacher in recommending books for the entire class, as well as books for small group and individualized reading.

The response theory in literature proposes that in order for the reader to derive satisfaction and pleasure from reading, there has to be an "experience" with the literature. When the situation and characters in the book are something readers can identify with, they will be more involved in the story and find the reading more satisfying. The more pleasure enjoyed by the reader, the more it will encourage further reading. An adult alert to such a response will guide the reader toward similar literature, or will know when it is time to nudge the reader toward other content.

Psychologists who specialize in adolescent behavior acknowledge the changes in our society that put additional pressure on young people. Despite the time lapse since Robert Havighurst first proposed his Developmental Tasks for Adolescents (1953), his general categories are still appropriate. The way society views the adolescent and its expectations of the adolescent are what has changed. Havighurst's tasks are identified here with a brief description of societal changes and examples of adolescent literature that could deal with each developmental task.

1. Achieving new and more mature relations with age-mates of both sexes. Adolescents move from groups of same-sex to opposite-sex interests at different ages. Some middle school students go to parties with dates, while others are still more comfortable with same-sex slumber parties, movies, or camping expeditions. Movies, advertising, and other media encourage young people to move into more mature relationships before they may be psychologically ready.

Many young adult books could be the basis for discussion of appropriate behavior and alternative choices for the characters. Cormier's *The Chocolate War* and *Beyond the Chocolate War* are stories about boys and their loyalty to their peer group. Judy Blume and Paula Danziger are authors whose novels typically portray girls and their concerns. Boy–girl relationships are especially important in books by Norma Klein, Richard Peck, Ron Koertge, and Todd Strasser.

2. **Achieving a masculine or feminine social role.** This task is complicated somewhat by the erosion of traditional role models, the feminist movement, and the evolution of the gay and lesbian movements. More men are house-husbands or involved with child care. Teenaged fathers are claiming rights to unborn children before marriage. Girls are involved in sports that were formerly considered for males only. Institutions that were formerly one-sex are now admitting both sexes. The role of women in the military is currently controversial. Gays and lesbians are more open about their life-styles. All of this puts pressure on young men and women to assume what they consider their roles, but the definition of the roles is elusive and may depend on the area in which people live and the media to which they are exposed.

Young adult literature reflects these role changes in addition to traditional roles. *Heartlight* (Barron) has a 12-year-old heroine and her astronomer grandfather on a space mission to save the universe. The heroine in Brooks's *Midnight Hour Encore* is an accomplished cellist, and *Standing Tall, Looking Good* (Miklowitz) describes the life of new recruits in the army, including a young woman.

In *No Kidding* (Brooks) a 14-year-old boy in the twenty-first century assumes responsibility for his young brother; eventually he has custody of their alcoholic parents. Kordon's *Brothers Like Friends* shows a more traditional relationship between two brothers and the importance of soccer in their lives.

3. **Accepting one's physique and using the body effectively.** At some point, everyone has to accept who they are and what they look like. The color of hair, the shape of the nose, the weight of the body can be changed to some degree, but eventually there has to be acceptance of the physical appearance. The adolescent years are especially difficult since physical changes occur rapidly, and adolescents are critical of themselves as well as of those around them. Lipsyte in *One Fat Summer* portrays a fat boy and his efforts to survive in a new community while his girlfriend has a "nose job" to feel more accepted.

In addition, there are any number of individuals who have physical impairments. Reading about the visual and/or hearing impaired and those with cerebral palsy, muscular dystrophy, and epilepsy can help young people understand their own conditions or those of friends who may be affected (Karolides, *Focus on Physical Impairments*).

Helen Keller is a classic example of an impaired person who achieved (*The Story of My Life*, Keller); Tom Sullivan is a more recent example (*Tom Sullivan's Adventures in Darkness*, Gill, 1976). Several novels for young adults on the subject of epilepsy have been written, such as *Child of the Morning* (Corcoran) and *A Handful of Stars* (Girion).

Focus on Fitness (Karolides and Karolides, 1993) is a resource book with information, fiction, and nonfiction reading suggestions designed to help young people work toward physical and emotional fitness, eat correctly, and care for their bodies.

4. Achieving emotional independence of parents and other adults. One obvious change in today's society is the structure of the family. The number of white single-parent households in 1991 represented 23.1 percent of all households, an increase from 10.1 percent in 1970. Although white mothers are most often the single parent (19.3 percent in 1991), the number of white fathers who are fulfilling this role has increased from 1.2 percent in 1970 to 3.8 percent in 1991 (Lewin).

In *Hey, Kid! Does She Love Me?* (Mazer), a teenaged boy finds out what it is like to care for a baby alone for a few days, while Ellie's father is head of her house in *Squashed!* (Bauer). Robby in *Nekomah Creek* (Crew) is afraid the school will find out that his father is a house-husband while his mother works.

In black families, the number of single-parent families grew from 35.6 percent in 1970 to 62.5 percent in 1991. Black women were responsible for 33 percent of the households in 1970 and for 58 percent in 1991, while black males were responsible for 2.6 percent of single-parent households in 1970 and 4.5 percent in 1991 (ibid).

Somewhere in the Darkness (Myers) portrays a young black boy living with a family friend until his father returns from prison and wants Jimmy to go with him. The Logan family in Mildred Taylor's books pictures a strong nuclear black family, supportive of the children and their activities (*Roll of Thunder, Hear My Cry* through *The Road to Memphis*).

The figures for Hispanic households were not available for 1970, but women were responsible for 28.7 percent of households in 1991, while Hispanic men were responsible for 4.4 percent (ibid).

The Hispanic family in *The Skirt* (Soto) is a strong nuclear family, while *Famous All Over Town* (Santiago) shows the disintegration of a Hispanic family.

The family structure influences adolescents in the home in many ways. Older children are more often caretakers of younger children in the absence of parents during working hours. Children are without adult supervision more hours of the day, and children without siblings are alone more hours. The number of children without brothers or sisters showed a 50-percent increase between 1965 and 1985, going to 13 million in 1985 (Cline).

In *Bridge to Terrabitha* (Paterson), Leslie is the only child in her family; *Moves Make the Man* (Brooks) compares the life-style of a family with several children and no father and a boy who is an only child but with both parents. *Summer of the Swans* (Byars) shows the agony of a 14-year-old girl who is responsible for taking care of her younger retarded brother. *Jacob Have I Loved* (Paterson) illustrates the rivalry between siblings, in this case twin girls, while Sleator shows the rivalry between twin boys in *Singularity. Dicey's Song* (Voigt) depicts a caring relationship in a family without parents. *Sarah, Plain and Tall* (MacLauchlan) portrays a frontier father in charge of two children and his efforts to find a female helper for the family.

Divorced families and the "blended" families that occur when partners bring their children into a new marriage are often traumatic events for adolescents. Many books portray these feelings, including *Blue Heron* (Avi), where 13-year-old Maggie becomes the "parent" to her stepmother during a crisis and *Home Before Dark* (Bridgers), when Stella resists moving into her new stepmother's house.

5. Achieving assurance of economic independence. Many adolescents have jobs after school, sometimes requiring long hours when they cannot study or read. These adolescents are part of our consumer economy, using their incomes for records, tapes, clothes, movies, cars, and books. But the jobs can also interfere with studying and make it impossible to be involved with extracurricular activities at school. Some families depend on the incomes of these young adults to augment the family income.

Teenagers today do more of the family shopping because they are more independent than they used to be. Fifty-two percent of girls between the ages of 12 and 19 shop for part or all of the family's groceries each week (Hauser, 1986). Another indicator of the independence of today's teenagers is their use of various forms of credit. Credit card companies court young people to get them to become credit card users.

Credit-Card Carole (Klass) shows how the family income drops drastically when the father changes careers and Carole has to curtail her shopping mall trips. Stephanie Tolan has written two books for young readers about the Skinner family as they reevaluate priorities when a job change lowers the family income and shifts their values: *The Great Skinner Strike* and *The Great Skinner Enterprise.*

6. Selecting and preparing for an occupation. Although young adult literature does not often focus on this topic, it is a subtheme in some books. The work ethic and satisfaction in the workplace are issues many adults struggle with and certainly should be part of our discussion with young people. *Focus on Careers* (Iglitzin) refers young readers to fiction, nonfiction, and nonprint sources on this topic. *Very Far Away from Anywhere Else* (Le Guin) portrays a young man who wants to become a great scientist and Natalie whose goal is to be an actress. In *The Haymeadow* (Paulsen), 14-year-old John is resourceful in fulfilling a man's responsibility while herding sheep in an isolated Wyoming area one summer.

7. **Preparing for marriage and family life.** With the rather grim statistics about the dysfunctional family in our society, teachers and caring adults can assist young people to understand the responsibilities of marriage and family life. The relationships between characters in any book can be highlighted in a discussion to point out what was effective and what was damaging to the other characters. Without positive role models, young people will continue the cycle. Child abuse is an example of this cycle: the number of abusers who were abused as children is very high.

Bless Me, Ultima (Anaya) depicts a young Chicano boy growing into manhood in a family that enjoys the wisdom and magic of Ultima, his Grande. An older book, *Mama's Bank Account* (Forbes), deals with a close-knit family during tough economic times. *Words by Heart* (Sebestyen) shows a close relationship between a black father and his young daughter, as well as the stepmother.

8. **Developing intellectual skills and concepts necessary for civic competence.** This task involves the skills necessary to be a thoughtful member of a democratic society. The study of literature helps young people to understand the actions and motives of characters in books. Transfer of this insight to the interactions in their own lives may help readers to be more tolerant of people with differing views.

The complex issues involved in censorship, for instance, can be looked at more objectively by reading and discussing Hentoff's book, *The Day They Came to Arrest the Book,* where complaints about teaching *Huck Finn* are the center of the plot. *Does This School Have Capital Punishment?* (Hentoff) shows the relationships between students in a private school in New York City and telling the truth, believing lies, and trusting others. *Motel of the Mysteries* (Macaulay) is a picture book satire on our society and its values that appeals to all age levels.

9. **Desiring and achieving socially responsible behavior.** Acknowledging the importance of peer pressure is crucial as adolescents develop. Often young people appear to have their own dress and hair codes; sometimes the code is simply that the dress and hair have to be outrageous. These styles are usually a point of conflict with parents and a symbolic gesture indicating independence; they are not necessarily a sign of irresponsible behavior.

In some instances, violent and unlawful gangs develop from the pressure to do what the peer group expects. Other young people may become involved in more socially accepted interests, such as music, sports, or hobbies.

Avi's *Nothing But the Truth* shows what happens when Philip doesn't tell his parents the whole truth about an incident in school. *The Runner* (Voigt) depicts the consequences for Bullet when he defies his father and chooses not to cooperate with his coach. Hinton's books *The Outsider, Rumble Fish,* and *Tex* are examples of young boys living on their own but learning what is expected of them in society. *Focus on Teens in Trouble* (Sander) is a resource book to help young people understand peer pressures and their relationship to the legal system.

10. Acquiring a set of values and an ethical system as guide. In novels, what guides the characters in the decisions they make? Is an ethical system obvious to the reader? Stories in which the protagonists are guided only by what people will think of them or whether they will be punished or rewarded for their actions represent a low level of moral development according to Kohlberg, whose work on moral education can be applied to literature.

Lena in *Words by Heart* (Sebestyen) shows a mature and charitable attitude toward her hard-hearted neighbors. Kate in *The Ancient One* (Barron) is guided by her desire to save the ancient trees for the good of mankind. Cloyd in *Bearstone* (Hobbs) learns that Walter cares for him and that vindictiveness is not an appropriate response. Questions of moral behavior in the power of an adult over the actions of a child are raised in Cormier's *Tunes for Bears to Dance To.*

Thinking with a class about the motives and actions of the characters is a good activity for a literature class. Why do the characters behave as they do? What alternatives did they have? What consequences would be likely to ensue from each of the actions? The decisions affect other people in the book and will help clarify some of the ethical issues.

Conclusion: The important goal for teachers is to know their students and help students find the books that will engage them and help them to grow as readers and people. Havighurst gives a structure to the psychological, mental, and physical goals for young people. Literature can assist young readers to know themselves and understand their world a little better.

References

Cline, Ruth K. J. *Focus on Families.* Santa Barbara: ABC-CLIO, 1990.

Hauser, Grady. "How Teenagers Spend Money: The Family Dollar," *American Demographics* 8, no. 12 (December 1986): pp. 38–41.

Havighurst, Robert. *Developmental Tasks and Education.* New York: David McKay, 1972.

Iglitzin, Lynne B. *Focus on Careers.* Santa Barbara: ABC-CLIO, 1991.

Karolides, Nicholas J. *Focus on Physical Impairments.* Santa Barbara: ABC-CLIO, 1990.

———, and Melissa Karolides. *Focus on Fitness.* Santa Barbara: ABC-CLIO, 1993.

Kohlberg, Lawrence. "The Child as a Moral Philosopher," *Psychology Today,* September 1968, pp. 25–30.

Lewin, Tamar. "Rise in Single Parenthood Is Reshaping U.S." *The New York Times,* October 5, 1992, pp. A1, B6.

Sander, Daryl. *Focus on Teens in Trouble.* Santa Barbara: ABC-CLIO, 1991.

Additional Reading Suggestions

Compiled by Ruth K. J. Cline

Character

Adler, C. S. *Mismatched Summer*. New York: Putnam, 1991. 174 pp.
Written in chapters that alternate between 12-year-olds Micale and Meg, in which the girls learn the importance of friendship and acceptance of other life-styles.

Avi. *Blue Heron*. New York: Bradbury Press, 1992. 186 pp.
Maggie, 13, spends her summer vacation in a remote cabin with her father, stepmother, and their 3-month old baby. As Maggie observes her father's changed behavior, she becomes the "adult" in whom the adults confide.

Buss, Fran Leeper, with Daisy Cubias. *Journey of the Sparrow*. New York: Lodestar (Dutton), 1991. 155 pp.
An illegal alien family from El Salvador by way of Mexico makes it to Chicago where they try to blend in with their host family. Poverty, cultural differences, and climate make the transition difficult for these children.

Charyn, Jerome. *Back to Bataan*. New York: Farrar, Straus and Giroux, 1992. 101 pp.
Set in 1943 in New York City, this is the story of Jack Dalton, whose father has been killed on Bataan. Jack lives with his mother, who works in a silk parachute factory. Jack, 11, has an overactive imagination, a flair for the dramatic, and a sense of the bizarre.

Cooney, Caroline B. *Twenty Pageants Later*. New York: Bantam, 1991. 192 pp.
Although her older sister has entered many beauty pageants, eighth-grader Scottie-Anne is persuaded to enter her first contest and learns about the nature of such competitions.

Cormier, Robert. *Other Bells for Us to Ring*. Illustrated by Deborah Kogan Ray. New York: Delacorte, 1990. 136 pp.

Eleven-year-old Darcy learns about war when her father goes into World War II, is declared missing in action, but eventually returns home; and she learns about friendship through Kathleen Mary O'Hara, who dies because of her alcoholic father.

Ehrlich, Amy. *The Dark Card.* New York: Viking, 1991. 178 pp.

Laura, 17, having a difficult adjustment to her mother's death, decides to visit the casinos, where she gets hooked on the games and meets some very strange characters.

Hobbs, Will. *Downriver.* New York: Atheneum, 1991. 204 pp.

Jessie, 15, involved in an outward-bound experience, changes as she understands the personalities and motives of her group of alienated young people who raft the Grand Canyon without adult guidance.

Irwin, Hadley. *Can't Hear You Listening.* New York: Collier Macmillan, 1990. 202 pp.

Tracy Spenser has been covering for some of her high school friends who have been using booze and drugs, but she realizes she is not doing them a favor to continue in this manner.

Mango, Karin N. *Portrait of Miranda.* New York: HarperCollins, 1993. 232 pp.

Miranda struggles to find her real identity, and almost loses the boy she likes because she plays "too many parts" without realizing the effect on those around her.

Sauer, Jim. *Hank.* New York: Delacorte, 1990. 260 pp.

As told by the 16-year-old brother, the focus of the story is really the unusual brother Hank, 9, who believes things should be done "the right way."

Soto, Gary. *The Skirt.* Illustrated by Eric Velasquez. New York: Delacorte, 1992. 74 pp.

Miata, who is distracted and forgetful, has forgotten her folklorico dance skirt on the school bus on Friday and worries about how she can get it for the Sunday performance.

Plot

Adams, Douglas. *Mostly Harmless.* New York: Harmony (Crown), 1992. 277 pp.

The fifth book in the *Hitchhiker's Trilogy,* this satire on our planet's culture and society includes strange characters, time travel, and plenty of puns in the life of Arthur Dent.

Carkeet, David. *Quiver River.* New York: HarperCollins, 1991. 236 pp.

Nate and Rickey are involved in a mystery at their summer camp, which includes Indian traditions and the rites of manhood as part of the plot.

Crichton, Michael. *Jurassic Park.* New York: Ballantine, 1990. 399 pp.
Excitement centers on a theme park featuring dinosaurs and other prehistoric animals created from a biotechnological process. Ignorance, greed, and carelessness cause disaster in this popular adult novel, which is read by all ages.

Crutcher, Chris. *Chinese Handcuffs.* New York: Greenwillow, 1989. 202 pp.
High school students cope with severe problems of suicide and sexual abuse against the backdrop of athletic competition.

Forman, James D. *Prince Charlie's Year.* New York: Scribner's 1991. 136 pp.
Colin MacDonald recalls his first experience with war as a 14-year-old boy in Scotland when Prince Charlie came out of Italian exile to reinstate the Stuart dynasty.

Hobbs, Will. *The Big Wander.* New York: Atheneum, 1992. 181 pp.
Searching for his uncle in the canyon country of Utah, Clay, 14, meets interesting people, and he and his stray pets have exciting adventures along the way.

Mazer, Norma Fox. *D, My Name is Danita.* New York: Scholastic, 1991. 163 pp.
Danita meets a young man at the mall and is surprised to learn that he is her half-brother, the result of her father's romantic, but forgotten, liaison some years ago.

Miklowitz, Gloria D. *Standing Tall, Looking Good.* New York: Delacorte, 1991. 149 pp.
Three young people join the army for different reasons and the reader follows them through basic training with their friends, fears, and trials.

Ogiwara, Noriko. *Dragon Sword and Wind Child.* Translated by Cathy Hirano. New York: Farrar, Straus and Giroux, 1993. 329 pp.
A fast-moving plot set in ancient Japan and based on Japanese myths. Saya is revealed as the Water Maiden and must accept conditions that are presented to her if the land and people she loves are to survive.

Thesman, Jean. *When the Road Ends.* Boston: Houghton Mifflin, 1992. 184 pp.
A strange group of children and one adult try to survive the pressures of traditional society by going to a family cabin in the woods. Acceptance of others and humor help them deal with circumstances that are often beyond their control.

Voigt, Cynthia. *The Wings of a Falcon.* New York: Scholastic, 1993. 467 pp.
The heroic efforts of Oriel and Griff to survive in medieval times and remain true to their values through stress and violence proves to be an imaginative plot.

Windsor, Patricia. *The Christmas Killer*. New York: Scholastic, 1991.
192 pp.
A mystery set in suburban New England using the psychology of
twins and the murders of teenaged girls, each with a plastic red
flower left beside her body.

Zalben, Jane Breskin. *The Fortuneteller in 5B*. New York: Henry Holt,
1991. 148 pp.
Alexandria and her best friend Jenny, both 11, let their imaginations
carry them away as they try to determine the identity and background of their new neighbor in the apartment building.

Theme

Avi. *Nothing But the Truth: A Documentary Novel*. New York: Orchard
1991. 177 pp.
The importance of communicating with each other, parents–child,
parents–teachers, teachers–administrators, is emphasized as Philip
tells his abbreviated version of a school episode that grows into a na-
tionwide controversy.

Barron, T. A. *The Ancient One*. New York: Philomel, 1992. 367 pp.
Saving the ancient forests of Oregon becomes the focal point for
Kate, 12, and her great-aunt Melanie, and results in a fantasy adven-
ture with "little people," magic, and a time tunnel.

Brooks, Bruce. *No Kidding*. New York: Harper & Row, 1989. 207 pp.
In this commentary on alcoholism in the twenty-first century, 14-
year-old Sam and his younger brother are AOs (alcoholic offspring—
that is, offspring of alcoholics) and have extraordinary attention, including special school courses and custody of their parents.

Brooks, Martha. *Two Moons in August*. Boston: Little, Brown. 1991. 199
pp.
Complex and intertwined family relationships are protrayed with a
family struggling to survive the mother's death and to maintain their
own friendships.

Christopher, Matt. *Tackle Without a Team*. Illustrated by Margaret Sanfil-
lippo. Boston: Little, Brown, 1989. 145 pp.
Scott has to defend himself against charges of possessing marijuana
and stealing, while wanting to play football on a special team.

Cormier, Robert. *Tunes for Bears to Dance To*. New York: Delacorte,
1992. 101 pp.
Questions of morality are raised through the pressure of an adult over
a child, the question of freedom of choice, and the consequences of
our actions. Henry struggles with sadness, loneliness, and guilt.

Guy, Rosa. *The Music of Summer*. New York: Delacorte, 1992. 181 pp.
Sarah, 17, is a talented pianist who is in conflict with her mother over friends and goals. She begins to understand other kinds of prejudice but becomes stronger for her trials.

Mango, Karin N. *Portrait of Miranda*. New York: HarperCollins, 1993. 232 pp.
Self-esteem is a missing element in Miranda's character, causing her to act in unpredictable ways as she tries out different identities and behaviors.

Qualey, Marsha. *Everybody's Daughter*. Boston: Houghton Mifflin, 1991. 201 pp.
After living in a commune in northern Minnesota, Beamer, 17, wants to make her own decisions and not have the extended family involved in every aspect of her life.

Shannon, Jacqueline. *I Hate My Hero*. New York: Simon & Schuster, 1992. 197 pp.
Sixth-grade girls are struggling to understand friendships and human relations when a video news program they are working on causes rivalry and disagreeable competition.

Taylor, Mildred D. *The Road to Memphis*. New York: Dial, 1990. 290 pp.
Continuing the Logan family story, Cassie and Stacey, now in their teens, deal with prejudice and inhumanity in the South just before the outbreak of World War II.

Setting

Avi. *The True Confessions of Charlotte Doyle, A Novel*. New York: Orchard, 1990. 210 pp.
The 1832 setting on the ship *Seahawk* provides a unique backdrop for Charlotte's adventures as a passenger who turns into a crew member on her unusual voyage from England to America.

Castaneda, Omar S. *Among the Volcanoes*. New York: Lodestar (Dutton), 1991. 183 pp.
Isabel, the oldest daughter, has the responsibility of her three siblings and ailing mother in this vivid story of life in a Guatemalan village. The volcanoes are symbolic of the forces of poverty and lack of education that mold the people living in their shadows.

Finkelstein, Norman H. *Captain of Innocence: France and the Dreyfus Affair*. New York: Putnam, 1991. 156 pp.
Based on the true story of Alfred Dreyfus, a young Jewish military officer in France in the 1890s, who is framed by anti-Semitic military officers and accused of treason.

Garland, Sherry. *Song of the Buffalo Boy.* Orlando: Harcourt Brace, 1992. 249 pp.
   Loi, a 17-year-old Amerasian girl, lives in a rural area of Vietnam and on the streets of Ho Chi Minh City, and struggles to survive the prejudice and poverty that surround her.
Laird, Elizabeth. *Kiss the Dust.* New York: Dutton 1992. 279 pp.
   Tara, 12, the daughter of Kurds, has the responsibility for her family when they have to leave their home in Iraq and risk their lives on a journey to Iran, where they live miserable lives as refugees.
Moore, Robin. *The Bread Sister of Sinking Creek.* New York: Lippincott, 1990. 154 pp.
   As set in 1776 in the sparsely settled mountains of western Pennsylvania, Maggie is a "bound-out" girl, helping families with their work and leaving the area on her wedding day, knowing the decision to marry the McGrew nephew is not a wise one.
Paulsen, Gary. *The Haymeadow.* Illustrated by Ruth Wright Paulsen. New York: Delacorte, 1992. 195 pp.
   Fourteen-year-old John, sent to the high country of Wyoming to tend the sheep in the summer pasture, survives many trials of the wilderness.
Paulsen, Gary. *Canyons.* New York: Bantam, 1990. 184 pp.
   In New Mexico, two boys tell their stories: Coyote Runs is a Native American who is killed in a horse raid, and years later Brennan Cole is camping in the same area and pieces together the story of the skull he found.
Paterson, Katherine. *Lyddie.* New York: Dutton, 1991. 182 pp.
   The textile factories in Lowell, Massachusetts, in the early 1840s is the setting for Lyddie's work and growing-up experiences.

Point of View

Arrick, Fran. *Where'd You Get the Gun, Billy?* New York: Delacorte, 1991. 132 pp.
   The saga of a gun that played an unfortunate part in many lives as it was used, thrown away, found, and used again. The narration follows the gun itself.
Cohen, Barbara. *Tell Us Your Secret.* New York: Bantam, 1989. 176 pp.
   Readers begin to understand the motives of twelve high school girls as they reach into their experiences for background for their writing, resulting in mysterious happenings. The chapters are each told from a different girl's point of view.
Crew, Linda. *Nekomah Creek.* Illustrated by Charles Robinson. New York: Delacorte, 1991. 191 pp.

Robby, a fourth-grader and the big brother of 2-year-old twins, is embarrassed because his father is a "house-husband." Robby is sure the school is spying on them and will not accept this role reversal. The humor is more obvious because the story is told through Robby's innocent eyes.

Hobbs, Will. *Bear Dance.* New York: Atheneum, 1993. 197 pp.

Cloyd learns about bears and himself in the wilderness of Colorado, with the story revealing insights as Cloyd discovers them for himself.

Hobbs, Will. *Bearstone.* New York: Atheneum, 1989. 154 pp.

When Cloyd is moved from a group home to live with a crusty old rancher, the reader learns about Cloyd's and Walter's motives, thoughts, and actions from Cloyd's point of view.

Riddell, Ruth. *Ice Warrior.* New York: Atheneum, 1992. 138 pp.

Rob, 12, learns that his step-family is trying to help him with his ice-boat while his biological father, about whom he dreams a great deal, is not dependable. As told from Rob's point of view, the reader agonizes with him as he tries to sort out his feelings.

Talbert, Marc. *The Purple Heart.* New York: HarperCollins, 1992. 135 pp.

Luke's father, who has been wounded, is returning from Vietnam, and Luke lives out his need to be a hero with his friends. Because Luke is telling the story, the reader sympathizes with his predicament.

Style

Barron, T. A. *Heartlight.* New York: Philomel, 1990. 272 pp.

Kaitlyn, 12, and her inventor, astronomer grandfather have an "other worldly" adventure with lots of symbolism and beautiful images included in the writing.

Peck, Sylvia. *Seal Child.* New York: Bantam Skylark, 1991. 192 pp.

A mystical winter experience in Maine for a young girl who meets a *selkie,* a seal turned into a human, which helps her to understand love and acceptance.

Rhodes, Judy Carole. *The King Boy.* New York: Bradbury Press, 1991. 168 p.

Benjy learns that he has to live with the family reputation in his rural wooded area of Arkansas, but he finally learns the truth. The language of uneducated rural folks and idioms of the area are important in setting the tone and style of the book.

Rylant, Cynthia. *Missing May.* New York: Orchard, 1992. 89 pp.

Whirligigs in the garden are the metaphor for 12-year-old Summer whose mother died when Summer was 6 and who lives with various relatives until Ob and May take her to their trailer in West Virginia.

Ob makes the whirligigs and calls them mysteries, like heaven, angels, fire, love, dreams, and death.

Salisbury, Graham. *Blue Skin of the Sea*. New York: Delacorte, 1992. 215 pp.

Sonny Mendoza changes from a 6-year-old with questions about his mother's death to a confident, self-assured young man who experiences the extended family, fishing, lava flows, and a tidal wave as he grows up in Hawaii. The author uses humor and the episodic narrative to build character and suspense.

Spinelli, Jerry. *Maniac Magee*. Boston: Little, Brown, 1990. 184 pp.

The prose is almost poetic when Maniac describes what he sees. An orphan white boy, Maniac integrates his multicultural city by crossing invisible boundaries, engaging in contests with all kids, and interacting with all ages.

Thesman, Jean. *The Rain Catchers*. Boston: Houghton Mifflin, 1991. 182 pp.

Living in a house with women, Grayling learns early about the importance of "story" that holds the extended family together. Use of sensory images enhances the enjoyment of the story.

Tone

Bauer, Joan. *Squashed*. New York: Delacorte, 1992. 194 pp.

The excitement and competition of who can grow the largest pumpkin is the basis for this Iowa story, with suspense as well as rural values portrayed. A tongue-in-cheek tone adds to the humor of the situation and characters.

Hobbs, Will. *Changes in Latitudes*. London: Pan Horizons, 1988. 162 pp.

Travis, 16, is trying hard to be "cool" and his narration reflects this attitude. But the events of the family in Mexico get him involved and the tone of his narration changes to show guilt, panic, and grief.

Kordon, Klaus. *Brothers Like Friends*. Translated by Elizabeth D. Crawford. New York: Philomel, 1992. 206 pp.

Set in Germany post–World War II, soccer, family relationships, and conscience are important to the two brothers who regret their mother's marriage to Uncle Willi. The tone conveys impending doom with the reader in suspense to see what happens.

Lutzeier, Elizabeth. *The Coldest Winter*. New York: Holiday House, 1991. 153 pp.

Set in Ireland in 1846 during the potato famine, the Eamonn family struggles to survive and to understand the destruction by the English soldiers and unexpected kindness shown by other people. Desperation and gloom are reflected in the tone of the story.

Myers, Walter Dean. *Somewhere in the Darkness.* New York: Scholastic, 1992. 168 pp.

Jimmy Little, 15, travels with his father, who has just come from prison, as the father attempts to show him people and places from his past, hoping to justify his life's decisions for his son. The tone conveys a feeling of doom.

Glossary of Literary Terms

Allegory   a literary work in which characters and actions represent abstractions

Alliteration   repetition of initial consonant sound

Allusion   indirect reference to something or someone outside the literary work

Antagonist   force in conflict with protagonist; usually designated as self, another person, society, nature

Anthropomorphism   the giving of human qualities to nonhuman animals or objects

Assonance   repetition of vowel sound in phrase

Backdrop setting   generalized or relatively unimportant setting

Ballad   verse narrative of love, courage, the supernatural. May be of folk origin

Biography   the history of the life of an individual

Cadence   rhythmic flow in prose

Character   human being, real or personified animal or object taking a role in literature

Character development   filling out a variety of character traits to provide the complexity of a human being

Chronological order   events related in the order of their happening

Classic   literary work that lives to be read and reread

Cliché   overused term that has lost meaning

Cliffhanger   unresolved suspense that concludes a chapter

Climax   action that precipitates resolution of conflict

Closed ending   conclusion leaving no plot questions unanswered

Coincidence   chance concurrence of events

Complication   early action; part of rising plot

Conflict   struggle between protagonist and opposing force

Connotation   associative or emotional meaning of a word

Consonance   repetition of consonant sound in phrase

Denotation   explicit or dictionary meaning
Denouement   final or closing action following climax
Dialect   language variation of a region
Diction   choice of words or wording
Didacticism   in literature, an instructive or moralistic lesson often at the expense of entertainment
Dramatic or objective point of view   third-person narration in which actions and speeches are recorded without interpretation
Dynamic character   one who changes in the course of the story

Echo   words repeated in familiar pattern
Epic   long narrative poem about a heroic figure whose actions reveal the values of the culture
Episodic plot   plot with independent, short storylike chapters linked by characters or theme more than by action
Explicit theme   theme stated clearly in the story
Exposition   presentation of essential information needed for understanding of the action

Fable   brief story, usually with animal characters, that states a didactic theme or moral
Falling action   final or closing action following climax; denouement
Fantasy   story about the nonexistent or unreal in which action may depend on magic or the supernatural
Figurative language   devices making comparisons, saying one thing in terms of another
First-person point of view   "I" narration in which a person's experiences, thoughts, and feelings are told by himself or herself
Flashback   return to event that occurred before present scene; retrospect
Flat character   one that is little developed
Foil   a character whose contrasting traits point up those of a central character
Folk epic   long narrative poem passed down by word of mouth; often about a hero
Folk rhyme   rhymes passed down by word of mouth
Folktale   story passed down by word of mouth
Foreshadowing   hints of what is to come

Genre   a kind or type of literature that has a common set of characteristics

High fantasy   a type of fantasy characterized by its focus on good and evil
Hyperbole   exaggeration or overstatement

Imagery   verbal appeals to the senses

Implicit theme   theme implied from the story's context

Inevitability   sense that it had to happen; in literature a sense that the outcome was necessary and inescapable

Integral setting   essential and specific setting that influences character, plot, and theme

Legend   a traditional narrative of a people, often with some basis in historical truth

Limerick   five-line humorous verse with traditional rhythm and rhyme pattern

Limited omniscient point of view   third-person narration in which story is seen through the mind(s) of one or a few characters

Lyric poem   songlike poem, compact expression of feeling

Metaphor   implied comparison

Meter   somewhat regular rhythm pattern of stressed and unstressed syllables in a line of poetry

Motif   recurring element in literary work, often found in traditional literature

Myth   story originating in folk beliefs and showing supernatural forces operating

Narrative order   sequence in which events are recounted

Narrative poem   poem that tells a story

Objective or dramatic point of view   third-person narration in which actions and speeches are recorded without interpretation

Omniscient point of view   an all-knowing writer tells the story in third person

Onomatopoeia   words that sound like their meanings, such as *meow, moo*

Open ending   final outcome of conflict unknown

Oxymoron   two contradictory terms brought together

Parody   limitation of known form for comic effect

Personification   giving human traits to nonhuman beings or objects

Phonetic intensives   lengthy duration of sounds for effect

Plot   sequence of events involving character in conflict

Poetry   distilled and imaginative expression of feeling

Point of view   the mind(s) through which the reader sees the story

Primary theme   major underlying and unifying truth of a story

Progressive plot   plot with central climax

Protagonist   central character in the conflict

Pun   humorous use of a word with several meanings

Realism   story based on the possible, though not necessarily probable

Resolution   falling action following climax

Rhyme   repetition of identical or similar stressed sound or sounds
Rhythm   recurring flow of strong and weak beats
Rising action   exposition and complications that lead to the climax
Round character   a fully developed or three-dimensional character

Sarcasm   irony that is personal and intended to hurt
Satire   a critical attitude blended with wit and directed toward human beings or their institutions
Science fiction   story that relies on invention or extension of nature's laws, not upon the supernatural or magical
Secondary theme   less important or minor theme of a story
Sensationalism   focus on the thrilling or startling
Sentiment   emotion or feeling
Sentimentality   overuse of sentiment; false arousal of feelings
Setting   the time and place in which the action occurs
Simile   stated comparison, usually using *like* or *as*
Static character   one who does not change in the course of the story
Stereotype   character possessing expected traits of a group rather than being an individual
Stock character   flat character with very little development; found in numerous stories, such as folktales
Style   mode of expression
Suspense   state of uncertainty that keeps the reader reading
Symbol   person, object, situation, or action operating on two levels of meaning—literal and figurative or suggestive
Synaesthesthia   concurrent response of more than one sense although only one has been stimulated

Theme   statement giving the underlying truth about people, society, or the human condition, either explicitly or implicitly
Tone   writer's attitude toward his or her subject and readers
Touchstone   example of excellence referred to for comparison

Understatement   reverse exaggeration or playing down

Verse   here used to denote rhyming metrical structure with less emotional intensity than poetry
Vicarious experience   experience available to readers through reading about it rather than living it

Acknowledgments

Art Acknowledgments

p. xv: Jacket illustration from *Jacob Have I Loved* by Katherine Paterson. Copyright © 1980 by Katherine Paterson. Jacket art by Kinuko Craft. Selection reprinted by permission of HarperCollins Publishers.

p. 6: Cover illustration from *Cat, Herself* by Mollie Hunter. Copyright © 1985 by Maureen Mollie Hunter McIlwraith. Jacket art © 1985 by Stephen Seymour. Selection reprinted by permission of HarperCollins Publishers.

p. 30: Jacket illustration from *Permanent Connections* by Sue Ellen Bridgers. Copyright © 1987 by Sue Ellen Bridgers. Jacket art © 1987 by Sheila Hamanaka. Selection reprinted by permission of HarperCollins Publishers.

p. 58: Jacket illustration from *I'll Love You When You're More Like Me* by M. E. Kerr. Copyright © 1977 by M. E. Kerr. Jacket art by Fred Marcellino. Selection reprinted by permission of HarperCollins Publishers.

p. 84: Cover illustration from *Julie of the Wolves* by Jean Craighead George. Cover art © 1985 by Wendell Minor. Interior illustrations copyright © 1972 by John Schoenherr. Selection reprinted by permission of HarperCollins Publishers.

p. 100: Cover illustration from *The Pigman* by Paul Zindel. Copyright © 1991 by Paul Zindel. Cover art © 1991 by Jeff Fisher. Selection reprinted by permission of HarperCollins Publishers.

p. 114: Jacket art from *The Moves Make the Man* by Bruce Brooks. Copyright © 1984 by Bruce Brooks. Jacket art © 1984 by Wayne Winfield. Selection reprinted by permission of HarperCollins Publishers.

p. 136: Cover illustration from *My Daniel* by Pam Conrad. Copyright © 1989 by Pam Conrad. Cover art © 1989 by Darryl S. Zudeck. Selection reprinted by permission of Harper-Collins Publishers.

p. 150: Jacket illustration from *Going Over to Your Place*, poems selected by Paul B. Janeczko. Copyright © 1987 by Paul B. Janeczko. Jacket painting by Neil Waldman, © 1987 by Bradbury Press. Selection reprinted by permission of Neil Waldman.

Literary Acknowledgments

Mary Baron. "Newborn Neurological Exam" from *Music of What Happens* edited by Paul B. Janeczko. Copyright © 1988. Reprinted by permission of the author.

Dave Barry. Excerpt from article by Dave Barry in the *Cincinnatti Enquirer*, June 3, 1992. Reprinted by permission of Tribune Media Services.

Janine Bossard. Excerpt from *A Matter of Time* by Janine Bossard. Copyright © 1988. Reprinted by permission of the author and Little Brown & Co.

Sue Ellen Bridgers. Excerpts from *All Together Now* by Sue Ellen Bridgers. Copyright © 1978 by Sue Ellen Bridgers. Reprinted by permission of Alfred A. Knopf, Inc.

Olive Ann Burns. Excerpts from *Cold Sassy Tree* by Olive Ann Burns. Copyright © 1984 by Olive Ann Burns. Reprinted by permission of Ticknor & Fields/Houghton Mifflin Company. All rights reserved.

Alice Childress. From *A Hero Ain't Nothin But a Sandwich* by Alice Childress. Copyright © 1973 by Alice Childress. Reprinted by permission of Coward, McCann & Geoghegan, Inc.

Robert Cormier. From *After the First Death* by Robert Cormier. Copyright © 1979 by Robert Cormier. Reprinted by permission of Pantheon Books, a division of Random House, Inc.

Robert Cormier. From *The Chocolate War* by Robert Cormier. Copyright © 1974 by Robert Cormier. Reprinted by permission of Pantheon Books, a division of Random House, Inc.

Paula Fox. From *The Slave Dancer* by Paula Fox. Copyright © 1975 Paula Fox. Reprinted with the permission of Bradbury Press, an affiliate of Macmillan, Inc.

Walker Gibson. "Advice to Travelers" from *Come As You Are* by Walker Gibson. Reprinted by permission of the author.

Seamus Heaney. "Mid-Term Break" from *Death of a Naturalist* by Seamus Heaney. Reprinted by permission of the author and Faber and Faber Limited.

Seamus Heaney. "Mid-Term Break" from *Selected Poems 1966–1987* by Seamus Heaney. Copyright © 1990 by Seamus Heaney. Reprinted by permission of Farrar, Straus & Giroux, Inc.

Christine Hemp. "To Build a Poem" by Christine Hemp. Reprinted by permission of Webster Review, Vol. XI, No. 1, Spring 1986.

H. M. Hoover. From *The Dawn Palace* by H. M. Hoover. Copyright © 1988 by H. M. Hoover. Used by permission of Dutton Children's Books, a division of Penguin Books USA Inc.

Langston Hughes. "Mother to Son" from *Selected Poems* by Langston Hughes. Copyright © 1926 by Alfred A. Knopf, Inc., and renewed 1954 by Langston Hughes. Reprinted by permission of the publisher.

Kathryn Lasky. Reprinted with the permission of Macmillan Publishing Company from *Beyond the Divide* by Kathryn Lasky. Copyright © 1983 Kathryn Lasky.

Ursula K. Le Guin. Excerpts from pages 2, 62–63 from *The Beginning Place* by H. M. Hoover. Copyright © 1980 by Ursula K. Le Guin. Reprinted by permission of HarperCollins Publishers, Inc.

Madeleine L'Engle. Excerpts from *A Wrinkle in Time* by Madeleine L'Engle. Copyright © 1962 and copyright renewed © 1990 by Crosswicks Ltd. Reprinted by permission of Farrar, Straus & Giroux, Inc.

Phyllis McGinley. "The Angry Man," from *Times Three* by Phyllis McGinley. Copyright © 1932–1960 by Phyllis McGinley; copyright © 1938–42, 1944, 1945, 1958, 1959 by The Curtis Publishing Co. Used by permission of Viking Penguin, a division of Penguin Books USA Inc.

John Marsden. From *So Much to Tell You* by John Marsden. Copyright © 1987 by John Marsden. Reprinted by permission of Little, Brown and Company.

Louise Moeri. From *The Forty-Third War* by Louise Moeri. Copyright © 1989 by Louise Moeri. Reprinted by permission of Houghton Mifflin Co. All rights reserved.

Robert C. O'Brien. Reprinted with the permission of Atheneum Publishers, an imprint of Macmillan Publishing Company, from *Z For Zachariah* by Robert C. O'Brien. Copyright © 1975 by Sally Conly.

Scott O'Dell. From *Island of the Blue Dolphins* by Scott O'Dell. Copyright © 1960, renewed 1988 by Scott O'Dell. Reprinted by permission of Houghton Mifflin Co. All rights reserved.

D. Randall. "Blackberry Sweet" from *New Black Poetry* by D. Randall. Reprinted by permission of the author.

Carl Sandberg. "Lost" from *Chicago Poems* by Carl Sandberg. Reprinted by permission of Harcourt Brace & Company.

Ian Serraillier. Excerpts from *Beowulf the Warrior* by Ian Serraillier. Copyright © 1954. Reprinted by permission of Oxford University Press.

Suzanne Fisher Staples. From *Shabanu: Daughter of the Wind* by Suzanne Fisher Staples. Copyright © 1989 by Suzanne Fisher Staples. Reprinted by permission of Alfred A. Knopf, Inc.

Mildred D. Taylor. From *Roll of Thunder, Hear My Cry* by Mildred D. Taylor. Copyright © 1976 by Mildred D. Taylor. Used by permission of Dial Books for Young Readers, a division of Penguin Books USA Inc.

John Hall Whelk. From *The Gardener and Other Poems* by John Hall Whelk. Reprinted with permission of Charles Scribner's Sons, an imprint of Macmillan Publishing Company. Copyright renewed 1989 by Sally Whelk Baritone.

Index